PRAISE FOR *A TIDAL ODYSSEY*

"The most thorough review ever written about Edward Ricketts's life leading up to the time he published *Between Pacific Tides*. It will immediately find its place in the lore and literature of that legendary, pioneering marine biologist."

—RICHARD C. BRUSCA, research scientist, University of Arizona; executive director emeritus, Arizona-Sonora Desert Museum

"Presents for the first time the captivating history of how *Between Pacific Tides*, one of the world's most enduring popular—and scientific—books on tidepool life and intertidal ecology came to be."

—JAMES T. CARLTON, professor emeritus of marine sciences, Williams College

"In 1945, John Steinbeck introduced readers to Ed Ricketts as 'Doc' in *Cannery Row*. Today, three-quarters of a century later, Astro and Kohrs bring the real Ed Ricketts back to life as a brilliant Renaissance person, a knowledgeable biologist largely self-taught, an incredible teacher and a compassionate individual. Astro and Kohrs trace the persistence shown by Ricketts through the nightmares of publishing *Between Pacific Tides*, now considered a classic of marine biology, and still in print.

As you read this book about Ed Ricketts and the making of *Between Pacific Tides*, you may wish you had known the man and were able to call him your friend.

Thank you, Richard Astro and Donald Kohrs, for sharing your knowledge of a fascinating person and an important happening in marine science."

—JOHN V. BYRNE, author of *Undercurrents*; former administrator of NOAA, US commissioner to International Whaling Commission, and president of Oregon State University

"We started at once to lay out plans, to write down lists of
things to do, to get, to take, to plan our itinerary and
activities . . . the idea of a book loomed up more and more
as the significant feature of the whole thing. We both
became quite sure that it could be a great thing,
maybe very great, a modern Odyssey."

E. F. RICKETTS

a tidal odyssey

Ed Ricketts and the Making
of *Between Pacific Tides*

Richard Astro & Donald Kohrs

OREGON STATE UNIVERSITY PRESS
CORVALLIS

The John and Shirley Byrne Fund for Books on Nature and the Environment
provides generous support that helps make publication of this and other
Oregon State University Press books possible.

Cataloging-in-Publication data is available from the Library of Congress

ISBN 978-0-87071-158-9 (paperback);
ISBN 978-0-87071-159-6 (ebook)

∞ This paper meets the requirements of ANSI/NISO Z39.48-1992
(Permanence of Paper).

First published in 2021 by Oregon State University Press
Printed in the United States of America

Oregon State University
OSU Press

Oregon State University Press
121 The Valley Library
Corvallis OR 97331-4501
541-737-3166 • fax 541-737-3170
www.osupress.oregonstate.edu

For Betty and Kelly.
And for Franklin, who was always at my side.
—RICHARD ASTRO

For Ed Jr. and Nancy Ricketts, who know why, or should.
And for my lovely wife, Leticia Medina-Kohrs, who
tolerates my endless staring at the computer screen.
—DON KOHRS

contents

a note from the authors

When writing about a book by two authors, it is sometimes difficult to state with complete certainty who wrote what. In fact, at this juncture in the process of our own composition, we'd be hard pressed to affirm unequivocally which of us wrote this or that paragraph in this book. Luckily it matters little in terms of our authorship, but it does suggest the need for clarification about two books that are central to our study: Ricketts and Calvin's *Between Pacific Tides* and Steinbeck and Ricketts's *Sea of Cortez*.

Ed Ricketts was the principal author of *Between Pacific Tides*. He was the marine biologist whose life work was the study of life in the intertidal zones of the central Pacific Coast. Jack Calvin was a talented writer who learned a good deal of science along the way, but his contributions to *Between Pacific Tides* were chiefly organizational and were largely confined to providing photographs of the animals Ed collected and perfecting Ricketts's imperfect prose. Accordingly, in this volume, we ascribe authorship to both men when we address large, overarching issues about *Between Pacific Tides*. We identify Ricketts as the author when we discuss material that is more detailed and chiefly scientific.

Sea of Cortez, published in December 1941, is the record of the Steinbeck-Ricketts expedition to the Gulf of California. The book has two parts: a narrative about the trip and a phyletic catalog of the animals they collected. Ed Ricketts compiled the phyletic catalog. Steinbeck composed the narrative based largely on a log that Ricketts kept during the expedition. The prose in the narrative is Steinbeck's (excepting the Easter sermon on non-teleological thinking that is almost entirely Ricketts), but in terms of content, the narrative is the product of both men. Four years after Ricketts's death in 1948, the book's publisher (Viking Press) published a stand-alone edition of the narrative titled *The Log from the Sea of Cortez*, to which was added an appendix that Steinbeck wrote in memory of and as a tribute to Ricketts. Therefore, although all the citations in this volume are from *The Log from the Sea of Cortez*, we often identify Ricketts as the source of a quote in the text.

preface

Cannery Row in Monterey in California is a poem, a stink, a grating noise, a quality of light, a tone, a habit, a nostalgia, a dream, . . . the gathered and scattered, tin and iron and rust and splintered wood, chipped pavement and weedy lots and junk heaps, sardine canneries of corrugated iron, laboratories and flop houses.

—JOHN STEINBECK, *Cannery Row*

Cannery Row lives on in John Steinbeck's memorable novel, a book that for so many readers supplies a nourishing grip—Mack and the boys, Lee Chong, Dora and her girls. And Doc, the center of the piece, American literature's most famous marine biologist.

'The canneries and flophouses are gone now. Lee Chong's grocery and the Bear Flag restaurant have given way to art galleries, boutique hotels, souvenir shops, and the Monterey Bay Aquarium. Ed Ricketts, the real "Doc," owner and operator of the Pacific Biological Laboratories at 800 Cannery Row, was killed in 1948 when his old car was hit by the Del Monte Express, the evening train from San Francisco. He was on his way to buy some steaks for dinner, but as he turned his noisy 1936 Buick sport coupe up the hill and across Drake Street, where the road meets the Southern Pacific Railroad tracks, the train edged around a warehouse and crashed into him.

Unlike the rest of old Cannery Row, though, Ed Ricketts will not die. "He haunts the people who knew him," Steinbeck wrote. "He is always present even in the moments when we feel his loss the most." Three-quarters of a century later, Doc still draws a crowd. Tim Wootton, a professor of ecology and evolution at the University of Chicago, while visiting Monterey, "took the time to wander down the alley next to Ricketts's lab, which I found to be a near-religious experience." Thousands come to Monterey and stand before his lab, searching for Ed's spirit.

What is it about Ed Ricketts that lives on? For those who knew him, it was his gift as a teacher. "Everyone near him was influenced by him, deeply and permanently," said Steinbeck. "Some he taught how to think, others how to see or hear." But for most of us he remained in the popular imagination as Steinbeck's sidekick, his drinking buddy, his coauthor of a book about a trip they made to the Gulf of California. And even then, most readers incorrectly attributed the narrative portion of *Sea of Cortez* solely to Steinbeck, relegating Ricketts's contribution to the catalog of animals they collected on their journey.

Gradually, this view began to change. First came the recognition that Ricketts had a substantial impact on Steinbeck's best fiction, that his science underpins the thematic design of Steinbeck's most important novels. Then there was the publication of Ricketts's essays, his journals, and his notebooks, which reveal his tremendous intellectual breath. And all the while a small number of marine biologists knew that Ricketts had changed the way we observe and understand marine life in the intertidal zones. Largely self-taught, unaffiliated with any university or established scientific laboratory, Ed Ricketts was in the vanguard of marine scientists who transformed our understanding of the seashore. In his writing about life in the intertidal zones, he joined the pantheon of America's best nature writers, that select group of women and men who have illuminated natural history information for us, who have demonstrated a personal response to the natural world, and who have interpreted nature philosophically—Thoreau, Muir, Burroughs, and Leopold. Combining science with natural history, and lacing all with an aesthetic appreciation of the world around him, Ricketts was wedded to scientific fact even as he conveyed the marvelous, the mystic, the poetry of the Pacific seashore.

We see Ricketts's science in the narrative portion of *Sea of Cortez*, which Steinbeck crafted from a log kept by Ed during the expedition. We see it in his unpublished notes, journals, and essays. And above all we see it in the masterwork that he authored with Jack Calvin, *Between Pacific Tides* (1939), the book about the habits and habitats of the animals who live on the rocky shores and in the tide pools of one of the richest life zones in the world—the Pacific Coast of North America.

Books about the invertebrates of the intertidal zones written before and during the first half of the twentieth century were organized on the basis of taxonomy. They were inventories of animals, of interest to taxonomic specialists at work identifying and classifying the critters of the seashore, and to laboratory biologists conducting controlled investigations, manipulating the particular factors under study to determine whether such manipulation generates changes in the subjects. By contrast, Ricketts and his coauthor, Jack Calvin, chose to arrange the animals they studied according to where they were found, in the mudflats, on sandy beaches, on wharf pilings, and on rocky shores. In addition, the authors focused on the relationships among the various animals and between the animals and their environments. Their treatment is ecological and inductive rather than taxonomic, and the animals are observed "in order of their commonness, conspicuousness, and interest." Ricketts and Calvin bring the wealth of life that occurs between the upper and lower limits of the tide to scientists and casual observers alike, even to the person who has little or no biological training.

In a foreword to the 1948 edition of *Between Pacific Tides*, John Steinbeck wrote, "This book then says: 'There are good things to see in the tidepools and there are exciting and interesting thoughts to be generated from the seeing. Every new eye applied to the peep hole which looks out at the world may fish in some beauty and some new pattern, and the world of the human mind must be enriched by such fishing.'" The reader will want to know, Steinbeck continues, "What is it called? What does it eat? How does it defend itself and reproduce its kind? Will it hurt me if I touch it?" "To supply such a person with as much as possible of the information that he wants," write Ricketts and Calvin, "is the chief aim of this handbook."

We are not suggesting that ecological investigations of animal life in the intertidal zones originated with Ed Ricketts and Jack

Calvin. In fact, the origins of ecology can be found in the writings of Aristotle, and in those of Thales and Plato. Ecology emerged as a distinct discipline during the latter part of the nineteenth century, from an array of different sources. The German explorer and scientist Alexander von Humboldt insisted that nothing in nature could be studied in isolation, that all phenomena were connected. Charles Darwin's theory of evolution by natural selection provided a mechanism not only for understanding how species arose, but also for interpreting patterns in their distribution and abundance. The German biologist Ernst Haeckel provided a name for the science, writing in his *General Morphology of Organisms*, "By ecology we mean the body of knowledge concerning the economy of nature—the total relations of the animal to both its inorganic and organic environment."

In the United States, Henry Chandler Cowles at the University of Chicago began a series of studies of ecological succession in the dunes around Lake Michigan. Cowles was followed by other scientists who established Chicago as the epicenter of ecological biology: Victor Ernest Shelford, Alfred Emerson, and Warder Clyde Allee. One of these Chicago ecologists, W. C. Allee, routinely traveled to the Marine Biological Laboratory at Woods Hole, where he conducted field research that complemented his laboratory studies. It was at the University of Chicago that Ed Ricketts spent most of his abbreviated college career.

Ricketts took courses from Allee and became an admirer, even an acolyte; in his own work he brought Allee's science out of the academy to a general readership. In a piece titled "Distribution of Common Littoral Invertebrates of the Woods Hole Region" that was published in the *Biological Bulletin* in 1923, Allee reports on his studies of the animals he observed by habitat, whether mudflat, sand, gravel, or "rocks or rockweed." In *Between Pacific Tides*, a volume designed for a general as well as a scientific audience, Ricketts and Calvin employ the same approach, "whether rock, sand, mud, or some combination of these." In fact, Ricketts goes beyond Allee, extending ecological benchmarks to include degree of wave shock and tidal exposure. Moreover, Ricketts and Calvin conducted their investigations on the shores of a different ocean, where such studies were previously unknown.

In their introduction to *Between Pacific Tides*, Ricketts and Calvin write that "the intertidal zone of the Pacific Coast of North America supports an extraordinarily rich assortment of plants and animals" and that "within this narrow strip of shore, colorful and intriguing representatives of nearly every group of invertebrates can be found." Writing in a style designed to popularize their science—to interest and engage the casual visitor to the seashore — Ricketts and Calvin captured the interest of the editors of the Stanford University Press, publisher of *Between Pacific Tides*. Generations of readers have read the book, which has been in print for more than eighty years. In *Sea of Cortez*, Ricketts and Steinbeck write, "The true biologist deals with life, with teeming boisterous life, and learns something from it, learns that the first rule of life is living." *Between Pacific Tides* is a book about teeming boisterous life.

In his foreword to *Between Pacific Tides*, John Steinbeck wrote of Ricketts and Calvin's process of discovery, noting that "a young, inquisitive, and original man might one morning find a fissure in the traditional technique of thinking. Through this fissure he might look out and find a new external world about him. In his excitement a few disciples would cluster about him and look again at the world they knew and find it fresh." Ed Ricketts was that young, inquisitive, and original man. He and Jack Calvin present the many readers of *Between Pacific Tides* with a world they can look at and, at once, find it new, find it fresh.

RICHARD ASTRO AND DON KOHRS
ORLANDO AND SANTA CRUZ
AUGUST 2021

kindling a flame

Education is the kindling of a flame, not the filling of a vessel.

—SOCRATES

T he art of writing scholarly nonfiction is for most a process of researching, collecting, sorting, and organizing material. We glean information from diverse sources: our own research, the contributions of other investigators, and letters, notes, and journals. Then, after a suitable period of maturation, we shape it all into the story we want to tell; such is this history. *Between Pacific Tides* is a classic work of marine biology that, since its publication by the Stanford University Press in 1939, has gone through four revisions and is still in print today. At the time of its writing, its authors challenged existing norms governing who should write science texts and how they should be written.

Edward F. Ricketts and Jack Calvin, an odd couple as authors of a science text, pioneered the study of life in the intertidal zones, where the lives of animals are shaped by their habitats and by their relationships with one another. The result was a book about marine life on the shoreline of the Pacific Coast of North America organized by the structural and functional relationships within and among living populations. This is marine ecology. It is what British zoologist Charles Elton defined as "scientific natural history," and what American biologist Eugene Odom would call "the study of the structure and function of nature." As a book about the Pacific seashore written and published in the 1930s, *Between Pacific Tides* was unique. Now, eighty years later, Ricketts and Calvin's understanding of life in these intertidal zones is the scientific norm. Decades ahead of its time, *Between Pacific Tides* remains a valued and valuable text for students and professionals in the various fields of marine biology, as well as for the lay reader who finds the seashore a place of enchantment, wonder, and beauty.

It is hard to find a richer and more interesting place to view living things than between the tide marks along the seashore. There one finds a tremendous number and variety of plants and animals, from the most common to the most unusual of species. On and under every rock, in every nook and cranny of the littoral (or intertidal) zone, even the scientific novice can find countless communities of animals to observe and study. As the place where the land meets the sea, the intertidal zone also offers the observer a continual variety of scenes, since what is submerged one hour is dry the next. And it is all accessible to the casual observer, who can find and observe marine organisms without any kind of underwater gear. For Ed Ricketts and Jack Calvin, visits to the various shoreline habitats, whether the rocky shores, the mudflats, or the sandy bottoms, were always interesting and enlightening. There, as the naturalist John Muir is alleged to have asserted, whenever they picked out anything by itself, they found it hitched to everything else.

Ed Ricketts, the lead author of *Between Pacific Tides*, was a marine biologist without portfolio. He attended college but never graduated. His collaborator, Jack Calvin, wrote adventure novels and was an English teacher with no formal scientific training. Though Ricketts and Calvin were not credentialed biologists, neither were they amateurs. Calvin was an accomplished writer, a naturalist, a fine photographer, and a lover of adventure. He and his wife sailed a seventeen-foot canoe from Tacoma to Southeast Alaska on their honeymoon. In his later years he was a fierce advocate for environmental protection in his adopted home of Sitka, Alaska. Calvin learned about the seashore from Ricketts and, in return, he smoothed Ed's often cumbersome prose, which was critical if their coauthored manuscript was to ever get published. His beautiful photographs of the marine specimens that he and Ed collected in the tide pools along the

Central California and Southeast Alaska coastlines help to account for the excellence of *Between Pacific Tides*.

Though Calvin's contributions to *Between Pacific Tides* were substantial and should not be undervalued, the primary authorship of the book belongs to Ed Ricketts. An accomplished student of animal ecology, though largely self-taught, Ricketts read widely in the field and became as learned as most credentialed marine educators. Ed communicated with many of them, in the United States and throughout the world. Over time, he became an experienced collector of marine invertebrates that he made available to scientists at many prestigious scientific institutions around the globe.

Ed Ricketts was as gifted a teacher as he was a student, albeit not in a traditional sense and certainly not in the classroom. In a tribute written by his closest friend, novelist John Steinbeck, as an afterword to the narrative portion of the book they wrote together, Steinbeck affirms that "no one who knew him will deny the force and influence of Ed Ricketts. Everyone near him was influenced by him, deeply and permanently. Some he taught how to think, others how to see or hear." [1] Among Ed's most accomplished students was Steinbeck himself. The holistic and relational view of life in *Between Pacific Tides* informs the thematic design of the novelist's best and most important fiction.

Ricketts had equally close friendships with artists, philosophers, poets, and novelists as with fellow scientists. The impact of his science—his understanding of the natural world—on the work of his artist and novelist friends was enormous. His relational view of life in the intertidal zones defines the plight of the striking migrants in John Steinbeck's *In Dubious Battle* and helps us understand the ordeals of the dispossessed tenant farmers in *The Grapes of Wrath*. It also informs the work of mythologist Joseph Campbell. Arguably the most distinguished comparative mythologist in American intellectual history, Campbell learned much from Ed, and readers can find clear connections between the ecological view of life in *Between Pacific Tides* and Campbell's *The Hero with a Thousand Faces* and *The Power of Myth*. Steinbeck and Campbell went on extended collecting expeditions with Ricketts, Steinbeck to the Gulf of California and Campbell to Southeast Alaska. They understood and embraced Ricketts's view of animal life in the tide pools; Steinbeck employs it in his memorable portrayal of the dustbowl migrants, as does Campbell in his saga of the archetypal hero.

In the preface Ricketts drafted for a handbook that he and Steinbeck planned to write about marine life in San Francisco Bay, Ed wrote,

> Who would see a replica of man's social structure has only to examine the abundant and various life of the tide pools where miniature communal societies wage dubious battle against equally potent societies in which the individual is paramount, with trends shifting, maturing, or dying out, with all the living organisms balanced against the limitations of the dead kingdom of rocks and currents and temperatures and dissolved gases. A study of animal communities has this advantage: they are merely what they are, for anyone to see who will and can look clearly; they cannot complicate the picture by worded idealisms, by saying one thing and being another; here the struggle is unmasked, and the beauty is unmasked.[2]

Steinbeck, who wrote an important novel about men and women waging a different dubious battle in the Torgas Valley—striking farmers, Communist organizers, and California agribusinessmen—speaks to Ed's vision in the foreword he penned for the 1948 edition of *Between Pacific Tides*. "The process of rediscovery might be as follows," he writes, "a young, inquisitive and original man might one morning find a fissure in the traditional technique of thinking. Through this fissure he might look out and find a new external world about him. In his excitement, a few disciples would cluster about him and look again at the world they knew and find it fresh. From this nucleus there would develop a frantic new seeing and a cult of new seers who, finding some traditional knowledge incorrect, would throw out the whole structure and start afresh."[3]

Steinbeck's "young, inquisitive and original man" was Edward Flanders Ricketts, a gifted scientist and a unique personality whose disciples in Monterey clustered about him and with him, looked again at the world they knew and found it fresh. Ricketts's circle included the aforementioned Jack Calvin, a high school English teacher from Mountain View, California, and Ritch Lovejoy, the artist and writer who illustrated Ricketts and Calvin's text. In the background is John Cage, the avant-garde composer who was Calvin and Lovejoy's brother-in-law (Cage, Calvin, and Lovejoy married three sisters); novelist Henry Miller, who wrote about sex as transcendence and who believed, like Ricketts, that "one's destination is never a place but rather a new way of looking at things";[4] and Joe Campbell, who signed on in 1932 and later referred to those days as a time when everything in his life was taking shape. During the years when Ricketts was working on *Between Pacific Tides,* an ever-changing community of artists, writers, and just interesting personalities passed through his lab and his life. They included Sasha, Tal, and Xenia Kashevaroff, the rather remarkable daughters of the archpriest of Alaska's Russian Orthodox Church; Bruce Ariss, the painter, muralist, and set designer who in later years built sets for *The Bing Crosby Show* and *I Love Lucy*; Lincoln Steffens, the journalist, political philosopher, and leading muckraker of the Progressive Era; psychiatrist Evelyn Reynolds Ott, who brought to the mix the thinking of Carl Jung; and Webster "Toby" Street, a Monterey original and a partner in the city's oldest and most formidable law firm. Steinbeck scholar Susan Shillinglaw writes that guests at the lab "found refuge in Ed's attentiveness and sweet temperament."[5] Like so many of Ed's visitors, Rolf Bolin, the ichthyologist from Hopkins Marine Station, said that he "went over [to the lab] for the purpose of feeling better."[6]

At the center of it all is the figure of Ricketts, whose influence reached well beyond the boundaries of marine biology to touch the careers of so many men and women, some of whom became far more famous than he did. While Ricketts was writing about the "pleasant and absurd hermit crabs," who he called "the clowns of the tide pools,"[7] Steinbeck was stoking the country's conscience about the exploitation of dust bowl refugees, and Miller was shocking the reading public with his novels of explicit language, surrealist free association, mysticism, and sex. Steinbeck and Miller, writing about life in their time, have much to teach us about our time, but no more so than Ricketts, whose studies of the ecology of the tide pools of Monterey Bay and the Straits of Juan de Fuca presaged the work serious marine biologists do today. An examination of the writing and publishing history of *Between Pacific Tides* is therefore long overdue.

Edward F. Ricketts. Photograph courtesy of San Jose State University, Martha Heasley Cox Center for Steinbeck Studies.

EDWARD FLANDERS RICKETTS

It is not uncommon for someone to achieve fame based on how their accomplishments are described by others. But it is rare and potentially regrettable when fame accrues based on a portrait of the person as a character in someone else's fiction. Such is the case with Ed Ricketts, who gained his notoriety first as a figure in John Steinbeck's novels: as the character of Doc Burton, who drops in and out of the action in *In Dubious Battle*; as Jim Casy, the ex-preacher whose dramatic life and death are central to the action of *The Grapes of Wrath*; as Dr. Winter in the novella-play, *The Moon Is Down*; as the unorthodox operator of Doc's lab in *Cannery Row* and its sequel, *Sweet Thursday*; and as Friend Ed in *Burning Bright*, the stage play written by Steinbeck in the aftermath of Ricketts's death. But Ricketts was neither a physician (*In Dubious Battle, The Moon Is Down*), a preacher (*The Grapes of Wrath*), nor a mystic (*Burning Bright*). There is some of each in Ed, but none are full representations of the original. The forgiving friend with the familiar nickname of Doc who grounds the narrative of *Cannery Row* and *Sweet Thursday*; the serious scientist who confronts the strange intruder in Steinbeck's short story "The Snake"; the passionate pilgrim who emerges from Steinbeck's essay "About Ed Ricketts"—these characterizations come somewhat closer to biographical fact.

The fictional hero of *Cannery Row* and *Sweet Thursday* drinks beer milkshakes, beds women, hires bums and misfits to collect frogs, reads Goethe's *Faust*, listens to Bach's *Art of the Fugue*, quotes from the Sanskrit *Black Marigolds*, and "tips his hat to dogs as he drives by and the dogs look up and smile at him."[8] Much in this picture of Ed Ricketts is true: the girlfriends, the all-night parties, the Bear Flag brothel, the Chinese grocer Lee Chong, the winos and assorted dropouts who collect specimens for the lab. Except for occasional hints, however, the hardworking field scientist is largely missing from Steinbeck's frame.

Complementing Ricketts's science was his love of music, history, philosophy, and literature. He studied the work of the German mystic Novalis, the historian Oswald Spengler, and poet Robinson Jeffers. Ed's personal library was vast. It included the work of the biologists, physicists, and chemists from whom he learned his science. It also included books of poetry, history, philosophy, and art, as well as scores of novels and volumes of short stories. He read copiously, and his letters and notebooks are filled with incisive commentaries about his reading that are as wide as the furthest horizon. He had a phonograph and radio receiver built for him by Pol Verbeck, who also built one for Steinbeck. Ed loved listening to music on Verbeck's machine—especially the Gregorian chants, the masses of Palestrina, compositions by Scarlatti and Monteverde, and always Bach's *Art of the Fugue*. Irene Longueira, a Ricketts neighbor who lived on nearby Wave Street, told friends that "on several occasions, I would look out my windows on the east side of my house and see Ed Ricketts and John Steinbeck sitting on a small patch of grass, drinking red wine and listening to classical music from his lab."[9]

Steinbeck celebrates the literary and music-loving side of Ricketts's personality in "About Ed Ricketts," written after Ed's death and published in 1951. Though warm and sensitive, Steinbeck's tribute is marred by exaggeration, error, and omissions of fact. For example, Steinbeck says that Ricketts graduated from the University of

Ritchie Lovejoy's woodcut portrait of John Steinbeck. From Carol Steinbeck's scrapbook. Photograph courtesy of San Jose State University, Martha Heasley Cox Center for Steinbeck Studies.

Chicago. In fact, Ricketts left college, as did Steinbeck, after taking a number of courses but without getting a degree. Steinbeck claims that he met Ricketts at a dentist's office in Monterey. Actually, they met at the Carmel home of Jack Calvin. More significant is

Steinbeck's failure to so much as mention *Between Pacific Tides.*
Steinbeck wrote "About Ed Ricketts" as a sort of postscript to *The Log
from the Sea of Cortez,* the 1951 reissue of the narrative portion of *Sea of
Cortez,* released by Steinbeck's publisher without Ricketts's name as
coauthor. Evidently, Steinbeck's agent (Elizabeth Otis) and Pascal
Covici at the Viking Press believed a book by John about science coauthored by a marine biologist would hurt sales. They were probably right.

Absent the full story, readers of Steinbeck's fiction, and viewers of
various stage and screen adaptations of his work, can be forgiven for
getting the wrong idea about Ed Ricketts. The 1982 movie cobbled
together from *Cannery Row* and *Sweet Thursday* by MGM starred
Nick Nolte as Doc/Ricketts and presented Nolte's character as a former major league pitcher who almost killed a batter by hitting him
in head with a fastball. Ed Ricketts was no Carl Mays, the Yankee
pitcher whose bean ball did kill Cleveland Indians shortstop Ray
Chapman in 1920.

The 1955 musical *Pipe Dream,* an adaptation of *Sweet Thursday* by
Richard Rodgers and Oscar Hammerstein, featured a young singer
named William Johnson in the Doc/Ricketts role. Initially written
for Henry Fonda, the tall, taciturn actor who was nominated for
an Oscar for his performance as Tom Joad in *The Grapes of Wrath*
(Fonda bowed out when Richard Rodgers realized that he could not
sing), the part was sanitized for Broadway, along with Steinbeck's
anti-middle-class message. As a result, the unhappy and uncertain
Doc who unburdened his heart in song on stage in *Pipe Dream* would
have been unrecognizable to Ricketts's friends on Cannery Row, as
well as to-fellow scientists in such faraway places as Sweden and the
Philippines. Eventually their living memories of the real Ed Ricketts
were eclipsed by the superior power of Steinbeck's books, and by
inferior adaptations of Steinbeck's Cannery Row–inspired fiction.

The misalignment of fact and fiction began to change in 1978,
when the appropriately named Mad River Press published *The Outer
Shores,* a two-volume collection of Ricketts's previously unpublished
essays, edited by Joel Hedgpeth. This compilation was followed by
the work of Katharine A. Rodger who, with help from Ricketts's son,
Ed Jr., edited two important books about Ricketts's work and his
person, *Renaissance Man of Cannery Row* (2002) and a collection of
his writings titled *Breaking Through: Essays, Journals, and Travelogues*

of Edward F. Ricketts (2006). Attention was finally being paid, by literary scholars, historians of science, and denizens of present-day Cannery Row, as Ricketts's life and work began to come into focus, independent of his involvement with Steinbeck.

Today, visitors to the Monterey Bay Aquarium can stop for a photo on the steps of Ricketts's lab at 800 Cannery Row, a small, brown, tenement-like building next to an upscale hotel where the sign still says Pacific Biological Laboratories and lucky tourists are sometimes treated to a tour. Plaques, busts, and murals populating the vicinity of Cannery Row now honor Ricketts and Steinbeck equally. A bit to the north, up in Moss Landing, the Monterey Bay Aquarium Research Institute operates a research vessel called *Western Flyer*, which serves as the platform for deploying, operating, and recovering a tethered ROV (remotely operated vehicle) named "Doc Ricketts." In 2017 the ROV Doc Ricketts made its one-thousandth dive at Sur Ridge in the Monterey Bay National Marine Sanctuary, twenty-three miles off the California coast, where it monitored deep-sea corals nearly 1,300 meters below the water's surface.

Just south of Cannery Row, on a spit of land near the Monterey–Pacific Grove city line, sits Stanford University's Hopkins Marine Station, where John Steinbeck and his sister Mary took a summer biology course. There the work and memory of Ed Ricketts are preserved, a tribute to the remarkable man who played a central role in the development of intertidal ecology on the Pacific Coast of North America. And rightly so, as scientists at the Hopkins Marine Station helped shape Ricketts's career, as both a collector and a pioneering ecologist of the intertidal zone. During a recent conversation in Sitka, with Ricketts's daughter Nancy, an interviewer remarked that she, Nancy, had a very famous father. After a lengthy pause, Nancy responded: "Yes, he is now. . . . But he wasn't, or he didn't feel like he was at the time."[10]

Within the international scientific community are professional men and women who discovered their passion and their vocation while reading *Between Pacific Tides*. Among them are Steve Webster, Chuck Baxter, and Robin and Nancy Burnett, all of whom helped establish the Monterey Bay Aquarium, where exhibits showcase the habitats of Monterey Bay and its splash zones, mudflats, sandy beaches, wharf pilings, and rocky shores. There is John Chapman, a member of the faculty of fisheries and wildlife at Oregon State University. Chapman teaches courses in invasion ecology at the university's Marine Science Center in Newport, and his introduction to marine science came from encountering *Between Pacific Tides* in high school. He stops short of saying that the book alone was the stimulus to a career in marine ecology, but surely it had an impact on the impressionable high school student. "I've been an admirer of Ricketts for a long time," said John Pearse, professor of ecology and evolutionary biology at the University of California, Santa Cruz. "Ed Ricketts was way ahead of people," he added. "It wasn't until the 1980s that scientists began to look at the intertidal the way Ricketts did."[11]

The best-known works to date about Ricketts, however, focus less on Ed's contribution to science and more on his passion for and writing about music, literature, and philosophy. Ricketts was not a great stylist—his prose is often tortured—and his essays on philosophy and poetry, particularly his lengthy piece on non-teleological thinking that, with Steinbeck's blessing, appears verbatim in their jointly authored *Sea of Cortez*, are dense and difficult to follow. But for those who take the time to study his essays, notebooks, and occasional pieces, the reward is a renewed appreciation of the range and depth of Ricketts's thinking about so many subjects: history, mythology, psychology, philosophy, art, music, and literature.

In a 1941 notebook he kept at his lab, Ricketts ranked dozens of writers, from famous figures like D. H. Lawrence and Virginia Woolf to less-familiar names like Louis Bromfield and Vardis Fisher. Ed's list is extensive; he knew the work of the famous and the not so famous. Always, though, there was particular praise for James Joyce, whom Ed wrote was a writer of true genius.[12] Katharine A. Rodger (*Renaissance Man of Cannery Row & Breaking Through: Essays, Journals, and Travelogues of Edward F. Ricketts*), Eric Enno Tamm (*Beyond the Outer Shores*), Michael Hanson (*The Philosophers of Monterey*), Michael Lannoo (*Leopold's Shack and Ricketts's Lab*), and others have surely increased our appreciation of the breadth and depth of Ricketts's thinking. But a fuller recognition of Ricketts's contribution to science has awaited this more systematic treatment of the writing and publishing history of *Between Pacific Tides*.

Beyond the community of scholars and scientists who hold Ricketts in high esteem is a growing entourage of fans and followers who call themselves "Ed Heads," as if Ricketts (or the idea of Ricketts) has been a sustaining inspiration and source of wisdom for their lives. Many of these enthusiasts can be found on Cannery Row, but they can also be encountered at outposts as remote as the west coast of Vancouver Island, where Ricketts and his longtime girlfriend Toni Jackson spent summers collecting marine specimens in 1945 and 1946. There, as on Cannery Row, Ricketts's name is spoken with reverence by devotees. We encountered one such Ed Head in the summer of 2019, on the Vancouver Island village of Ucluelet. Bill Morrison, a central player in the founding of a small nonprofit catch-and-release aquarium that, Ricketts-like, is organized by habitat, is a charming, middle-aged man whose day job is teaching First Nations peoples at a local community college. He smiles when Ricketts's name comes up, as if he were recalling a conversation with a man he could never have met. Many Ed Heads have trouble distinguishing the man from the myth: the mythic dimension obscures their understanding of the principal author of *Between Pacific Tides*.

Also contributing to the rebirth of interest in Ricketts is a renewed focus on the 1940 expedition he and Steinbeck took to Baja, California, and on the resulting book, *Sea of Cortez: A Leisurely Journal of Travel and Research*, which distills the central focus of Ricketts's worldview. Scientists and scholars have retraced the route of the original *Western Flyer*, the commercial fishing vessel that Steinbeck rented (with crew) for the expedition. Missing for many years, it resurfaced in Port Townsend, Washington, a submerged and stripped-down shell in need of total repair. The discovery became a cause célèbre for a cadre of Ricketts-Steinbeck enthusiasts led by John Gregg, a marine geologist and entrepreneur who is spending millions of dollars to restore and equip the boat before returning it to Monterey for use as a floating classroom and laboratory. *Sea of Cortez* remains a seminal source in other ways, too, telling us a great deal about the marine life of the Gulf of California and, in the narrative portion of the book, providing a lively mix of science and philosophy laced with social observation, cultural commentary, and earthy humor not found in most scientific travel writing. The written record of a unique collaboration and meeting of minds, *Sea of Cortez* reiterates ideas already expressed, less elegantly perhaps, in *Between Pacific Tides*. Many of the philosophical musings depicted aboard the *Western Flyer* in *Sea of Cortez* are refined versions of the conversations between Ricketts, Joseph Campbell, and Jack and Sasha Calvin during their ten-week expedition to British Columbia and Southeast Alaska on Calvin's boat, the *Grampus*, nearly a decade before the publication of *Sea of Cortez*.

Some Ed Heads and other disciples remain convinced that Ricketts's insights and illuminations resulted from a series of eureka moments, as if Newton's apple struck Ed on the head repeatedly, over time, in a sequence of sharp epiphanies. They point to his essay "The Philosophy of Breaking Through," wherein he writes that "there can be rare moments when one achieves things which are not transient by means of things which are"; "such a thing," he continues, "objectively seems to exist, even collectively, and it characterizes, is influenced by, and influences or at least indexes a trend reflected philosophically in holism, that the whole is more than the sum of its parts; that the integration or relation of the parts is other than the separate sum of the parts."[13]

The fact, however, is that scientific discovery develops incrementally, building on the observations and ideas of many yesterdays. With Ricketts, the building process started at a young age, before he even finished high school. Ricketts and Calvin's method of organizing *Between Pacific Tides* on the basis of habitats rather than taxonomies was unconventional. But Ricketts's insights into the interaction between the habits and habitats of marine animals owed much to a lifetime of reading natural history. He knew Thoreau and Muir. He read Agassiz and Austin. He reveled in conversation with fellow scientists and with nonscientist friends like Calvin. John Steinbeck was neither the first nor the last to benefit from lengthy conversations with Ed Ricketts.

Steinbeck understands the force and impact of Ricketts's person and his thinking when he writes, "Everyone near him was influenced by him, deeply and permanently."[14] Ed influenced a tremendous number of science popularizers and credentialed marine scientists who were never "near him." That influence extends beyond the First Nations teacher we found in Ucluelet to a popular instructor of natural history at the University of Arizona; to highly respected marine ecologists from Woods Hole, Harvard, and the Scripps Institution; and to Bill Clinton and Al Gore. That's right—the former president and vice president of the United States.

BEGINNINGS

Born on the west side of Chicago in 1897, Ed was one of three children of Charles Abbott and Alice Flanders Ricketts (there was a brother, Thayer, and a sister, Frances). His childhood and adolescence were unremarkable, though there were early signs of aptitude. As Katharine Rodger notes, Ricketts's interest in the natural world started when his family spent a year in Mitchell, South Dakota, before returning to Illinois. Frances recalled that he was "interested in zoology from birth"; in a letter discovered by Joel Hedgpeth, Ricketts wrote, "At the age of six, I was ruined for any ordinary activities when an uncle who should have known better gave me some natural history curios and an old zoology textbook."[5] That uncle was Robb "Roy" Ricketts, a prominent art dealer and a longtime member of the Union League Club of Chicago.

As head of the Chicago firm of Moulton and Ricketts, Roy Ricketts operated art galleries in Chicago, Milwaukee, and New York, exhibiting and selling paintings by some of the most renowned European and American artists of the late nineteenth and early twentieth centuries. Roy Ricketts employed Ed's father in his Chicago gallery for a time, and Ed spent time with his father exploring the world of fine art. Roy specialized in showing and selling the work of the Tonalists, a school of landscape painters who used color tones, shading, and light to create atmosphere. Chief among them was George Inness, the prominent landscape painter of his time, whose work, in his own words, should show the "reality of the unseen." Young Ed was struck by Inness's paintings since, as he could read in a Moulton and Ricketts catalog, "there is no Art in the world that better expresses the sentiment of landscape in all its moods; who perceive that the exact painting of individual objects is of less importance than the massing together of larger parts; that the light that develops all things, that the atmosphere that permeates them, and the trembling vibration which suggest life is the reality of landscape; that George Inness, A. H. Wyant and Ralph Blakelock were the men who best appreciated these great truths and the greatest exponents of them."[6]

Robb Roy Ricketts. Photograph courtesy of Chicago History Museum, DN-0062323, Chicago Daily News Collection.

In that same catalog, the North Carolina artist and art critic Elliott Daingerfield describes George Inness as "your true 'Impressionist.' While taking all sorts of liberties with the Nature he saw and painted so superbly, he could only express himself well when he had actually seen it. He had to have the inspiration of a true impulse, an actual impression in order to start the workings of his imagination. . . . As we study Inness's exquisite paintings, nothing is more evident than their truth to Nature. . . . His pictures were enveloped in poetry as the hills are in glorious mystery."[7]

The influence of this impressionistic style of American nature painting would be visible, years later, in Ricketts's perception and understanding of nature. But he was struck by it early, and it sparked his curiosity about a wide range of other subjects. Once lackadaisical about schoolwork, he became academically precocious. At Chicago's John Marshall High School he was named one of the notable alumni of the class of 1914, along with the future Admiral Hyman Rickover, father of the nuclear navy, and the troubled high school basketball player Arthur Agee, best known as a character in the award-winning basketball documentary *Hoop Dreams*.[18] As Katharine Rodger tells us, he enjoyed studying the sciences and the humanities, reading widely in both and, as noted by Steinbeck's biographer Jackson Benson, finding connections within and across discipline boundaries that made his later approach to his chosen field of biology "as much philosophical as it was scientific."[19] Benson and Rodger are necessarily vague on this point, since there is no life of Ricketts comparable to Benson's life of Steinbeck, and some of the conclusions they draw about the young Ed Ricketts remain a matter of conjecture. But one book Ed was known to have read and found impressive as a high school student was William Temple Hornaday's *Campfires on Desert and Lava*. Published in 1908, Hornaday's book fueled Ricketts's interest in nature and wilderness and complemented his appreciation of George Inness's landscapes.

William Hornaday was a zoologist, conservationist, taxidermist, author, and the first director of the New York Zoological Park, known today as the Bronx Zoo. He had a particular interest in preserving endangered species, and he wrote several books about the environmental and human threats to certain animal species. A pioneer in the wildlife conservation movement in the United States, Hornaday published a comprehensive study of the subject, *Our Vanishing Wildlife*, in 1913, followed a year later by *Wild Life Conservation in Theory and Practice*. Whether or not Ricketts was familiar with all of Hornaday's conservation writings, he cared enough about *Campfires on Desert and Lava* to write eleven lines of notes on the pastedown of his personal copy.

Campfires is the story of Hornaday's expedition with a group of friends to what he calls "a genuine terra incognita"—the Pinacate region of northwest Mexico, which, though it may have been known to the Tohono O'Oodham people and "half a dozen" Mexicans, is to "the reading and thinking world . . . totally unknown; and the more we gathered maps and inquired about it, the less we knew. On all available maps the space around the Pinacate dot was a blank."[20] Hornaday had a multifaceted interest in the Pinacate. Noting that "the animal and plant life of the Pinacate region was as much unknown as its geography," he says that its exploration calls for a "combination

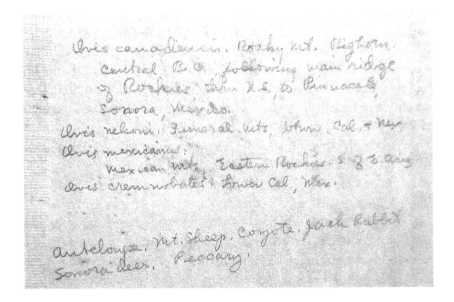

Eleven lines of notes scribbled by E. F. Ricketts in his copy of William Temple Hornaday's *Campfires on Desert and Lava*. Photograph courtesy of John Gregg.

of botanist, zoologist, sportsman and geographer," [21] the four fields of activity of Hornaday's friends who accompanied him on the expedition. Hornaday's account of the trip unfolds as he moves through the American Southwest, from El Paso to Tucson, then south across the US-Mexico border to the Pinacate.

Hornaday's expression of wonder at the Mexican wilderness enhances his travel narrative, which, in an intriguing way, anticipates Steinbeck and Ricketts's expedition to the Gulf of California. Once Hornaday and his companions reached the mystical peaks of the Pinacate, they had an unobstructed view of that same body of water. Unlike Steinbeck and Ricketts, however, Hornaday had little interest in exploring it, noting that "the shore of the Gulf at this particular point has few zoological attractions" and telling his friends that, "if I may be excused, I think I will watch the rest of you make the journey while I hunt mountain sheep." Hornaday writes that only one member of the party, a Mr. Sykes, the group geographer, traveled from the Pinacate down to the Gulf, where he "collected at tide-water, and brought back to me the following shells: *Murex, Arca pacifica, Pectunculus gigantea, Cardium procerum,* and *Ostrea lurida*." [22]

Of his Pinacate adventure Hornaday concludes, "All's well that ends well; and may the Reader someday make the journey himself."[23] Ed Ricketts would take this advice, with a solo tour of his own in the American Southwest in 1916, a decade of annual collecting trips to and near Ensenada beginning in 1925, and, later, with John Steinbeck on the 1940 expedition to the Gulf of California that produced *Sea of Cortez*.

Ed's reading of Hornaday's *Campfires*, while still in high school, likely sparked his interest in a multidisciplinary exploration of science and his fascination with the previously unknown. His eleven lines of notes penciled in Hornaday's book list various subspecies of bighorn sheep that Hornaday describes in the Pinacate. Note-taking became Ed's habit. For the rest of his life, he penciled notes in his books, on reprints, on cards, and on other writing surfaces. And later, Ed's note-taking became part of his approach to observing and collecting animals. He consistently made lists of what he saw, and those lists, along with information he wrote on note cards and in notebooks, help organize the narrative structure of *Between Pacific Tides*.

After graduating from high school, Ed enrolled at Illinois State Normal University, 130 miles southwest of Chicago, where he had little interest in his classes and was a rather mediocre student. After a year at Normal, he dropped out, traveling alone to the American Southwest, vagabonding through parts of New Mexico and Texas. His adventure was quite possibly inspired by *Campfires* and William Hornaday's trip to Pinacate. Ricketts stayed in El Paso for upward of a year, working as a bookkeeper at that city's country club. In June of 1918, he was sent on another adventure that was not his choice and about which he had little interest.[24] He was drafted into the US Army Medical Corps for a tour of duty that ended in March 1919. He hated the military bureaucracy, but, curiously enough, according to Steinbeck, "In appearance and temperament Ed was a remarkably unmilitary man, but . . . was a successful soldier."[25]

Seeking a more expansive educational environment than he had found at a normal college, in the summer of 1919 Ed enrolled at the University of Chicago, in that city's Hyde Park, where, for more than two decades, faculty from the departments of geology, biology, and geography had been developing the concept of ecology as a focus for science education and research. In 1892, Thomas Chamberlin, a geologist with an early and abiding concern about climate change, left the presidency of the University of Wisconsin to head the University of Chicago's geology department. He was followed by a former student named Rollin Salisbury, who went on to create the first PhD-granting department of geography in the country at the school. Together Chamberlin and Salisbury worked with other faculty members who were thinking along similar ecological lines, especially Henry Chandler Cowles, a botanist whose principal interest was "the relationship between [the] physical environment and the environed organism."[26]

Prior to World War I and Ricketts's arrival on the scene, the Chicago group had not viewed the relationship between the organism and its environment as mutually interactive. For them, as historian Gregg Mitman notes, "the physical environment was the driving force behind organic change,"[27] and their understanding of how changes in the physical landscape shape the development of organic life constituted a version of environmental determinism that can be traced back to Darwin. Chamberlin and Salisbury believed that the physical environment changed because of climatic fluctuation and the effects of geographical isolation. Confronted with these changes, organisms had to adapt or face extinction. It was only later that this deterministic view of relationships was revised by Charles Otis Whitman, head of the University of Chicago's zoology department, who recognized and understood behavior as an interactive and adaptive response that aided organisms along their evolutionary path.

Such a worldview, in which the task of the ecologist is to discover the laws governing developmental change, demanded a field-based approach to science teaching and research. It became the focus of life scientists at the University of Chicago, who spent summers doing field study, and it informed science teaching at John Dewey's Laboratory School, which gained a reputation as one of the best private schools in the country. In fact, Dewey took Whitman's ideas to the next level by extending findings in animal behavior to human behavior, focusing on how humans and other organisms develop because of changes in their environment, and how their responses, in turn, affect that environment. This synergistic approach was embraced by Victor Shelford, the University of Chicago zoologist who took Dewey's notion even further by working to preserve important ecological communities as

a means of enhancing nature conservation. Shelford, who became
the first president of the Ecological Society of America, was a gifted
teacher, with a talented graduate student named Warder Clyde Allee
whose ideas would, in turn, influence the young Ed Ricketts.

By the time Ed arrived at the University of Chicago and registered
for classes in the summer of 1919, no serious student of science at
the university could have escaped what had become the faculty's
sociological orientation to ecological investigation. After commut-
ing to school during the fall quarter, Ricketts joined two other
students, James Nelson Gowanloch and Albert Edward Galigher,
in the spring of 1920 in an apartment they shared on Chicago's
South Side that they called "the Boar's Nest." Then suddenly, a few
months later, Ricketts left the university on a walking trip through
the American South. He kept a record of his progress of his walk,
first through southern Indiana, then south through Kentucky,
North Carolina, and Georgia, which he distilled into an essay,
"Vagabonding through Dixie," that appeared in the June 1925 issue
of *Travel* magazine. Ricketts's trip may well have been inspired in
part by John Muir's *A Thousand-Mile Walk to the Gulf* (1916), which
he came across while lounging in the Savannah city library. Muir's
volume is an intellectual coming of age, laced through with a rhap-
sodic youthfulness much like Ed's piece in *Travel*. Whatever the
inspiration, "Vagabonding through Dixie" is essential reading for
an understanding of Ricketts's person and his intellectual development in the years before his arrival in California.

In "Vagabonding," Ricketts's descriptions of the Georgia and
Carolina landscapes are highly impressionistic, a way of seeing nature
that would continue throughout his entire life: "The whole landscape
melts into a bluish-brown haze, very restful, but at the same time
a little discouraging to one who would gain an idea of the country. The mountains themselves bear a varied and luxuriant flora: oak,
hemlock, pine and laurel, with underbrush of several types. Even
the rocks are covered with mosses and ferns. Distant mountains are
black with timber and stand out sharply against the sky. Down in
the valley, hemlock and pine contrast with the brown, earthy tones
of winter oaks and tilled soil."[28] And then, about three-quarters of
the way through his essay, Ricketts writes, "Near Millen [a small
town in rural Georgia], I camped in a clump of pines that continually

reminded me of George Inness's 'Path Through Florida Pines.'"[29] This painting is among Inness's lesser-known works but is the first artwork in the 1913 catalog of Moulton and Ricketts.

Combining a sensitivity to the beauty and intrigue of nature with knowing references to the landscape painting of Inness, Ed's essay forecasts the combination of science, art, and philosophical inquiry that came to characterize so much of his thinking and writing. Hiking through the Great Smoky Mountains of North Carolina, he climbs an outcropping called Doggett Gap, where

> there is as fine a lookout as I have ever seen. . . . Mountains, mountains everywhere, stretching for miles around; the whole surface of the earth crumpled and tumbled, as far as eye can reach. Take fifty mighty mountains, a hundred ridges clothed in oak and laurel and pine, narrow canons and icy mountain streams, cliffs and crags and towering peaks, veil it all in a thin purple haze, and you have the Smokies, the mightiest range in all eastern United States. These Carolina mountains are no playthings; they approach very nearly the great, age-wrinkled ranges of New Mexico, Arizona or Northern Mexico. There is the same deep-blue sky, the same blue haze cloaking distant ranges, the same sawtooth skyline, all in the blazing glory of a noonday sun.[30]

"Vagabonding through Dixie" is the record of a careful observer who sees clearly and feels deeply; these habits of observation and note-taking would serve Ricketts in his future work in California, and in his friendship with John Steinbeck, who shared Ricketts's appreciation of nature as holistic, poetic, and mystical. Returning to Hyde Park in 1921, Ricketts landed back at the Boar's Nest, enrolling in classes in science, philosophy, and Spanish and resuming his friendship with Gowanloch and Galigher, whose influence on his future life merit further attention.

J. Nelson Gowanloch was a gifted scientist who taught at four different colleges around the United States and in Canada, where he conducted successful research programs in botany and zoology.[31] Two years older than Ricketts, he had already completed his undergraduate degree at a Canadian college before beginning advanced study

Frank R. Lillie and James Nelson Gowanloch, 1920. Photograph by Walter K. Fisher. Photograph courtesy of Harold A. Miller Library, Hopkins Marine Station, Stanford University Libraries.

at the University of Chicago. As a graduate student, he spent time in the company of such distinguished scientists as his adviser, Frank R. Lillie, and in January 1920, he traveled to Pacific Grove with Lillie, where the two men spent three months conducting research. Details of his visit are recorded in the *Annual Report of the President of Stanford University* for 1920: "From January 7 to March 10, Dr. Frank R. Lillie, Professor of Zoology, University of Chicago, and Director of the Marine Biological Laboratory, Woods Hole, worked on problems of fertilization using the two species of common sea urchins. Dr. Lillie was assisted by Mr. J. Nelson Gowanlock [*sic*], University of Manitoba, an assistant in Zoology, University of Chicago."[32]

After finishing his PhD at Chicago, Gowanloch taught biology at Wabash College near Indianapolis before moving on to Dalhousie University in Nova Scotia, where he taught until 1930. He was a lively lecturer and a ready raconteur who loved a good time. One morning after a dance, when he did not arrive for his class, some students went over to his house on Le Marchant Street where they found him asleep in full evening clothes. Awakened, he came to class and gave the lecture as he was.[33] His work was eclectic; in 1928 he broadcast a series of fascinating lectures on biology over Halifax radio. At about the same time he published an essay in the *Dalhousie Gazette*, "The Unicorn, and the Childhood of Biology," an intriguing blend of myth, history, and science. Gowanloch mixed well with students, too well in the case of one co-ed. His wife filed for divorce, and Gowanloch left for New Orleans, where he served as chief biologist of the Louisiana Department of Wildlife and Fisheries, a position he held for the rest of his life. The bulletin that Gowanloch wrote, *Fishes and Fishing in Louisiana*, was recognized for excellence by the American Association for the Advancement of Science.[34] In it, as in almost everything he wrote, Gowanloch was a scientific popularizer who managed to render technical language into everyday English, comprehensible to the layman lacking special training or knowledge.[35] He and Ed did not live together for very long, but it certainly seems likely that Gowanloch exerted a formative influence on the younger Ricketts. In addition to his knowledge of Monterey Bay and his interest in making science accessible to laymen, a review of Gowanloch's scientific publications suggests that he had taken the animal ecology course from W. C. Allee that would later make such a profound impression on Ed.[36]

Ricketts met Albert Galigher when Galigher arrived at the University of Chicago to pursue a master's degree in zoology. The third member of the Boar's Nest circle, Galigher worked with the invertebrate zoologist Libbie Hyman, with whom he coauthored his first published paper. Hyman was another Chicago scientist who spent time at the Hopkins Marine Station. Galigher attended Hyde Park High School and the Lewis Institute, graduating with a Bachelor of Science. He enrolled at the University of Chicago in 1919 and roomed with Ricketts and Gowanloch until he met and married Doris June Kingsley. In the summer of 1922, Galigher set off with Doris and his mother on the "Lincoln Highway," 3,400 miles of two-lane, gravel-topped roadbed running from New York City's Times Square to San Francisco's Lincoln Park.[37] By early 1923 the trio had settled into the small coastal community of Pacific Grove. Soon thereafter, Ricketts contacted Galigher and began making plans to join them.

Galigher may have discussed his plans to start a biological supply company with his roommates before leaving for California. Joel Hedgpeth and others have speculated that the idea for Pacific Biological Laboratories was suggested to Galigher in Chicago by Libbie Hyman. There is also the possibility that the suggestion came from Gowanloch's mentor, Frank R. Lillie, who, in 1918, along with his brother-in-law Charles Crane, had purchased controlling interest in a Chicago biological supply company. According to a company statement in 1919, "The Chicago Biological Supply Company incorporated in the name of The General Biological Supply House, with Dr. Morris Wells as President and Dr. Frank R Lillie head of the Zoology Department of the University of Chicago and director of the Marine Biological Laboratory of Woods Hole Massachusetts, acting as Vice-President, so as to represent the interests of the Marine Biological Laboratory in the new firm."[38]

It is likely that Galigher knew about Lillie's interest in the biological supply business. Although it's not clear that he went west specifically to open a similar business of his own, it most certainly provided him with an attractive option. Mary Galigher Groesbeck, Galigher's daughter, suggests that her father hoped but failed to get a job at the Hopkins Marine Station and that his decision to open a biological supply house was his fail-safe.[39]

While the Galighers were getting established in Pacific Grove, Ricketts continued on at the University of Chicago, but with both of his roommates gone, he grew impatient with the undergraduate curriculum. The one course about which he was not critical was W. C. Allee's Animal Ecology.[40] The work Allee was doing on animal aggregations appealed to Ricketts's emerging ideas about the environment, so much so that after moving to California, he employed Allee's thinking about how animals aggregate as he studied the marine life of the central Pacific Coast. Allee's influence on Ricketts and, through Ricketts, on Steinbeck and other members of Ed's circle, deserves more than brief mention.

THE MENTOR

After completing his doctorate at the University of Chicago in 1912, Warder Clyde Allee taught and carried out research at several schools.

Warder C. Allee. Photograph courtesy of University of Chicago Photographic Archive, apf1-00296, Special Collections Research Center, University of Chicago Library.

He regularly spent his summers at Woods Hole, where he taught classes in invertebrate zoology that included a substantial fieldwork component. For nine consecutive summers, from 1913 through 1921, Allee and his students conducted systematic surveys of the nearby littoral, dividing the sites they studied into four major habitats: rocks and rockweeds, flats, wharf pilings, and the deepwater sea bottom.

They recorded data about the invertebrate species they found according to the habitat from which the animals were collected (mud, sand,
gravel, eelgrass, rocks and rockweed, pilings, dredging, and plankton), surveys that allowed Allee to investigate the primary physical
factors controlling animal distribution, along with species associations, within and among habitats. In 1934, Allee made the observation that "in the waters about Woods Hole, where Verrill worked [A.
E. Verrill, a marine zoologist, authored an important study of the
animals in Vineyard Sound near Woods Hole, 1874] and where my
own marine experience was largely gained (Allee, 1919, 1923, 1923a,
1923b), the physical factors of the habitat appear to be the obvious and
controlling agents in delimiting ecological communities. Tidal zones
are relatively narrow, especially so in Vineyard Sound, and the
inshore communities are much subdivided by physiographic forces."[41]
Allee's unusual practice of repeating surveys of the same littoral over
successive years, though pioneering, would not become standard
practice for scientists conducting intertidal ecological research in the
United States until the late 1960s.[42]

In 1921, Allee returned to the University of Chicago as a faculty
member, establishing the field that would become, under his leadership and that of his colleagues, Robert Park and Alfred Emerson,
the "Chicago school of ecology." In his first year at Chicago, Allee
submitted his findings from his surveys at Woods Hole for publication in the *Biological Bulletin,* and there is a strong likelihood that he
talked about his work in classes attended by Gowanloch, Galigher,
and Ricketts. Years later, Allee remembered Ed, remarking, "I first
met him [Ricketts] on becoming a staff member at the University of
Chicago in 1921. He was a member of a small group of 'Ishmaelites'
who tended sometimes to be disturbing, but were always stimulating."[43] In that same communication, Allee said that he was "pleased
that Mr. Ricketts lived up to the promise he showed in those years of
having great ability. . . . I know Edward F. Ricketts and Jack Calvin's
Between Pacific Tides and respect it."[44]

When Allee came to the University of Chicago, he was already
interested in the animal associations that eventually led to the pathbreaking studies of animal ecology that he published in his 1931 book
Animal Aggregations, wherein he argues that all animals, humans
included, cooperate in nature, instinctually aggregating into what

amounts to a communal life. By documenting patterns of aggregation in "organisms whose interrelations have not reached the level of development usually called 'social,'"[45] Allee was developing a form of population biology that has more to do with the interactions among animals than it does with the relationships between them and their environments.

The field of ecology is distinctive in the way it bridges the professional lives of scientists with the broader social worlds in which they live and work. A Quaker and a pacifist, Allee rejected the quasi-Darwinian rhetoric used in the buildup to and justification for World War I, embracing instead a model of animal behavior based on cooperation rather than competition. His study of the social behavior of animals provided him with a window to ethical problems in human society. His theories, which proved to have staying power, were incorporated by those who followed him at Chicago. So, for example, Eugene Odum, one of the leaders of the "Chicago school" after World War II, championed the ideas about group selection, cooperation, and aggregation theory developed by Allee. Odum's 1953 book, *Fundamentals of Ecology*, exemplifies the legacy of Allee's thinking on the development of ecosystem ecology as a field of academic study.[46] In fact, Allee was so influential in the development of ecology research and education that the University of Chicago named a building in his honor. The W. C. Allee Laboratory of Animal Behavior on South Fifty-Seventh Street remains today a major research facility for biopsychology.

In *Between Pacific Tides*, Ricketts references Allee's study of the Atlantic Ocean ophiuroids known as brittle stars, comparing his teacher's findings with his own research in the tide pools of Monterey Bay.[47] Some years later, in an outline for a guidebook about the marine invertebrates of San Francisco Bay that he and Steinbeck had planned but never written, Ed noted that "most zoological studies have been based on the fundamentally necessary systematic or taxonomic plan. . . . A more recent tendency, not yet widely accessible because so much systematic work has still to be done, interests itself in the relation of given organisms and societies of organisms to other nearby organisms and societies, and in the relations of this complex to the almost equal complexity of the physical environment." "This," concludes Ricketts, "is the method of sociology . . . [and the] physical

architecture of [the planned guidebook] derives thru the latter method."[48] Allee's ideas inform much of the architecture of *Between Pacific
Tides* and, by extension, the etiology of *Sea of Cortez* as well. Put
simply, W. C. Allee "provided a philosophical foundation and a
direction for a man [like Ricketts] given to speculation, analysis, and
synthesis."[49] In the outline for the aforementioned San Francisco Bay
guidebook, Ricketts writes, "The beginning student, the tourist, the
nostalgic layman who respects Novalis['s] dictum [that] 'Philosophy
is properly homesickness, the wish to be everywhere at home,' but
who has no zoological training to facilitate his acquaintanceship with
the seashore, all will find this method more convenient, and certainly
more interesting."[50]

John Steinbeck learned Allee's theories about animal aggregations, about what amounted to a grand unifying theory of sociality,
from Ed Ricketts. He combined them with the somewhat similar ideas of William Emerson Ritter, which he encountered when
he took a biology course at Hopkins during the summer of 1923.
Like Allee, Ritter emphasized a holistic view of ecology, and he
extended his ideas beyond shoreline biology into philosophy and
human social systems. Ritter argued that nature in all its separate parts and in its aggregate is "one gigantic whole," the parts of
which support and nurture one another. Steinbeck applied Allee
and Ritter's views about group behavior in human beings in his
most important fiction. The roots of *The Grapes of Wrath* are best
found in Allee's biological humanism and in Ritter's organicism,
the notion that life is best defined by the interrelationships among
living things.

The intellectual friendship between Ricketts and Steinbeck was
symbiotic. Steinbeck learned about Allee and animal aggregations
from Ricketts, but in the process, he fueled Ed's developing interest
in human behavior as a corollary to and an extension of his work
on marine invertebrates. *In Dubious Battle* and *The Grapes of Wrath*
are underpinned by the novelist's belief that social cooperation and
the phalanx—what in *Grapes* he defined as the "I" to the "we"—are
enabling; that group solidarity is the way his impoverished migrants
can manage "their environments."

For Steinbeck, a straight line led from Ed's tide pools to Tom
Collins's Farm Security Administration camps. He was thinking

about and writing these books during a time when he and Ed were seeing each other almost daily, and it is certainly likely that together they explored connections between human and animal behavior. Ricketts shares his preference for the latter, writing that "a study of animal communities has this advantage: they are merely what they are, for anyone to see who will and can look clearly. . . . Here the struggle is unmasked and the beauty is unmasked." [51] Ed Ricketts believed that "everything is an index of everything else . . . and that to understand nature means to discern the relationship of its constituent parts."[52] This inheritance from Allee, who provided the philosophical basis for a humanistic view of the world that transcends science, becomes for Ed Ricketts an occasion for poetry.

THE WAY WEST

Back in Chicago in the summer of 1922, Ricketts followed Albert Galigher to the altar by a month, marrying Anna "Nan" Barbara Maker, a close friend of Galigher's wife Doris.[53] The Galighers wanted the newlyweds to join them in California right away, but the move was delayed by the birth of Ed Ricketts Jr. in August of 1923. Soon thereafter, Ricketts left Chicago to join Galigher as a partner in Albert's Pacific Biological Laboratories, which was housed in a one-story board-and-batten building at 165 Fountain Avenue in Pacific Grove. Nan and Ed Jr. joined Ed a few weeks later.[54]

For Nan Ricketts, from gritty Pittsburgh, the Monterey Peninsula was an earthly paradise. In her unpublished "Recollections," she writes that "the California Poppies and Blue Lupines covered the ground. The acacia trees were blooming, and the Monarch Butterflies were drinking the nectar. There were oranges and lemons on the trees. It was all so beautiful." [55] For Ed, the attraction was the interesting people in the lively communities along Monterey Bay, and the rich intertidal zones where he could collect all sorts of specimens to sell at Pacific Biological Laboratories. Joel Hedgpeth notes that "when Ed Ricketts came to the Pacific coast in 1923 . . . .there was no guide to the rich fauna and flora of the shores upon which he had to depend for specimens for the supply business."[56] Seizing an

Pacific Biological Laboratories with Ed Ricketts's father's Model A Ford parked outside. Photograph by Fred Strong. State University, Martha Heasley Cox Center for Steinbeck Studies.

opportunity to fill this void, Ricketts traveled up and down the California coast on collecting trips, an activity that occupied him for the rest of his life.

Intertidal zones, where the land meets the sea, house uniquely rich communities of flora and fauna. The nature of those communities depends on their sizes and locations, and what Ed Ricketts found on the Monterey Peninsula was one of the richest and most varied intertidal zones in North America. Its rocky intertidal areas tend to be dominated by several "key" species, which often form distinct vertical bands or zones along the California shoreline. In 1923, the same year Ed and Nan came to California, Walter Fisher, the director of the Hopkins Marine Station in Pacific Grove (who we meet later in this narrative), wrote an interesting commentary about Monterey Bay that appeared in *Science*. In the article, Fisher noted that "visiting biologists at Monterey profess themselves astounded at the wealth of shore life—the multitudes of anemones (of eight or nine species), sea urchins, sea stars, bryozoans, annelids (the largest a yard long and an inch or even more in diameter), flatworms, nemerteans, sipunculids, mollusks, crustacea, compound ascidians. The Asteroid fauna of the west coast of North America is the richest in the world." There are, he continued, "fifty-odd species of Monterey chitons (the largest upward of fifteen inches long) [and] ninety-five species of Monterey hydroids. . . . Need I mention that the climate is never uncomfortably hot, and that irises bloom in the station's grounds at Christmas?" [57]

The first months of business at Pacific Biological Laboratories were a struggle, but Ed and Albert divided their labors and kept it going. Galigher was good at preparing microscope slides, and Ricketts loved collecting and preserving specimens. Ed had worked part time as a clerk and a lab assistant at Anco Biological Supplies in Chicago, a company that sold microscopic slides as well as frogs, white rats, and a number of other "preserved materials for the biological sciences."[58] We suspect that Albert worked there as well, so at least one and perhaps both men had experience working in a biological supply business, even though neither had run one. But their prospects seemed good. There wasn't another biological supply house on the west coast, and Pacific Biological Laboratories would fill a local and a regional need, if only Ed and Albert could manage it effectively.

Ed brought the kind of ecology that he had learned from Allee with him to California, and he took it to the spatially and temporally variable habitats of the intertidal zone. In the sand and mudflats and in the rocky reefs of the Central California coast, he watched as members of marine communities adapted and adjusted to the many and frequent changes caused by the ebb and flow of the tides. Back in the lab, he learned the rudiments of microscopical techniques as he prepared the specimens that Galigher mounted on slides. He and Galigher learned from each other. Albert thoroughly enjoyed going on collecting expeditions with Ricketts. Socially and professionally, they enjoyed each other's company, and their families got along well. As Nan recalled many years later,

> Ed and Albert were friends for a long time before this, and Doris and I were friends for a long time, so we were not strangers to one another, and it was easy to adjust. Each family had a baby, so Doris and I had no trouble working out a plan. One week one of us took complete care of the babies, bathing and feeding and putting them to bed, while the other one took care

of the meals. We both did the dinner dishes and the men built the fire in the fireplace and had their time together, until Doris and I were finished with our work. Then we would all sit and chat or play bridge and enjoy the evening and make plans for the next day.[59]

But bridge and potluck didn't pay the bills, and after a time it became clear that an infusion of cash and marketing know-how were required to keep the business going. The Ricketts family had moved into a small cottage on Cedar Street, across Lighthouse Avenue from the Galigher home, where Ed and Albert spent evenings drinking wine and considering their future. As the months passed and too few orders for slides and specimens came in, both men grew frustrated and discouraged, and sometime in 1924 they dissolved the partnership. Nan Ricketts recalls that "each had the opportunity to buy out the other, on certain conditions. It happened that Ed was the one who was able to raise the money, and Albert and Doris went to Berkeley."[60]

Fortunately for Pacific Biological Laboratories, a distant relative on Ricketts's mother's side named Austin Flanders stepped in to help with an infusion of cash. Flanders was the president of University Apparatus Company in Berkeley, which supplied scientific equipment to schools. Established in 1904, the business was quite successful. According to a local high school principal who knew Flanders and purchased supplies from University Apparatus, by 1910 it was "doing an annual business of many thousand dollars. They [sic] own a factory which is the largest on this coast devoted exclusively to the manufacture of their specialties. Their apparatus is well known on the Pacific Coast and they also make shipments to Eastern cities and to foreign countries."[61] With Austin's financial help, and now free to make operating decisions, Ricketts shifted the business of Pacific Biological Laboratories from developing prepared microscope slides to supplying biological specimens to the high school, university, and natural history museum market already primed by Flanders's University Apparatus Company.[62]

The Flanders connection remained critical to Ricketts's business. Thanks to Austin's financial support, Ricketts was able to organize and streamline his lab's operation. By 1925, he had confidently put his stamp on the lab's marketing material and prepared a catalog listing slides and specimens available for purchase from Pacific Biological Laboratories. Most of the specimens offered were collected locally in the intertidal zone, though several were nearshore pelagic and muddy-bottom creatures caught at depths ranging from 20 to 500 fathoms. Beyond his gatherings from the intertidal region, then, Ricketts collected from inland ponds, streams, and fields. In the introduction to his 1925 catalog he wrote,

> Monterey Bay is the fusion point of faunas from the North and South, and the ranges of a number of characteristic species of both regions overlap in these waters. Here we have the 1000 fathom line swinging close to shore on the open coast, with plenty of shallow water in the bay proper. One can find almost any combination of rocky coast, sand beach, or mud flat within a few miles. Rich pelagic hordes approach the shore and enter Monterey Harbor, where a large fishing fleet finds shelter. A short distance to the north, the still water, estuary conditions of Elkhorn Slough are encountered. The local boat bottom and piling fauna is very rich. Located in such a region, it is rather in the order of things that the Pacific Biological Laboratories should be unsurpassed for western marine specimens.[63]

In her unpublished memoir, Nan expressed gratitude to Flanders for his timely assistance. "We have to thank the late Austin Flanders for showing us much of California," she wrote.

> Shortly after we met him, after the two firms were incorporated, Austin made many trips to Pacific Grove to see us. Austin was a major stockholder and president of University Apparatus Co. He had lived in Berkeley for many years, and knew the state well, and all the interesting places. We took various trips. One of these was to Big Basin in the Santa Cruz mountains, where the giant Redwoods grew. One tree had a hollow large enough for a car to go through. . . . Another one of the trips Austin took us on was to the Pinnacles, close to King City. The Pinnacles were spectacular. There were caves all through the area, and bats by the hundred. I would not-go near them. I had heard

that they got in one's hair. And that they bite. . . . Yosemite was
another of the places he took us to. We rented an outdoor can-
vas covered cabin, with a wood cook stove just outside, where
we cooked most of our meals. Sometimes we would eat our din-
ners at the Inn. We stayed about a week.[64]

Thanks first to the Galighers and then to the Flanderses, Ed and Nan
became Californians.

In Berkeley, Galigher was hired to work in the Department of
Zoology at the University of California, but, lacking an academic
temperament, he soon left the position to start the A. E. Galigher
Inc., Laboratory of Microtechnique in the back bedroom of a rented
house.[65] Like Pacific Biological Laboratories, this was a family affair.
Albert taught his wife and mother how to do lab work, and Mary
Galigher Groesbeck says that the enterprise was profitable throughout the 1930s, filling a stream of orders from academic institutions
only marginally affected by the Great Depression. Besides running
the business, Galigher wrote and published an important text, *The
Essentials of Practical Microtechnique in Animal Biology* (1934), one of
the earliest and most comprehensive sourcebooks for training in
microscopy in the United States. Mary Galigher Groesbeck paints
a happy picture of the period: "After the publication of *Essentials
of Microtechnique* the publisher always wanted him to update it, but
[Father] was too busy making a living, playing the violin, teaching
himself the flute, being President of the Albany Rotary Club, taking
pictures and developing and printing them in his home darkroom.
My dad was kind of a one-man band, did every job needed to keep
the lab going, with the help of my mom, my grandmother and some
part-time grad students."[66]

One of the part-timers was George Payne, a young pre-dental student at UC Berkeley who worked for the Galighers in the early 1950s.
Payne remembered Galigher as a genius, but "also something of a
maverick, having first fled the University of Chicago after a dispute,
and much later, the marine biology lab in Monterey he operated with
Ed Ricketts. . . . He was also a raconteur, philosopher, and concert
violinist, who introduced his young employee to new worlds: music,
radically new ideas, and an array of unusual and fascinating people."
During Payne's three years at the lab, the two men often chatted

late into the night, engaging "in mammoth intellectual bull sessions where we talked about everything under the sun."[67]

Ed and a group of his new friends were having similar conversations in Pacific Grove during the same period, and one can only imagine what might have been if he and Galigher had remained together. Albert Galigher and J. Nelson Gowanloch were intelligent and articulate young men with career interests that paralleled those of Ed Ricketts. They undoubtedly provided much of the impetus that Ricketts needed as he came to California and fashioned his own future.

With Galigher gone, Ricketts needed help if the business had any chance of becoming successful. There was simply too much work involved with collecting all the specimens, preparing them for sale, and marketing the business. To help gather specimens, Ricketts hired William J. Martin, a member of the California Academy of Sciences and a collector for the Steinhart Aquarium in San Francisco. Ricketts and Martin were adventurous; in May 1925, they traveled down to La Jolla and Mission Bay, near San Diego, then on to Tijuana and Todos Santos Bay in Northern Mexico. Nan recalls a trip the two men took to Death Valley in search of frogs, and another collecting expedition closer to home, in Big Sur. "A man named Martin collected frogs for Ed," she recalls.

> He and Ed drove down the coast to Big Sur. At this time the road was still very rough. They parked the car and hiked to a little cabin near the sea. In this remote place lived a very old woman, and her cabin was filled with all sorts of shells and dried starfish. She was friendly and cheerful and contented. Her husband had died and she was living alone. Ed asked her how she got her food. They had lived there many years, her husband had been a fisherman. So he must have had a boat, or worked on one. There was no boat there though. She told Ed and Martin that she lived mostly on the fish and abalone that she caught and had a vegetable garden with lots of flowers. [68]

In addition to his longer trips, Ricketts routinely collected at sites between Pacific Grove and Santa Cruz, thirty-five miles to the north, and in just a few years his collecting had taken him all around

Monterey Bay: Stillwater Cove in Pebble Beach, Pacific Grove, Point Cabrillo, Monterey Harbor and the Monterey wharf pilings, Del Monte Beach, the Whaling Station in Moss Landing, Moss Landing Beach, Elkhorn Slough and Bennett Slough, and the Santa Cruz municipal wharf.[69] Shortly after returning from Mexico with Martin, Ricketts rented space on the wharf to store the specimens he and Martin had collected, along with those provided by the fishermen Ricketts befriended along the northern edge of the bay.[70]

A newspaper article that appeared in the *Santa Cruz News* in 1927 mentions Martin's presence: "Rare Biological Specimens: Prof. William Martin of the Pacific biological laboratories at Monterey, with a branch in Santa Cruz, came over from Monterey yesterday looking over his branch. Professor Martin stated that he would spend a good part of next summer on this side of the bay, pursuing his interesting work of gathering marine specimens for biological research study.[71]

William Martin was immensely helpful to Ricketts, working for Ed several years after Pacific Biological Laboratories had stopped leasing space on the Santa Cruz Wharf in 1928. Ed had an uncommon ability to attract and keep friends, and Martin was certainly among them.

Joel Hedgpeth provides an important reminder of a different set of obstacles Ricketts faced: "On the Monterey coast most invertebrates had yet to be described in monographs, and the only general work, Johnson & Snook's *Seashore Animals of the Pacific Coast*, was not to be available until 1927. . . . He was thus confronted by a new and generally unstudied fauna, and he had to set about learning something about them, which meant careful collecting, labeling, and, if necessary, shipping to the National Museum in Washington for identification and description."[72]

As early as 1925, Ricketts, drawing on his time at the University of Chicago, had become seriously interested in the relationships between the animals he collected and their habitats. He surveyed the rocky coasts, sandy beaches, mudflats, and wharf pilings surrounding Monterey Bay, familiarizing himself with the invertebrates of the nearshore pelagic and benthic communities, and studying those communities individually where he found them.

Ed was a fine collector, an astute observer and a quick learner, but he was not a traditionally educated zoologist, and so he had to depend on more conventionally trained scientists to help him identify unfamiliar species. The most immediate source of help was at the Stanford University's Hopkins Marine Station, a five- or six-minute walk from Ed's lab on Fountain Avenue. By the mid-1920s, the facility hosted an impressive array of residential and visiting faculty, a cohort of talented graduate students, and a director with a diversified skill set that included art along with writing and administration. Both the institution and the director of Stanford's seaside laboratory would be critically important to the writing and publishing history of *Between Pacific Tides*.

western shores

The question is not what you look at, it's what you see. A person has not seen a thing who has not felt it.
— HENRY DAVID THOREAU

THE STATION

Founded in 1892, the Hopkins Marine Station is the oldest marine biological laboratory on the Pacific Coast and the third oldest in the United States. Only the Marine Biological Laboratory (MBL) at Woods Hole in Massachusetts (1888) and the Cold Spring Harbor Laboratory on the north shore of Long Island (1890) have been in operation longer. Founded by Stanford University, Hopkins was also the first marine station to be chartered by, and function within, a single university. Originally named the Hopkins Seaside Laboratory, the facility was first located near Lovers Point Park in Pacific Grove. The laboratory's namesake was Timothy Hopkins, the adopted son of Mrs. Mark Hopkins and the founder of the city of Palo Alto. A prime mover in the making of Stanford University, Hopkins funded the seaside laboratory with a modest gift of one thousand dollars.

The Stanford annual register of 1892 printed an extended announcement of the new station:

> The Hopkins Laboratory of Natural History—A seaside laboratory of natural history has been founded as a branch of the University by the liberality of Mr. Timothy Hopkins, of San Francisco. The laboratory is located on Point Aulon, a headland

projecting into the sea near the town of Pacific Grove, on the Bay of Monterey. It will be provided with aquaria and with all apparatus necessary for carrying on studies in the structure, development, and life history of marine animals and plants, and will be open during the summer vacation of each year to naturalists wishing to carry on original investigations, and to students and teachers who desire to make themselves familiar with methods of study in marine zoology and botany. The work of the laboratory will be under the general direction of Professors Gilbert, Jenkins, and Campbell, the committee of the University Faculty in charge. The general purpose of the laboratory is similar to that of the Marine Zoological Laboratory at Woods Holl [*sic*], Mass., and to the seaside and marine laboratories established by Johns Hopkins University at different places along the Atlantic coast. The Bay of Monterey is peculiarly favorable for investigations of the kind contemplated, being exceedingly rich with life, and the life history of the peculiar animals and plants of the Pacific Coast has for the most part received little study from naturalists.[1]

Lovers Point proved to be a less-than-ideal site for Stanford's station. The position of the plateau provided wonderful views of Monterey Bay, and there was a protected cove with a small sandy beach, allowing for the safe landing of small boats. Unfortunately, the building was too close to the crashing surf; it was severely damaged during a winter storm in 1893. Beyond the threat of storms, Stanford's leadership grew increasingly troubled as Lovers Point became overcrowded by local businesses and amusement facilities that brought tourists onto their property, thereby limiting the usefulness of the site for instructional and research purposes.

In 1918 Stanford moved the Hopkins operation to China Point (sometimes referred to as Mussel Point or Cabrillo Point), the site of an abandoned Chinese fishing village just west of the Pacific Grove–Monterey town line. With additional funds from Timothy Hopkins, Stanford built a three-story reinforced concrete structure on the new site and renamed it the Hopkins Marine Station in honor of its benefactor's ongoing support. The opening coincided with Stanford's 1918 summer quarter, and from the beginning, a remarkable level of

Hopkins Marine Station, 1920. Photograph by Walter K. Fisher. Photograph courtesy of Harold A. Miller Library, Hopkins Marine Station, Stanford University Libraries.

energy and enthusiasm characterized its teaching and research programs. Courses were offered to graduate and undergraduate students (including John Steinbeck, who, as noted earlier, took summer courses in zoology), and access to research facilities was extended to resident faculty and visiting scientists throughout the year. This was significant since, when it opened at China Point, Hopkins was the only marine laboratory operating on a twelve-month calendar.

By the time Ricketts and Galigher arrived in Pacific Grove, Hopkins was attracting a good many visiting oceanographers, fisheries experts, and invertebrate zoologists. Some came for brief stays, giving talks and meeting with resident faculty; others remained for longer periods and conducted important research projects. Unlike MBL, which operated only during the summer months because of the cold New England winters, Hopkins was as busy during the winter months as during the summer. Gradually Ricketts and the Hopkins community got to know one another, and Ed, still something of a novice as a working scientist, grew increasingly comfortable drawing on the expertise of Hopkins' scientists. Many were taxonomic specialists in various fields of invertebrate zoology, and they helped Ricketts identify and classify the marine invertebrates he collected. Once he could confirm the identity of those animals, Ed would return to the same collecting sites at intervals and learn which species spend most of their lives in the intertidal zone and are integral parts of the intertidal ecosystem, which use it only at high tide to extend their subtidal homes, and which employ it as a nursery or spawning ground. Though the primary objective of his collecting expeditions was to secure the animals he could sell to the customers of Pacific Biological Laboratories, Ricketts became increasingly interested in observing the relationships of marine species to one another and to their environments.

Some biologists, the idiosyncratic but accomplished Joel Hedgpeth chief among them, have suggested that Ricketts was rejected by the scientific community at Hopkins because he lacked traditional academic training and was something of a scientific outlier, since his interests were ecological rather than taxonomic. In *The Outer Shores,* Hedgpeth writes, "It was an odd quirk of fate that Ed should establish himself in a community where there was so little intellectual stimulation for a field naturalist, despite the presence of a marine station."[2] Hedgpeth blames what he calls the old guard at Hopkins, "staunch conservatives of another day, whose concerns were for the most part with the identification and cataloguing of species."[3] This seems unfair, or at least exaggerated, since not all the Hopkins faculty were "old guard." Some fit Hedgpeth's bill, such as the rigid embryologist and zoologist Harold Heath. But others, like the electrobiologist and plant physiologist Lawrence Blinks, and the ichthyologist Rolf Bolin, were anything but old-fashioned. A review of Ricketts's correspondence suggests that even during his first years in Pacific Grove, he was working with them and with other Hopkins scientists in cooperative relationships. Hopkins scientists helped Ricketts identity unfamiliar marine invertebrates. Ricketts provided those same scientists with specimens that they could describe taxonomically in their own writings. The central member of the Hopkins group, the man largely responsible for establishing and nurturing the supportive culture of the marine station, was its director, Walter K.

Fisher, who would become a central player in the developing history of *Between Pacific Tides.*

THE DIRECTOR

Walter Fisher was Stanford through and through. From the time he enrolled as an undergraduate in 1897 to the day, nine years later, when he completed his doctorate in invertebrate zoology, Fisher was a fixture on the campus founded in 1891 by Mr. and Mrs. Leland Stanford in memory their son, Leland Jr. While still a graduate student, Fisher was appointed to a faculty position as an assistant instructor; he was promptly promoted to full instructor when he finished his degree. Moving quickly up the academic ladder, he became a full professor of biology in 1925. In 1918, Stanford's president, Ray Lyman Wilbur, appointed Fisher to the post of director and first full-time resident faculty member at Hopkins. For seven years he was the only full-time member of the staff, working on his own with responsibility for every aspect of the station's operation and administration. Gradually, he was able to attract colleagues from Stanford's main campus in Palo Alto as well as visiting scientists from universities in the United States and in other countries.

Walter Fisher was ebullient about the prospects for Hopkins. As he assumed the directorship, he wrote,

> The extraordinarily rich fauna and flora of the Monterey Bay region offer exceptional opportunities to investigator and beginning student alike. There are a surprisingly large number of marine animals and plants readily accessible. The student of land forms will encounter a varied assemblage of species, since there are very few regions of equal extent which offer such a curious combination of widely diverse ecological formations. There are probably a greater number of endemic plants than in any other similar continental region. Investigators in the fields of general experimental work, taxonomy, anatomy and embryology will find a wealth of material to choose from, while those concerned with a study of animals or plants from the special standpoint of their "marineness" will naturally be exceptionally favored.[4]

In 1925, Harold Heath, an expert on chitons, moved his research program from Palo Alto to Pacific Grove. At Hopkins, he taught

Walter K. Fisher. Photograph courtesy of Harold A. Miller Library, Hopkins Marine Station, Stanford University Libraries.

courses in embryology and invertebrate and vertebrate zoology while supervising graduate research in embryology, morphology, and zoology. Tage Skogsberg joined Fisher and Heath in 1926. He developed research programs studying marine ostracods and amphipods, and he served for eight years as supervisor of the Hydrobiological Survey of Monterey Bay.

In 1929, the group was joined by Cornelius Bernardus van Niel, who taught a celebrated course in microbiology that was offered during all but two summer sessions for more than thirty years, attracting hundreds of students, many of whom became prominent in their own right. Two of van Niel's students, Paul Berg and Arthur Kornberg, became Nobel laureates. C. B. van Neil was the first biologist to receive the American National Medal of Science and today is recognized as having introduced the study of general microbiology to the United States; his key discoveries explain the chemistry of photosynthesis. Professor Lawrence Blinks signed on in 1933, with parallel research interests in photosynthesis and electrophysiology. Rolf Bolin followed and taught courses and conducted research in ichthyology and the ecology of marine animals. The teaching and research programs at Hopkins developed incrementally, so that by 1934, Fisher had assembled a world-class residential faculty and an array of distinguished visiting scientists. He continued to develop the education and research programs at Hopkins until his retirement in 1943.

Fisher was truly a multifaceted man. Originally planning a career as a botanist, he shifted gears in the summers of 1902 and 1904 while working as a field naturalist for the US Biological Survey aboard the USS *Albatross* on behalf of the United States Fish Commission. In 1906 he published *Starfishes of the Hawaiian Islands,* an account of the specimens he collected during the 1902 *Albatross* expedition. This led him into the field of invertebrate zoology, with a particular interest in echinoderms.[5] In 1911, as he was working on papers about starfish species from the Philippines to Kamchatka, he wrote *Asteroidea of the North Pacific and Adjacent Waters,* a four-hundred-page monograph published by the United States National Museum, for which he also drew the illustrations. An avid bird-watcher, he was an active member of the American Ornithologists' Union by the time he finished college. He wrote articles about birds from all over the world; many appeared in *The Condor,* the official publication of the American Ornithological Society. Fisher served as editor-in-chief of that journal during its early years and remained an active contributor throughout his career.[6]

Beyond his scientific publications on birds and starfish, Fisher was an accomplished writer on a variety of subjects of interest to non-specialists.[7] He wrote a fascinating piece on the Shantung province of China that appeared in the June 1917 issue of *Scientific Monthly*. Titled "A Pilgrimage to the Home of Confucius," the article concerned the bird life of what he calls the "small but remarkable island" of Laysan, eight hundred miles north-by-northwest of Honolulu.

From adolescence forward, he was interested in painting and sketching, and for a time he considered pursuing art as a career. After committing to the study of marine biology, Fisher combined his skills as an artist and scientist, beautifully illustrating his own books and papers. He drew and he painted, illustrating the book his wife Anne wrote for the Rivers of America series, *The Salinas: Upside Down River*. Anne (and, perhaps, Fisher himself) had been struck by the fact that the river Steinbeck made famous in such novels as *East of Eden* flows north rather than south and goes underground for much of its course, making it one of the largest subsurface flows of any river in America. Fisher was a prominent member of the Carmel Art Association and frequently exhibited his paintings there and elsewhere on the Monterey Peninsula. In a tribute to chemist Edward Burgess, he wrote that his subject "was not only a scientist; he had a wide and eager knowledge of many subjects and an especially deep appreciation of the finer things in the literature and art of many lands. . . . A man of rare charm and unassuming manner, he chose always to elucidate, never to impress; gentle, selfless, kindly, he gave unstintingly of his time and energy to his students and to his chosen field of work."[8] Walter Fisher was writing his own epitaph.

Joel Hedgpeth and others have argued that Fisher criticized the way Ricketts did biology—that Fisher, more than anyone or anything, was responsible for the lengthy delay in the publication of *Between Pacific Tides*. This notion has become so widespread among Ricketts enthusiasts as to require examination. That the two men possessed very different personalities is undeniable. To his students and colleagues, Fisher was the consummate gentleman scientist-teacher. Consider, for example, the experience of Ruth Andresen, a remarkable geologist who, after graduating from college, found herself in the center of the action with the Military Geology Unit of a terrain-intelligence group helping to plan D-Day. Andresen attended Stanford, and in the summer of 1938, she took the summer invertebrate course that Fisher taught at Hopkins. In an interview with the ecologist and evolutionary biologist John Pearse, she recalled that Fisher always taught "in three-piece suits and in shirts with starched collars. . . . With his steel framed eyeglasses on. He did not touch a thing. He had his probe and he would show you where it was in the Petri dish. He had big drawings. He was the most immaculate, pristine looking person and so dignified. We were very much in awe of him. He was all gray, gray hair, gray suits, white shirt. I can still remember him standing there. He looked like something out of a magazine. He was so well groomed."[9]

According to Andresen, Fisher never took his students outside the lab. By contrast, Ricketts was always in the field, touching everything he saw. In 1930, his mentor, W. C. Allee, had written that he was "tired of working with man-made, degree-hunting graduate students in zoology." He insisted that "I want students with a love for field work which even the handicap of living in the city of Chicago cannot quench. . . . I welcome the natural naturalist who cannot be kept out of field work."[10] Ed was such a natural naturalist. But contrary to the commonly held assumption that Ricketts was unkempt, the reality is decidedly otherwise. A handsome man, Ed traveled all the way to San Francisco for haircuts, and when not collecting or preparing specimens, he was quite a stylish dresser. He simply never wore three-piece suits and shirts with starched collars.

To insist that Walter Fisher disdained the study of animals in their natural habitats and that nothing other than taxonomy was important to him is not accurate. In fact, the reverse is true. Walter Fisher was very interested in large, inclusive pictures. In a 1919 edition of the *Stanford Review*, Fisher wrote, "Life began in the sea, and in the sea still is found the greatest variety of animal life. It is everywhere, not alone, along the shores, but far and wide over the surface, in the intermediate depths, and over the bottom to the greatest abysses."[11] As he assumed the directorship of Hopkins, he defined the station's mission and the goal of its research, writing that "it is within the scope of a marine station to find out everything possible about the animals and plants of the ocean, as well as about the physical characteristics of the ocean itself. It is concerned with the life history of animals and plants—whence they come, their behavior and interrelationships, what they eat, what eats them, where they live, what controls their diurnal and seasonal wanderings, when they spawn, and so on." [12]

Fisher continues:

> No animal or plant is independent of other animals or plants. It is the study of such problems of relationship as applied to animals which are either directly or indirectly valuable to man, that makes up the general subject of economic zoology. Although its final object is to ascertain something of benefit to man, yet its beginnings are always in pure science and distant from the goal. Usually the solving of the problem, however simple it may seem, is the result of the effort of many, carried on through a series of years until the story is pieced together bit by bit. It is our hope that each one who works at the station may add his definite contribution to the solution of some one of Nature's riddles. [13]

This is precisely the kind of marine ecology that we find in *Between Pacific Tides*. And it is what John Steinbeck and Ed Ricketts sought in the Gulf of California: "to see everything our eyes could accommodate." [14]

Over time Fisher developed respect, even affection, for Ricketts's person and his unconventional but appealing way of doing science. Consider a recently rediscovered 1964 letter that Steinbeck sent to John Bivins in response to a question he received from Bivins about the authorship of *Sea of Cortez*. Assuring Bivins that the "thinking and observation" in the book was a collaboration between himself and Ricketts (though Steinbeck penned the narrative), Steinbeck informs Bivins that "Dr. Fisher of the Hopkins Marine Station once said that Ed Ricketts and I together were the best single speculative zoologists in the world. . . . And if he couldn't separate us, I would suggest that you do not try." [15]

While Walter Fisher was growing Hopkins, Ricketts was developing Pacific Biological Laboratories. Austin Flanders continued to support PBL financially. He helped Ricketts organize and manage the business so that it could become profitable. He remained involved with the lab for several years; his signature appears in the 1929 PBL

FOREWORD

A revision of the P B L catalog has been in the offing for some time, necessitated by increases in our stock of specimens and by the various slight price adjustments, but most of all by a change in policy best reflected by the new catalog itself.

We have to determine considerable ecological and zoological data for our own purposes. There seemed to be no reason why these facts should not be incorporated into the body of a catalog that would interest the instructor (and his students) quite as much from the scientific standpoint as from the commercial angle.

Thus we have given characterizations, thought to be fairly accurate, of phyla, classes and orders, inter-preted especially in terms of the forms we supply, and accompanied by structural diagrams. In general, the idea has been to have at least one representative of each order. This has not always been found possible; and we have sometimes thought it wise to include several. Among the Dis-cophora (Scyphozoa) for instance, an instructor might devote useless time, in the otherwise excellent Chrysaora, trying to demonstrate the radial canals so obviously apparent in Aurelia. In such cases, both forms have been listed and stocked.

In such a way, a considerable variety of animals has been listed, allocated properly in the phylogen-etic sequence, and roughly sketched. Possibly this list in itself, with the specimens backing it, will have value. Certainly it will if, as we suspect, an increasing number of instructors are coming to believe that a too close application of the principles system of teaching is not without disadvantages, and had best be supplemented by an attempt at acquainting the students with a variety of the animals themselves. This follows if it be granted that one of the cultural aims of biology is to cultivate a feeling of at-homeness with one's environment.

From the practical standpoint, possibly our innovation of free delivery ought to be regarded as most important. Without changing materially any of our prices (many of which are already lower than those of other houses), we are absorbing all container and transportation charges unless otherwise stated. Thus an instructor may figure in advance exactly what each item will cost laid down at the school.

These three phases indicate a plan virtuous at least in its novelty. Certainly an attempt has been made to increase the usefulness of a list to which most instructors must refer at least occasionally. If your careful inspection reveals discrepancies that even the greatest effort sometimes permits, it is hoped that you will value the total contribution as much from the standard of what has previously been done in the way of catalog making, as from the standpoint of what we set out to do. In any thing departing so radically from previous efforts in the field, one could justly expect results open to criticism: constructive comments will be most welcome.

The appended copy has to be regarded as the first section of a catalog to be published in parts: ad-ditional sections, uniform with this, will be issued as completed; we expect eventually to supplement the present illustrations with plates of halftones from photos.

Pacific Grove, California, U. S. A.
September, 1929

A.F.Flanders

President University Apparatus Co., Berkeley
Vice-President Pacific Biological Laboratories,
Pacific Grove

Foreword to Pacific Biological Laboratories 1929 catalog.

catalog. By 1927, Ed's sister, Frances, and his parents, Charles and Alice Ricketts, had moved to California. Frances helped at the lab for a brief time, and Charles became Ed's chief assistant, managing orders and ensuring that specimens were properly packaged and shipped on time. With this newfound help, Ricketts had time to do more than collect, organize, and ship specimens. This is evident in his foreword to the 1929 PBL catalog, in which he says that he changed the format of the catalog to include ecological and zoological data about the animals he had for sale. The additional information would be useful, Ricketts suggests, because it might help teachers "fulfill the cultural aims of biology which is to cultivate a feeling of at-homeness with one's environment."[6] By the time Ed wrote this catalog, he clearly had the outlines of what would become *Between Pacific Tides* in mind.

Several years later, Walter Fisher had health issues that affected his work; he suffered from eye problems as early as the 1930s. According to an April 8, 1933, article in the *Monterey Peninsula Herald*, this was the result of "too close application to his scientific work at Hopkins Marine Station [which] has compelled Dr. W. K. Fisher, Director of the station, to take a prolonged rest at his Carmel Valley home. Dr. Fisher, carrying on special research in growth of corals, has spent long hours at the microscope, resulting in a condition of nervous exhaustion that necessitates complete rest. He cannot receive visitors but hopes, in the near future, to be able to resume his work."[7]

There is no evidence that Ricketts was aware of Fisher's health problems; he regularly wrote to Fisher about his collecting expeditions, and when the first draft of *Between Pacific Tides* was nearing completion, he asked Fisher to write a foreword to the book. Even after learning that Fisher had given a less-than-glowing review of his manuscript to the editors at the Stanford University Press, Ricketts continued to send the Hopkins director friendly letters about the various marine species he collected.

Ricketts loved the natural world and the science that makes that world intelligible. The young man—who a few years earlier had walked through Georgia enchanted with the landscapes before him—was now a working scientist. He had learned that knowledge and understanding rely not just on observation, but also on experimental evidence, rational argument, and even skepticism. Combining his growing knowledge of science with an expanding appreciation for art, music, philosophy, and literature, he turned to the sea as the most accessible means of understanding the natural world. In so doing, he joined a lengthy line of men and women—artists, writers, musicians, and mystics—for whom the seas were a source of inspiration. In particular, his work anticipated that of Rachel Carson who, in *The Edge of the Sea* (1955) wrote that "to understand the shore, it is not enough to catalog its life. . . . Understanding comes only when, standing on a beach, we can sense the long rhythms of earth and sea . . . the surge of life beating always at its shore." In his work, Ricketts combined the drama and wonder of the seashore with factual information about the life he found there. Asked about the poetry in her books about the sea, Carson affirmed that "it is not because I deliberately put it there, but because no one could write truthfully about the sea and leave out the poetry." Ed Ricketts would surely have agreed.

CANNERY ROW

In 1928, the owner of the row of buildings that housed the Pacific Biological Laboratories decided to demolish the existing structures and construct a new and fashionable "business block" for the fifty-year-old town.[18] As a consequence, Ed needed to find a new location for his lab, and he needed to do so quickly. Fortunately, he found a desirable site along Monterey's Ocean View Avenue that had room for his laboratory, a small but serviceable living space, and outdoor holding tanks for the animals he collected. Some years later, after the breakup of his marriage, Ed moved into the building; he lived there for the rest of his life. This was Cannery Row, the street Steinbeck called "a poem, a stink, a grating noise, a quality of light, a tone, a habit, a nostalgia, a dream"[19] and that he made famous in his 1945 novel of the same name. For Ed Ricketts, it was everything that his friend described and more; it was also just around the corner from the Hopkins Marine Station.

When Ricketts opened his lab at 740 Ocean Avenue (when the street was renamed Cannery Row, the address changed from 740 to 800), the surrounding area was inhabited by an eclectic collection of vagabonds, Chinese and Italian fisherman, sardine canneries, small grocery stores, and whorehouses. At first, Ricketts's neighbors did not know what to make of him or Pacific Biological Laboratories. They were curious about the young man who left the lab at dawn most mornings, drove south, past Lovers Point, and returned in the afternoon with bags of marine specimens he collected in the "Great

Tide Pool." In time, as Ed got to know the characters on the Row, he hired some of them to help collect butterflies, frogs, and stray cats. Once they got to know Ed, the locals decided that, although he was eccentric, he was harmless and a very friendly fellow. Nan notes that, as Pacific Biological Laboratories became familiar to Hopkins professors, children, and curious citizens, "it turned out to be more like a museum than a commercial biological supply house."[20] Welcoming scientists and bums alike, Ed assumed the role of intermediary between the Hopkins scientists and the characters of Cannery Row. As his reputation grew, visiting scientists at Hopkins came to meet him. Nan writes about "a professor from a British university, a very formal type, who came to the Lab asking to see Mr. Ricketts if indeed he could spare the time. Ed said, 'I'm Ed Ricketts.' The professor was embarrassed and apologized, saying that he expected a much older man to be Ed Ricketts. To make himself look older Ed at once started to grow a beard."[21]

Shortly after Ricketts moved onto Ocean Avenue, Waldo Schmitt, the distinguished biologist from the Smithsonian Institution, visited him after concluding meetings with scientists at Hopkins. Nan writes that "he took us to lunch and told us many interesting stories about his recent trip to the Galapagos Islands, and he brought back a Gila Monster in his suitcase. How very typical of a biologist."[22] There were visits by Deogracias Villadolid, a Stanford PhD student from the Philippines who was working at Hopkins. Ed and Nan befriended him, and he occasionally came to dinner. "He seemed so lonesome and homesick," Nan recalls. "I don't remember just how long he was in this country, but it seemed a long time."[23] Before leaving to return home, he presented Ed and Nan with a poem by Li Po that he had written out on parchment. This was Ricketts's introduction to the Tang-dynasty poet whose work he came to love. He often read it to friends who gathered at the lab. Some years later, Villadolid became known as "the father of fisheries education" in the Philippines; the former Hopkins student became the first director of the Bureau of Fisheries in that country.

Remembering these and other visitors to Ed's lab, Nan confirms,

> The waterfront laboratory created much interest to all sorts
> of people, unemployed, drifters, winos, and children. Mostly

young boys who wanted to help "Doc" and liked to see the babies in jars—pig, human or shark embryos. And they always had to take a look at the white rats in the cages upstairs. Ed's father was working at the Lab at that time and just loved showing off all the specimens. The boys hoped that the snakes needed to be fed while they were visiting, so they could see the snake swallow one of the rats whole. It was not only the children who liked to see that performance; there were lots of adults too.[24]

One such snake-on-rat encounter, observed by a female visitor who paid for the privilege, is the subject of Steinbeck's short story "The Snake," which provides as accurate a picture of Ed Ricketts as anything Steinbeck ever wrote.

Once settled in his new lab, Ricketts had the time—unless interrupted by visitors like the anonymous woman in Steinbeck's story—to preserve and catalog the marine invertebrates that he and his Cannery Row "employees" had collected. Some of Ed's collecting trips had unintended or unfortunate consequences. Nan recalls one such expedition that Ed and Martin took "to Death Valley to get frogs (a wild goose chase to find frogs in the desert! I guess they just wanted a trip to Death Valley). They were gone for some time, and there was no one to tend the Lab." A group of Ed's local collectors broke in and made themselves at home, drinking denatured alcohol and, in their drunkenness, breaking up some things (that is where Steinbeck got the idea for the party in *Cannery Row*). Returning home, Ed was fuming and forbid them ever to come near the lab. "They stayed away for a while, and then, of course, they came back with frogs and promises to not repeat the incident."[25] In real life as in Steinbeck's fiction, Ed always relented.

One might, and with good reason, question Nan's remark about the Cannery Row characters drinking denatured alcohol. For anyone consuming such a beverage, the consequences are certainly toxic and could well be lethal. But Nan is certain about the matter:

> There were the drifters who came to the Lab, bringing frogs or eels to raise money for their wine and just enough food to keep them alive. But first came the wine. They discovered that Ed was using precious denatured alcohol for animals, and

Gabe and the boys. Photograph courtesy of the California History Room, Monterey Public Library.

kept their eyes open and stole it whenever they had the chance. Ed warned them that they could kill themselves, but Gabe [Gabe Bicknell was the prototype for the character of Mack in Steinbeck's *Cannery Row*] said that they could distill it. Then too, they said they were used to drinking vanilla extracts and cough medicines. I guess they stole those too, for they were not cheap items. [26]

Ed Ricketts enjoyed people, and he particularly relished talking about his work, whether his listeners were the locals along Cannery Row, Hopkins scientists, or passersby who saw him collecting in the tide pools of Monterey and Pacific Grove. Nan notes that, at some point,

He had an idea that he could conduct tours to tide pools for hotel guests [from the nearby upscale Hotel Del Monte] who might be interested in local color or biology or both. We used to see a lot of people gathered around Ed when he was collecting at low tides, asking questions. That is where he got the idea. He would have made an excellent tour guide. He loved telling the people around him about the animals he uncovered and about their habits. Tourists loved coming to the tide pools and sometimes it was not easy to watch them turning over rocks to see the animals underneath and then not turning the rocks back again, leaving the animals exposed before the tide turned to protect them.[27]

Nan often accompanied her husband on his collecting trips around Monterey Bay. It was one activity they enjoyed together, if for somewhat different reasons. She loved everything about the outdoors: the beauty of the tide pools, the annual arrival of migrating monarch butterflies attracted by the area's acacia trees. "They cling to the blossoms as they drink the nectar, and are so easy to pick off," she recalls "especially if the fog comes up very suddenly. Then they get trapped and very few get back to their pine trees where they stay for the season. I have seen them hang onto the trees in long clusters, in strings as long as two feet, like grapes. A beautiful sight to behold. . . . We collected gallon jars full for the Lab."[28] (More about the monarchs later.)

Ricketts collected all sorts of different species of marine animals, some of which, as noted earlier, scientists from Hopkins helped him identify. To keep track of his data about each animal, Ed started a system of organizing the notes he made during his collecting trips. In addition to a series of notebooks, he designed eight-and-a-half-by-eleven-inch sheets of paper with the heading "PBL Collecting Report" and three-by-five-inch index cards that he titled "PBL Collecting Report Card." Ricketts also created "Species Identification Reports," to be completed by the scientists to whom he sent species for identification. Ed diligently recorded reams of information about the species he collected, no small task since he was trying to become familiar with upward of two thousand invertebrates that live along the shores of the central Pacific Coast.

Steinbeck wrote that "Ed loved paper and cards. He never ordered small amounts but huge supplies of it."[29] Reviewing Ricketts's collecting and species identification reports housed in the Special Collections at Stanford University, the reader can quickly determine the individual who identified the species. Almost always, individuals who identified for Ed more than a single species within a particular taxonomic group were specialists in that specific area. Ed's notebooks, cards, and collecting reports also contained information about the bottom type in which he found the animals he collected, as well as the time and intensity of their exposure to wave shock. In fact, Ricketts had become very interested in the effect of wave shock, tidal patterns, and habitat on marine invertebrates. He was as interested in these interlocking environmental factors about life in the tide pools as he was about the animals themselves.

Given the nature of the data about the animals he collected, it's clear that Ed was not only thinking about the kinds of specimens that he could sell to high schools, colleges, and museums, but he was also considering the prospect of compiling a handbook about the marine invertebrates of the central Pacific Coast. It seemed the natural next thing to do. Ed's mailing list was diverse. It included the names and addresses of his current and prospective customers as well as those of the scientists to whom he had sent specimens specific to their research interests and whose help he might secure as he began writing his handbook. Ed's mailing list was also enormous. It spanned the globe, from Argentina to South Africa and throughout the United States and Canada. As examples, his card index contained the names and addresses of more than sixty schools in Massachusetts, and forty-seven high schools and colleges in the city of Chicago.

Activity at Pacific Biological Laboratories increased rapidly, and Ed needed additional assistance for the business to remain successful. Happily, help was readily available. Besides his father, his mother, and his sister Frances, Ed received support from Martin and from John Steinbeck's wife, Carol, who worked in the lab as his assistant. Ed's mother (Alice) and his sister helped at home, where Nan was often overwhelmed caring for her son, Ed Jr., and two daughters, Nancy Jane and Cornelia. All of this assistance enabled Ed to take extended collecting trips to Oregon, Washington, and throughout British Columbia as far north as the Alaskan border. His notes about those trips commingle scientific data with personal and anecdotal reflections. So, for example, in *Between Pacific Tides*, Ed mentions an early trip to Washington: "On one Puget Sound beach, in the summer of 1929, we found a small boy capturing fish for food, using a method that must have seemed, to the fish, to violate Queensbury rules."[30]

During July and August 1930, Ricketts was joined on a collecting expedition by Jack and Sasha Calvin, whom he had recently met and who, after spending time with Ed, grew to share his interest in the seashore.[31] The trio spent six weeks exploring the intertidal zones of Washington State and Vancouver Island. After completing his reports about this trip, Ricketts provided Hopkins director Fisher with a number of sipunculan specimens that he'd collected. Along with the specimens he included a PBL Identification Report (dated July 26, 1930), which provides a glimpse into the range and scope of Ricketts's developing understanding of intertidal ecology. According to this report, Ricketts collected specimens "near [the] mouth of the Pysht River on Washington State's Olympic Peninsula and along the shore of the Straits of San Juan de Fuca." He found tidelands more than half a mile wide, "filled with boulders and rocks on a substratum of muddy gravel, with Fucus, Corralines [Corallines], Marcocystis, Laminaria, and in some places, eel grass."[32] He found the sipunculan "in sandy mud under boulders, different in habitat as well as in appearance from the Monterey Bay Physcasoma ag. [*Phascolosoma agassizii*]. They are larger, stouter, rougher in texture and darker in color," Ed wrote. "The physiology is also a bit different; they 'went under' nicely with only a few hours methanol whereas a long and complicated methanol narcosis is required to get a good percentage of expanded [Pacific Grove] specimens."[33] Ed also noted that "there is little or no wave shock at this point, but currents are strong and tides a bit bigger than at P. G. Wilderness country and no beach pollution from campers and industry other than that incident to floating log rafts."[34] Increasingly, we see Ricketts's developing interest in the interlocking factors of wave shock, degree of tidal exposure, and bottom type that determine the zonation of intertidal life within a specific habitat.

On occasion Nan and the children came along on Ed's excursions to Puget Sound. Nan writes that a trip to Hoodsport, on the Washington coastline, was especially enjoyable: "The first year that we went north to Puget Sound was our most exciting. Ed and I planned for a long time, at night when the children were asleep. For them to know would mean the never ending 'When are we going?' The day school closed for the summer vacation we were packed and ready to go, and then we told the children we were going on a long trip to Puget Sound. Which meant little to them at the time, except that we were going on a trip."[35] Hoodsport was among Ricketts's favorite collecting sites; he frequented the area often over the course of the next decade.

Sometimes Ed had company other than Martin or family members on his collecting expeditions. Among his companions were Hopkins graduate students who shared his interest in the distribution of seashore animals. George MacGinitie was one of those students, a native Nebraskan who had recently completed his bachelor's degree at Fresno State and enrolled in the master's program at Hopkins along with his not-yet wife, Nettie (they met at Hopkins, where Nettie was taking summer classes after finishing her undergraduate degree at Oregon State). Ricketts also became friendly with Swedish zoologist Torsten Gislén and his wife. The MacGinities and Gisléns developed strong personal as well as professional friendships with Ricketts, their conversations fueling Ed's desire to write a comprehensive manual about the habits and habitats of Pacific Coast shore invertebrates.

In 1926, Ricketts and the MacGinities traveled together on trips along the California coast, collecting and identifying species. George MacGinitie worked extensively at Elkhorn Slough near Moss Landing, a biologically rich estuary where, incidentally, Ricketts had been collecting for some time. MacGinitie's study of the Central Coast estuary resulted in his master's thesis, "Ecological Aspects of Elkhorn Slough," which he completed in 1927 and published in the journal *American Midland Naturalist*, in 1935.

Elkhorn Slough is habitat for a wide array of resident and migratory birds, plants, marine mammals, and fish that today are protected by California conservation agencies and by the National Oceanic and Atmospheric Administration. At the time, though, there was a rendering station nearby that served the whale hunters who made a living harvesting the dwindling population of gray whales. Nan recalls, "Ed would go there and climb [over] all of them, scraping barnacles or any other animals that were lodged on the whales, and put them in his Stetson hat which he used to wear at that time. However, he never could wear that one anymore. The whale oil was very strong and impossible to get off your shoes and clothes. But because he was not prepared, he used what he had."[36]

Shortly after completing his master's thesis, MacGinitie was offered a position as an instructor at Hopkins. Two years later he became the assistant to the director and taught introductory and advanced graduate and undergraduate courses. A representative

George MacGinitie. Photograph courtesy of Harold A. Miller Library,
Hopkins Marine Station, Stanford University Libraries.

catalog entry for his class on shore ecology reads, "A course primarily
for biology majors designed to give an understanding of animal communities and the life activities of individual members of these communities in response to certain environmental factors."[37] Whether
cause and effect was at play or not, MacGinitie and Ricketts's scientific perspectives had become very similar.

In 1930, the MacGinities accompanied Ricketts on collecting
trips south to Newport Bay, Corona Del Mar, Balboa, and Laguna
Beach, and then to Tijuana, Ensenada, and Estero de Punta Banda
in Northern Mexico. Besides the opportunity to do good science,
the trips enabled Ed to more than balance the books at Pacific
Biological Laboratories; he gathered large numbers of what he called
his "bread and butter" animals, which included several species of the
genus *Octopus*. In *Between Pacific Tides* he talks about securing a large
quantity of *Octopus bimaculoides* during trips to Mexico: "At various

points between Tijuana and Ensenada we have found octopuses very numerous in April, May, and December, in several different years. In December 1930 they were so abundant that one could count finding a specimen under at least every fourth rock overturned."[38]

In 1933, George MacGinitie, who aspired to an administrative position at a marine station but for whom there were no further opportunities at Hopkins, resigned his position and accepted the directorship of the Kerckhoff Marine Laboratory at the California Institute of Technology. Though he no longer saw the MacGinities regularly, Ricketts visited George and Nettie at their lab in Newport Beach when he traveled south, and he sometimes relied on them for supplies of the locally available *Renilla* (sea pansy), the ubiquitous octopod, or *Velella* (by-the-wind sailor) that he could sell to schools and colleges. For almost a decade Ricketts made annual collecting trips as far south as Boca de la Playa, usually stopping to see the MacGinities on the way. On one such trip in the winter of 1931, Nan and her younger daughter, Cornelia (usually called by her nickname, Rickie), accompanied Ed on a trip to Southern California and Northern Mexico. They were joined by Torsten Gislén and his wife. It was the beginning of a friendship between the two men that continued for the rest of Ricketts's life.

A zoologist at Lund University in Sweden, Torsten Gislén was on his way home from Japan when he arrived on the Monterey Peninsula in 1930. The purpose of his visit was to conduct a study of the ecology and zoogeography of the Central and Southern California coasts, showing that different shorelines affect the productivity of the same species of littoral fauna and flora in different ways in different parts of the world. During the first several weeks of their stay, the Gisléns visited Hopkins, reconnecting with Torsten's former colleague Tage Skogsberg, who was on the station's faculty. They also met other Hopkins scientists, including Fisher and the MacGinities. During his time in Monterey, Gislén spent time with the MacGinities exploring the rocky shoreline of Point Lobos and the mudflats of Morro Bay.[39]

At some point early in his visit he met Ricketts, and the two men discovered their shared interests in intertidal ecology. They became inseparable. Nan writes,

There were some wonderful collecting areas around Laguna Beach, La Jolla, and Newport Beach. . . . They [the Gisléns] were so excited. We were collecting octopi. I kept looking under the rocks and could not find any. The others were collecting dozens. I told Ed that I was not finding any, so he went 'along with me. As I turned over the rocks he would say: "Do you see one now?" I did not. Then he touched it. It slid off the rock into the water and spewed ink in the water to protect itself. They are the color of the rocks and can turn to a dirty gray color. Some were small enough to hold in the palm of one's hand. Dr. Gislén found one that was pure white. I guess these were the ones that were canned. I saw some served at a cocktail party. They were smoked. Most people ate and liked them. But after seeing them alive I could not eat them. Then I did eat a slice of a very large one. I did not know that it was octopus, but it was delicious, different from anything else I had eaten. [40]

Nan continues,

When we crossed the Mexican border, the guards took Dr. Gislén to the office because he was from Sweden. Ed went with him to help (since Ed was well known by the guards, as the funny Californian who carries a lot of empty jars in his car and fills them up with animals). Another guard was inspecting the inside of the car, and Mrs. Gislén and I were in the back. He looked in and asked if we had any fruit or vegetables in the car. Mrs. Gislén said "Yes," and I said "no" at the same time. The poor man was puzzled, and asked again, and I said "no." Mrs. Gislén said nothing. We did have potatoes, onions and carrots. Also canned tomatoes. But we needed those for our chowder. I don't remember just why we were not able to purchase these foods in Ensenada the time we were there before, but I did remember that we did not have it for the chowder then. [41]

Satisfied that they weren't criminals, the Mexican authorities sent them on their way.

Initially trained as a botanist, Gislén had gone on to study frogs, reptiles, and, from there, echinoderms (starfish, sea urchins, and sea cucumbers). Like Ricketts, he wrote vivid personal reflections as well as scientific observations on his many journeys. One of his

Torsten Gislén. Photograph courtesy of Hagblom Photo Collection, Lund University Library.

books, a study of crinoids in Japan, enjoyed a good deal of critical acclaim; a reproduction of that volume remains in print today. Also, like Ricketts, Gislén studied the relationships among marine animals and between animals and their environments.

Armed with the basic tenets of ecological thinking that he had gleaned from W. C. Allee at Chicago and enhanced by his field studies and in discussions with faculty, students, and visiting scientists at the Hopkins Marine Station, Ricketts became very knowledgeable about the relationships between the animals he collected and the habitats in which he found them. Increasingly, he moved toward an understanding of the essential oneness of the natural environment even as he classified his animals into families, genera, and species. As the range of Ed's explorations expanded, south to the western coast of Northern Mexico and north to the inlets, protected waters, and open coastlines of southeastern Alaska, he broadened his knowledge and understanding of wave shock, tidal exposure, and bottom type in different locales and the part played by these forces in determining the distribution of marine life. He recognized that these factors were, in part, responsible for the adaptations of form, function, and life history that he observed among the intertidal organisms he investigated and collected. And, in the process, he rediscovered the poetic voice he first heard on his walking trip throughout the American South.

When Ricketts was taking courses from Allee and other biologists at the University of Chicago, his mentor was already investigating a sort of middle ground between ecological studies of a single organism (autoecology) and those on communities of organisms. He called these "aggregations"—"intermediate units between individual animals and the larger ecological community."[42] By studying aggregations, Allee came to understand how biotic interactions help structure animal communities. He expanded his focus, from the effect of the abiotic environment on animal life to the effect of group life on individuals. As Gregg Mitman points out, these kinds of investigations would provide insights into issues of community integration, biotic relations, and the origins of sociality. Put simply, at the level of the aggregation, the same forces operating within a community were present, but they behaved in a way that was simpler and more accessible to study. Allee's early focus on the importance of aggregations paved the way for his complete analysis of the subject in his landmark volume, *Animal Aggregations* (1931).[43]

Recalling Allee's studies of marine life at Woods Hole that led that scientist to conclude that "social units of this type have distinct survival value for their members," Ricketts observed that "the fragile and beautiful brittle stars, whose delicacy requires the protection incident to the under-rock habitat, [are] bountifully represented, as to both number of individuals and number of species." These, he notes, are "invariably found in aggregations of from several to several dozen, so closely associated that their arms are intertwined."[44] For Allee, observations like this were in a sort of "border-line field where general sociology meets and overlaps general physiology and ecology."[45]

It was, for Allee, the ecologist's "responsibility for interpreting [this] scientific point of approach to human problems."[46] Looking back to Allee's investigation about the importance of aggregations and forward to a personal philosophy of "breaking through," Ricketts and Calvin conclude that this process of science "leads us to the borderline of the metaphysical." As he developed an aesthetic awareness to match his scientific understanding, Ed wove aesthetics and ecology in a way that enabled him to help his readers see beyond the level of isolated details and so perceive their underlying cohesion.

As he examined one shoreline habitat, Ricketts observed that when animals (the specific critters in this instance were anemones) aggregate together, "an actual protective material was given off by the aggregations, . . . a material similar to antibodies, such as are familiar to the general public in vaccine," so that "certain animals can confer immunity on other taxonomically unrelated animals."[47] Astounded by this discovery, proof of which Ed found in a variety of animal aggregations other than anemones, Ricketts and Calvin wrote in *Between Pacific Tides* that this will "open new and unexplored vistas to students of biology. It will certainly throw some interesting light on animal communities in general and may conceivably make understandable the evolutionary background behind the gregariousness of animals, even human beings."[48]

Discussing the behavior of the brittle star *Amphiodia* as it aggregates in its natural state, Ricketts concludes that "it may be assumed that it is for protection against some usual environmental factor, probably oxygen suffocation."[49] Although it would be a mistake to overstate the sociological implications of the aggregation thesis and its benefits for species survival, there is certainly a correspondence between Ricketts's ideas about community cooperation and themes in Steinbeck's most important writing during the 1930s.

Ricketts's work collecting and selling marine specimens continued throughout the last years of the 1920s and even after the stock market crash of 1929. Unlike so many enterprises that failed almost immediately, the business at Pacific Biological Laboratories remained unaffected for several years. Schools still had money to buy laboratory supplies, and Ed was able to juggle his business interests while planning the outline of what would become *Between Pacific Tides*. By late 1930, however, the situation had begun to worsen. Sales to institutions in India and Japan continued, but orders from schools and colleges in the United States fell off. Ed became increasingly concerned that he would lose his business; he needed to find an additional source of income that would insulate him from financial ruin.

One possibility seemed a natural. As we have already seen, Ed enjoyed talking to passersby as he was collecting in the tide pools along Monterey Bay. For years, curious onlookers watched with interest as he collected specimens. Nan noted that "people would follow him around and he would explain to them what the animals were, and how they existed. The children were mostly interested in the crabs, starfish, especially the brittle starfish, because if they picked them up, they would drop an arm or two. Then there were the purple urchins, which the Italian people would break open on the rocks and pull the insides out and place them on their garlic bread and eat them right there."[30]

As more and more laypersons became interested in Ricketts's work in the tide pools, he considered the possibility of offering them a field course about marine invertebrates. The degree of his enthusiasm for the idea is unclear, but sometime in 1930, he wrote to the owners of the upscale Hotel Del Monte soliciting funds to get his layman-learning project under way. Nan was unsure whether the letter was ever sent, and nothing further came of it. We do know, though, that Ed liked the idea of a book about marine invertebrates for lay readers. He didn't understand why such a book couldn't be of interest to them as well as to working scientists. It was, in fact, an interest that he maintained for years. In *Sea of Cortez,* he and Steinbeck talk about biologists who write exclusively for specialists. They call such scientists "dry balls"—custodians of their little corner of the woods who can identify a tree or two but never see the forest. This disdain for academic "dry balls" was something of an obsession for Ricketts, and it informs the writing and publishing history of *Between Pacific Tides.* In a letter to Lucille Lannestock in February 1937, as he was waiting for the Stanford University Press to finally publish *Tides,* Ricketts wrote that there is "no reason why a scholar shouldn't be a dear good man." But, he laments, "not many are. Most are pedantic; most are more interested in scrupulous accuracy of small details than in the more difficult honesty of large pictures."[31]

By 1930, even as he seems to have abandoned his layman-learning project, the idea for a book about marine invertebrates that would be of value to laypersons as well as scientists had taken shape. It was then, just as the Rickettses were settling into a new house on Fourth Street in Pacific Grove, that Ed met Jack Calvin.

the collaborators

Look deep into nature, and then you will understand everything better.

—ALBERT EINSTEIN

JACK CALVIN

John Thornton "Jack" Calvin was born October 17, 1901, to James and Fannie Thornton Calvin in Miles City, Montana. When, in 1908, Jack's father, then the foreman of the famous W Bar Ranch of Wibaux, Montana, died of internal injuries sustained in a saddle horse accident, Fannie, widowed with two boys, Jack and his brother Frank, moved to California.[1] Jack started high school in the Bay Area, but his mother moved the family to Seattle sometime around 1915, and Jack graduated from high school there. Not yet ready for college and seeking adventure, he traveled to the Alaskan frontier, where he canned salmon and sardines at the Wakefield Cannery in Little Port Walter and worked in a sawmill in Wrangell.[2]

By 1920, he was ready for college, and with limited educational options available in Alaska, he went to Seattle and enrolled at the University of Washington, where he graduated in 1924. He then returned to California, earning a master's degree in English literature from Stanford University. During summers Jack worked for the Alaska Packers Association, owners of the steel-hulled, square-rigged *Star of Zealand*, on which he sailed each June from San Francisco to

Jack Calvin. Photograph courtesy of the California History Room,
Monterey Public Library.

Bristol Bay. Like Ricketts, Calvin had no interest in a traditional
academic life; his Alaskan adventures had thoroughly captured his
imagination.

After completing his education at Stanford, Calvin got a job teaching English at Mountain View High School, located just south of Palo Alto and three miles inland from the southern wash of San Francisco Bay. Among his best students at Mountain View was Ritch Lovejoy, who loved to write and had by the age of sixteen produced several near-professional-quality drawings. Calvin believed Ritch had real promise as a writer as well as an artist. Jack maintained contact with him after leaving his teaching position and moving to his mother's house in Carmel. It was there that he began writing novels.

In 1928, Jack invited Ritch to join him in Carmel. According to Lovejoy's son, John, his father "got a job at the *Carmel Pine Cone* newspaper as a cub reporter. Ritch also earned a reputation for making woodcuts, a way of creating images by cutting them into blocks of wood and using the blocks the same way one uses rubber stamps."[3] In late 1928 or early 1929, Calvin and Lovejoy met their future wives, the Kashevaroff sisters from Alaska.

By 1930, Calvin had published two novels, *Fisherman 28,* an adolescent adventure story set in the salmon cannery town of Nushagak, Alaska, and *Square-Rigged,* a suspense story based on his experiences on the *Star of Zealand.* Both books capture Calvin's love affair with Alaska, a passion that years later was confirmed by his granddaughter, Mary Purvis: "He never again felt home unless he was in Alaska. This was the place for him, his love for wild places and his wife and being able to be close to the land."[4]

Square-Rigged, originally published by Little Brown in 1929, was out of print for three-quarters of a century until it was republished in Alaska in 2017. Lisa Busch, the director of the Sitka Sound Science Center, who was instrumental in the effort to bring *Square-Rigged* back to life, writes,

> It's a very authentic book. It is what a square-rigged boat is like and (Calvin) names everything perfectly. That is special about the book. He describes life aboard a square-rigged vessel back in the day. It is a slice of history that I think sometimes we're a little bit removed from in Alaska, but that was definitely part of our history. Square-rigged boats were here . . . It's a really fun read. Every chapter ends with suspense and there's so much authentic maritime history here, in terms of how they went up

the stays, how they set the yardarm sails. . . . It captures the period and shows off Jack Calvin's writing style. He was a really good writer. . . . He was an incredible writer and storyteller.[5]

In 1931, a reporter for the *Carmel Pine Cone* noted that "*Square Rigged* held interest for all lovers of adventure. . . . Calvin promises to go far as a writer of fiction."[6] Little did that reporter know that Jack's talent would shine most prominently in a text about marine biology.

Fisherman 28 was republished in the summer of 2020. A sequel to *Square-Rigged*, *Fisherman 28* is the story of Bert Lindsay (aka Fisherman 28), a novice at sea who embarks on a summer of salmon fishing for his father's business, where he learns life lessons about hard work and all kinds of people. In the background is the story of the culture of the Alaskan fishing industry and the majesty of Alaskan frontier. *Fisherman 28* and *Square-Rigged* were republished by the Sitka Sound Science Center "to celebrate Sitka's important chapter in the History of Science and remember an author that captured the spirit and culture of west coast tall ship sailing and fishing at the turn of the last century."[7]

In Carmel, Calvin and Lovejoy became friendly with a good many residents of what was rapidly becoming known as "the Seacoast of Bohemia," best known through Franklin Walker's excellent account of the writers and painters who found refuge there earlier in the twentieth century. These were people like Mary Austin, Jack London, Upton Sinclair, and Sinclair Lewis. Among more contemporary writers, Jack and Ritch met and became friendly with the as-yet-unknown John Steinbeck. Richard Astro talked at length with Calvin in 1971. He expressed no great fondness for Steinbeck (in fact, he didn't like him at all), but he "lit up" when the subject changed to Ed Ricketts. He talked at great length about how he and Ricketts decided to work together on what Ed told him then was his book project about the animals in Monterey Bay. Calvin indicated that when Ed first told him about the project, it was very modest by comparison with what *Between Pacific Tides* would ultimately become. [8]

Ricketts may have been short of cash because of declining sales at Pacific Biological Laboratories, but he had plenty of space in the lab to study and catalog the marine invertebrates he collected in tide pools up and down the Pacific coast. Because of the amount of time required to collect, prepare, and ship animals to schools and museums had shortened so substantially, he had more time to study the physical factors that drive ecosystems, the communities of organisms found in the mudflats and rocky shores of the Pacific littoral. No longer just a collector, Ed studied animals in their natural habitats, recording data about them in his large "New Series Note Books."

Calvin met Ricketts shortly after coming to Carmel, and he occasionally joined Ed on his collecting trips. At some point their conversations during and after such expeditions included discussions about coauthoring the book that had already taken shape in Ed's mind. Talking with Jack enthused Ricketts, and in his mind the scope of the book would cover marine life considerably north and south of Monterey Bay—from Northern Mexico to Southeast Alaska—and its focus would be not only on the animals but also on their relationships to one another and to their various intertidal environments. In an interview for the *Daily Sitka Sentinel* in 1979, Calvin recalled some of the details:

> "We found we had similar tastes in wine, music, and attitudes toward life," Calvin noted. "Ed was always looking for someone to go along with him on his collecting trips, and that's since filled in how I got involved. Unintentionally, I was in training with the best marine biologist in the world," Calvin said. "Everywhere we went we were bothered by people wanting to know more about the creatures we were collecting," Jack notes, "So I suggested Ed put together a little pocket manual for people to carry along on the beach as a handy guide to the marine life of California beaches." "He said, 'I'll do it if you'll help me.'" Picking up the 500-page *Between Pacific Tides*, Calvin said, "This is what our little pocket guide turned out to be."[9]

What began as a casual friendship defined by wine, music, and conversation led to one of the most important authorial partnerships in the history of marine ecology. Calvin was a fine writer and a talented photographer. Ed, who struggled to turn his ideas into good prose, needed and certainly appreciated Jack's writing skills. Calvin was also knowledgeable about the outer shores of Washington, British Columbia, and Alaska, and he was eager to go with Ed on collecting trips to the Pacific Northwest. They traveled together extensively during the summers of 1930 and 1931. In December 1931, a writer for the *Carmel Pine Cone* wrote that "Jack Calvin, with Mrs. Jack, is again on his adventurous way. . . . The old kit-bags are being packed for travel [in 1932]. This time the train will lead to Seattle first, then a cruise that looks, at the moment, permanent [?] through the inner passage of the British Columbia and Alaska coast."[10] Jack and his wife, Sasha, were planning to revisit the haunts they had encountered during a honeymoon canoe trip of two years earlier. But this time their plans included buying and outfitting "a boat rigged for sailing, or for motor cruising with a comfortable cabin built to house a typewriter as well as the Calvins."[11] The *Pine Cone* writer affirmed that Jack was working on *Between Pacific Tides* with Edward F. Ricketts, for publication by the Stanford University Press and for which Ritch Lovejoy, a former artist for the *Pine Cone*, had completed more than a hundred illustrations. This was the first public announcement of the Ricketts-Calvin book project. "It will be a textbook upon the subject it covers. . . . It will be out in the spring." The *Pine Cone* writer was correct about *Between Pacific Tides* becoming a textbook. His estimate of the book's publication date was off by seven years.

RITCH LOVEJOY

Ritch Lovejoy has been and remains today known almost exclusively as the needy recipient of the $1,000 Pulitzer Prize money that John Steinbeck was awarded for writing *The Grapes of Wrath*. This is unfortunate, because the money was not a handout by the novelist to a struggling friend. Steinbeck gave Ritchie (known as both Ritch and Ritchie) the money to help support his work as a writer. Lovejoy died more than sixty years ago and remained an obscure member of the Steinbeck, Ricketts, and Calvin circle until recently, when we came to know him far better from a lengthy article penned by his son, John, "The Man Who Became a Steinbeck Footnote," published in 2008 in the *Steinbeck Review*. John's intent in writing this article was "to set the record straight," though he is quick to admit that "I'm biased since I am Ritch Lovejoy's son."[12] John Lovejoy fills in many of the gaps

Fred and Genevieve Lovejoy behind the counter of Lovejoy's Candy Store and Ice Cream Parlor (1909), which the couple owned and operated in Mountain View, California. Photograph courtesy of Mountain View Public Library.

about Ritchie, some of which bear directly on *Between Pacific Tides*. John, by the way, was named by his parents, he and Tal, for John Steinbeck.

"Ritchie Lovejoy was born on the first of January 1908, in what was then a little farming town—Mountain View, California, the son of a fruit farmer and Jack-of-all-trades named Joseph Winfred 'Fred' Lovejoy," John tells us. "During his early years, the family home had no electricity; gaslight was the norm. And Ritchie learned early in life how to drive a buckboard. Eventually, Fred bought a one-cylinder car, and then one with two cylinders. As a child, my dad used to ride in one of those topless cars standing up."[13]

Ritch attended the local high school for which, at age fifteen, he designed the cover of the school yearbook. He was already a talent as an artist, and in Mountain View he met Jack Calvin, whom he later joined in Carmel. John Lovejoy writes, "My father later told me he fled because he had worked all summer in his father's rock quarry,

Ritch Lovejoy. Photograph courtesy of John Lovejoy.

but his dad refused to pay him." He also writes that "Calvin did tell me in the early 1960s, at his home in Sitka, that he had 'seen promise' in my father, and so had persuaded him to come to Carmel. . . . Calvin seemed to imply that my father had subsequently not lived up to his full potential."[14]

In either 1929 or early 1930, Ritchie met and married Natalya (or "Tal") Kashevaroff, one of five daughters of Andrew Kashevaroff, the famous and sometimes infamous Russian Orthodox priest from Alaska. The elder Kashevaroff was a remarkable fellow; not only a priest, but a language teacher (Tlingit, Aleut, Russian, and English), a violinist, and the curator of the Alaska State Museum. Tal was no slouch herself. She was a talented pianist, taught herself to play the accordion, and knew a thing or two about performing ballet. "The first time that my mother—who I surmise was in Carmel to visit Sasha and Jack—saw Ritch Lovejoy," John writes, "he was washing dishes in a restaurant. Apparently, it was love at first sight."[15]

Another member of the Kashevaroff clan, Sasha, married Jack Calvin. A younger sister, Xenia, would marry the American music experimentalist John Cage. Artistically the most talented of the group, Xenia was a painter, bookbinder, musician, and a sculptor noted for her mobiles that were on the cutting edge of a new surrealism. Cage was enthralled with Xenia. Sometime in 1935, he wrote to composer Adolph Weiss, telling him that Xenia "is a marvelous creature. Her world is almost without limitation: for she includes, from her mother (an Eskimo), an animal, pre-historic, primitiveness; and from her father (a Russian priest), the rich and organic mysticism and instinctiveness of Russians; and of herself she has found our own American insistence upon being contemporary and intensely speculative of the future."[16]

John Lovejoy recalls that, some years later, Xenia came to live with Ritch and Tal. That was after Cage "decided that he was gay and went to live with dancer-choreographer Merce Cunningham." During the time that Xenia was with us, John writes, "she made several mobiles that hung from our ceiling."[17] In addition to Tal, Sasha, and Xenia, the family included two more sisters and a brother. The Kashevaroffs were a very interesting clan. But we're getting ahead of ourselves; more about them later.

It is not clear exactly when Ritchie joined the Ricketts-Calvin project, but we surmise from several of the Round and About columns that he wrote for the *Monterey Peninsula Herald,* and the aforementioned article in the *Carmel Pine Cone,* that it was sometime in

Formal group portrait of Mrs. Andrew Kashevaroff and her five daughters.
Photograph Courtesy of Alaska State Archives, ASL-Kashevaroff-Family-03.

1931. In a 1948 column for the *Herald,* Ritchie wrote that "in about
1931-1932 the book [*Between Pacific Tides*] was already begun. I did a
year's work on the line drawings for it, and Calvin besides writing did
exceptional photographic illustrations."[18] In another Round and
About column published in 1952, Lovejoy wrote, "I worked about a
year part-time, quite a lot of microscopes, and my eyes became a
beautiful crimson."[19] Ritch did the line drawings at Pacific Biological
Laboratories, where he had access to a microscope and to the animals
he needed to illustrate. He did excellent work; one reason for the
enduring popularity of *Between Pacific Tides* is his high-quality
illustrations.

Like so many financially insecure newlyweds, Ritch and Tal suffered during the early 1930s. The Great Depression hit Carmel hard,
and it became increasingly difficult for them to eke out a living.
Seeking new income possibilities, in 1932, they moved to Eagle Rock,
a working-class neighborhood northeast of Los Angeles where
Steinbeck and his wife Carol were living at the time. The Steinbecks
were also struggling financially (John was still unknown), and Ritch
and Carol came up with a plan for a new business—a plastic molding

Ritch and Tal Lovejoy. Photograph courtesy of John Lovejoy.

process making three-dimensional reproductions for department stores, where there was a need for lifelike mannequins. Ritch and Carol convinced themselves that their product would appeal to Hollywood types who would pay to have their faces reproduced. They called their molding business the Faster Master Plaster Casters, and Ritch went to work making molds. It happened that their first customer was the brother of then-famous actor Adolphe Menjou. All was going well during Menjou's visit to the Plaster Casters studio. The actor's brother was talking with Tal Lovejoy in Russian as Ritch was mixing the goop for the mold. And then a slapstick event occurred: a loud and very drunk Lovejoy acquaintance arrived—a naked and obscene landlord of one of Ritch's friends. Menjou left in a huff. After that auspicious beginning, the business collapsed.

Ritch and Tal left Southern California in late 1932 or early 1933, and John recalls that "my parents later lived in San Francisco where my father scratched out a living painting gold leaf lettering on glass windows and doors of area companies. Then, in the mid-1930s, my parents were back in my mother's home in Sitka, Alaska, where they decided to start a newspaper. They called it *The Arrowhead*, and it was printed by hand and by muscle. . . . My dad made the front-page picture for each issue by means of a wood block that he carved himself."[20]

Another series of misadventures undid *The Arrowhead*, and by 1937, Ritchie and Tal were back in California. John writes, "My dad got a job as advertising manager at Holman's Department Store in Pacific Grove, California, and also went to work reading the news on radio station KDON in Monterey, where he immediately discovered he had terrible stage fright. So much for a career on radio."[21]

Next came a stint working for the Farm Security Administration, a New Deal agency created in 1937 to combat rural poverty that replaced the failing Resettlement Administration. Ritch ran a labor camp in the Mojave Desert town of Blythe, where he became very knowledgeable about and sympathetic toward the dust bowl refugees seeking new lives in the expansive agricultural gardens of California. It was undoubtedly Ritch's experience with the FSA that cemented his friendship with Steinbeck who, by the time Ritchie went to Blythe, was already in the field himself, working with FSA camp administrator Tom Collins in Arvin, California, compiling background material for *The Grapes of Wrath*.

By 1939, Ritchie and Tal had returned to Pacific Grove, and it was during that year that Lovejoy's poem "The Swamp" was published in the *New Republic*, no small achievement for an unknown writer. He was also at work on *Taku Wind*, a six-hundred-page novel about fishermen, Native Alaskans, businessmen, drunks, Russian Orthodox priests, and artists who lived in the town of Karluk on Alaska's Kodiak Island. The title refers to a mountain wave phenomenon of powerful winds generated over Gastineau Channel near downtown Juneau, a city with which Ritchie was familiar. This was the book project that prompted Steinbeck to give Ritch his Pulitzer Prize money. There are those who have dismissed Lovejoy as a hanger-on, a ne'er-do-well who couldn't finish anything, let alone a six-hundred-page novel. The fact is that Ritchie did finish *Taku Wind* and, at

Steinbeck's suggestion, sent it to the novelist's editor, Pat Covici at the Viking Press. Covici rejected it, and while Ritchie talked about sending it to other publishers, there is no evidence that he ever did. Still, the fact remains that, in addition to being a fine illustrator, Ritch Lovejoy was a writer of substantial energy and something more than modest ability.

THE KASHEVAROFF OUTFIT

The Kashevaroff outfit, so named because that was the appellation given to the group by Ed Ricketts, were minor players in the writing and publishing history of *Between Pacific Tides*. But because members of "the outfit" married two of the three *Tides* contributors, and because another member of the "outfit" knew Ed well and helped compile the book's index, their involvement in the process, though tangential, seemed worthy of inclusion. We have mentioned Tal, Sasha, and Xenia, three of five daughters of Archpriest Andrew Petrovich Kashevaroff. Born in Kodiak in 1863, four years before the Alaska Purchase, the elder Kashevaroff was of Russian and Native Alaskan heritage and served the church as a teacher, choir director, inspector, deacon, and priest for more than a half century in locations throughout the Alaska Territory. All of five feet two inches tall, Andrew played the piano, the organ, and the violin. He was more than a competent musician.

After years of traveling long distances on church business, Archpriest Andrew became the first librarian and curator of the Alaska Historical Museum and Library (now the Alaska State Museum), a position he held for twenty years and during which he proposed and then supervised the facility's relocation to what would become the Alaska state capital of Juneau. During his tenure at the museum, he collected thousands of items, providing interesting and previously undocumented information about Alaskan history. Humorist Will Rogers visited the museum on a trip to Alaska and later wrote, "There is a little Russian man . . . Father Kashevaroff. . . . He has made a great study of Alaskan customs, relics, languages, its history, and everything, and if ever a fellow fit in a museum, it's him in this one."[22] Years later, a writer for the *Milwaukee Sentinel* wrote about a visit to Juneau in 1930, remarking that "our favorite refuge from the

Rev. Andrew P. Kashevaroff standing outside the Alaska Historical Museum.
Photograph Courtesy of Alaska State Archives, Skinner Foundation. Photographs,
Alaska Steamship Company, 1890s-1940s. ASL-PCA-44-03-003.

rains was the Territorial Museum, whose most interesting 'exhibit'
was its curator, Father A. P. Kashevaroff. There was an old-world
charm about him that seemed incongruous in that lusty mining town.
His dark, clerical garb accentuated his snow-white Van Dyke. He
was small and retiring, but to talk with him for a minute was to feel
the force of an extraordinary personality."[23]

Much of what we know about Father Kashevaroff and the Kashevaroff family we learned first from John Lovejoy, who traveled to Kodiak to discover everything he could about his mother's family. John and his wife, Diane, explored the Kashevaroff family history, discovering that John's great-great-great-grandfather, Artamon Kashevaroff, and great-great-grandfather, Filipp Kashevaroff, came to Kodiak from Russia in a two-masted sailing vessel named the *Three Saints* during the summer of 1774. After establishing a vibrant fishing industry in Yakutat, a former Russian colony in the isolated lowlands along the Gulf of Alaska, almost everyone who arrived on the *Three Saints* was killed by a Tlingit war party. Filipp miraculously escaped the attack and apprenticed himself to James Shields, a Russian-American Company shipwright. He later worked as a storekeeper and a teacher, marrying Alexandra Petrovna, a native Alaskan and a member of the Alutiiq tribe. The couple had two children, Alexander and Peter. Filipp died in Sitka, and he is likely buried there.

Alexander Kashevaroff headed the Russian Navy's Hydrographic Department and managed the Russian-American Company outposts in Siberia. His brother, Peter, studied for the priesthood and, once ordained, remained in Kodiak after the 1867 sale of Alaska to the United States. He married Mariia Arkhimandritov, daughter of the captain of the bark *Kad'y*, a vessel that shipped ice from Woody Island to San Francisco. Over time, the Kashevaroffs became one of Alaska's most prominent and influential families. Andrew, the father of the Kashevaroff girls and the son of Peter and Mariia, was a child prodigy. He was sent by his parents to Russian and American schools in San Francisco where, by the age of eighteen, he mastered the organ, the violin, and the piano. After attending the Russian Orthodox seminary in San Francisco, he returned to Alaska to assist the priests at Sitka's Greek-Russian church, Cathedral of St. Michael the Archangel. in In Sitka, then the capital of the Alaska Territory, he met and married a Tlingit woman named Martha Bolshanin. The Kashevaroffs had the aforementioned son and five daughters.

Xenia Kashevaroff, who had already spent a good deal of time on the US west coast, moved with John Cage to Chicago and then to New York, where she mingled with the likes of Max Ernst and Peggy

Cathedral of St. Michael the Archangel (Sitka, Alaska). Alaska State Archives, Early Prints of Alaska. Photographs, ca. 1870-1920. ASL-PCA-297.

Guggenheim. Her sisters Natalya and Sasha stayed closer to home—traveling back and forth between Sitka and Monterey with Jack and Ritchie. When in Monterey, they frequently visited Ricketts lab and spent long days and evenings with Ed and with John Steinbeck, by then a regular lab visitor. Sasha shared Ricketts and Calvin's love for the sea. She thoroughly enjoyed her honeymoon paddling a seventeen-foot canoe with Jack from Tacoma up the Inland Passage to Alaska, about which adventure, in July 1933, the *National Geographic* published Calvin's written record. In this fine piece of writing, the author, without bravado, recounts the work of the two-person crew of the *Nakwasina* as they navigate their way north to Juneau. Calvin writes that "there was no motive for our voyage except the fun of the thing,"[24] yet some of the fishermen who they encountered on their trip were sure he and Sasha were doing it on a bet, that some unknown rich person was offering them a $25,000 prize if they could complete their trip. This recalls Steinbeck's account of Ricketts's walking tour

Jack and Sasha Calvin paddling their canoe, *Nakwasina.* Courtesy of Alaska State Archives (ASL-P425-31-25).

through the American southeast when, Steinbeck writes, Ed found it far simpler to tell people that he was doing it on a bet rather than just for fun. If we accept Steinbeck's story, Ed Ricketts and Jack Calvin had similar experiences before they ever met.

Sasha sometimes accompanied Jack and Ed on collecting expeditions. In 1930, the three went collecting along the shore of Puget

Sound, with Xenia joining them for the return trip to Monterey. Two years later, Sasha joined her husband, Ricketts, and a newcomer to the Ricketts-Calvin circle, an attractive young man who would become America's best-known mythologist, on their thirty-three-foot boat for an extended collecting trip from Tacoma to Juneau. During that trip, Calvin and Ricketts collected specimens, some of which Ed would prepare for sale for Pacific Biological Laboratories and others they would study and then catalog for inclusion in *Between Pacific Tides*. The boat was the *Grampus*; the soon-to-be famous mythologist was Joseph Campbell.

JOSEPH CAMPBELL

Arguably the most famous and accomplished comparative mythologist in American history, Joseph Campbell arrived in Monterey/Carmel in February 1932. Shortly thereafter, he met Ed Ricketts. They became close friends, and Joe was with Ed during a critical period when Ricketts was working on *Between Pacific Tides*. In a 1983 interview with Pauline Pearson at the John Steinbeck Library in Salinas, Campbell recalled that in the summer of 1932 Ricketts was going on a collecting expedition to Alaska "in a boat a friend of theirs had. A chap name of Jack Calvin and his wife who is the daughter, one of them, gorgeous daughters of a Russian priest in Juno [*sic*]." Campbell was invited to join the expedition, and during that ten-week trip, he and Ricketts bonded. Campbell told Pearson, "I came to know Ed very well and admired and loved him. This was a loveable man."[25] Reviewing Ricketts's notes at the time, as well as numerous comments over the years by Campbell, it is clear that no one, including Steinbeck, was closer to Ed during the early 1930s than Joe Campbell. They were truly kindred spirits.

Though Campbell was unknown when he met Ricketts, his was an inquiring mind and had been almost from birth. When he was seven years old, his father took him and his younger brother, Charlie, to New York City to see *Buffalo Bill's Wild West* show. The evening was a high point in Joe's life. Although the cowboys were the show's stars, Joe would later write that "I early became fascinated, seized, obsessed, by the figure of a naked American Indian with his ear to the ground, a bow and arrow in his hand, and a look of special knowledge in his eyes."[26] The young Campbell was consumed by Native

Joseph Campbell. Photograph courtesy of the Joseph Campbell Foundation.

American cultures. By the age of ten, he had consumed every book on American Indians in the children's section of the White Plains, New York, library. He sought and was granted admission to the adult stacks, where he eventually read the entire multivolume *Reports of the Bureau of American Ethnology*. As it was with Native Americans, so it was with everything that interested him: he dove in with abandon. His interests were wide and varied, as much as, and perhaps even more than, those of Ricketts.

As a college student at Columbia (he transferred there after finding the intellectual life at Dartmouth less than stimulating), Campbell excelled in everything he tried—studying medieval literature, playing in a college jazz band, starring as the fastest half-miler at the university, and running at championship levels throughout the country. He was a voracious reader, and when, years later, he became a college instructor at Sarah Lawrence College, he expected the same from his students. On the Joseph Campbell Foundation website, we find his reading list, the books he routinely assigned in his mythology classes at the college. It is exhaustive.

After graduating from Columbia, Campbell was at loose ends. He became a Kerouac-like figure, drifting first south and then westward,

to New Orleans and then to Los Angeles. Finding those cities unin-
teresting, at least by comparison with New York, he drove up the
California coast to San Luis Obispo, then inland through the Salinas
Valley, and finally to Carmel, about which he had heard much but
knew little. Considering the impact that living there and in nearby
Monterey and Pacific Grove had on him, Campbell wrote in a journal that he kept during those years, "It is not at all unlikely that the
least clearly foreseen way in the end may be the most important."[27]

Campbell's introduction to the Steinbeck-Ricketts circle began
when he reunited with a young woman named Idell Henning, whom
he had met in 1925 on a passenger ship returning to California from
Hawai'i. In an interview with Donald Newlove for an article titled
"The Professor with a Thousand Faces" in a 1977 issue of *Esquire*,
Campbell recalled that it was Idell who "introduced me to John and
Carol Steinbeck, in Pacific Grove."

> I just fell in love with the pair of them. I stayed and got a lit-
> tle place called the Pumpkin Shell. And again, here I am, try-
> ing to pass John Dewey and Bertrand Russell, Adelle [Davis,
> Campbell's first serious girlfriend] bringing me vitamins and
> Steinbeck and I trying to write. There was a little fellow with
> a goatee at John and Carol's, Ed Ricketts, who was Doc in
> *Cannery Row*. His laboratory is the place *Cannery Row* is all
> about. Oh, four months of just something glorious. Wonderful
> people. And I was in the Carmel library—sort of, what am I
> gonna read now?—and my right hand went up to a book that
> was the beginning of everything. Spengler's *Decline of the West*.
> I read the first page and knew I'd found it—Dewey and Russell
> just blew away—I read nothing but that for two years. Two vol-
> umes. And I read it in German, too—this was it! It brought
> back everything I had had in Germany, and added, added,
> added, made sense of it, put it in play in the contemporary sit-
> uation. When I finished Volume One, I gave it to Steinbeck.
> Well, next I see Steinbeck—he was a ponderous guy, walk-
> ing around like a bear, rubbing his side thought-fully (people
> thought we were brothers) he's rubbing his side and I ask him,
> "what's wrong, John?" "Can't read this, can't read this." "Why
> not?" "My art! My art! This thesis that now we're to put down
> the pen and paint brush and pick up the monkey wrench and
> the law book-technology and law!" "John, you can't just shut

your eyes to things. You gotta take it and beat it." So he gave me the book back and I went on in rapture. A beautiful time; we were all in heaven. The world had dropped out. We weren't the dropouts; the world was the drop out.[28]

In their biography, *Joseph Campbell: A Fire in the Mind,* Stephen and Robin Larsen write that Campbell noted in his journal, "I learned from John that there was a house right next to Ed's that was vacant, a smaller, cheaper house—because the one main thing was we didn't have any money. I would then be closer to this whole little combo. So I came over to Pacific Grove, to this little house that was called Canary Cottage."[29] Campbell moved close to the Rickettses' cottage on Fourth Street, and the two men grew very friendly. Cannery Row and the neighboring communities of Monterey, Pacific Grove, and Carmel constituted the artistic capital of the west coast. There was Steinbeck and poet Robinson Jeffers and, a few years later, Henry Miller. There were artists of various stripes—painters and sculptors, musicians and Jungian psychologists, and Louis Terman's gifted children—even as fishermen and cannery workers were establishing Monterey Bay as the sardine capital of the world. Joe fit in perfectly. It was, as he raptured, a beautiful time.

Free to explore everything that intrigued and interested him, Campbell read widely and, in evening gatherings with Ed, John and John's wife Carol, during which they drank cheap wine and consumed communal stews, he explored with them the meaning of what he had read. At some point, Joe came upon Oswald Spengler's *Decline of the West* in the Carmel community library. He read it through and was mesmerized. He would "read the entire opus seven times over the next decade (his preference was for the original German) and draw major inspiration from it. It was not only the mythological foundation of Spengler's ideas but also the scale of Spengler's intellectual purview that appealed to Campbell, and which he would in some ways carry forward in his own work."[30] During one of their evenings together, Campbell introduced Ricketts to Spengler; Ed read and talked about the German philosopher's science and his notions about history for the rest of his life.

When he arrived in Carmel, Campbell knew next to nothing about marine biology. At Ed's invitation, he joined in on some collecting expeditions and was struck by and impressed with the way Ricketts was developing a new and, for Campbell, an interesting way of seeing the animals. Even more interesting to Campbell was how Ed drew connections between what he saw in the tide pools and human behavior, moving through animal biology to human sociology. Nearly a decade before Steinbeck and Ricketts told readers of *Sea of Cortez* to look from the tide pools to the stars and then back to the tide pools again, Ed and Joe Campbell were doing precisely that. As the Larsens note,

> It was an extraordinary matrix of destiny, then, into which Joseph Campbell had stumbled in Monterey in 1932. If he had searched the country over, he could not have found a circle of acquaintances more suitably matched—not only to his own inquiring mind and blossoming talents, but to the next task of growth which awaited him. It was in speaking of this time and these people that he confirmed he had encountered here not only the Earthly Paradise but the "great death and rebirth," one of the primary personal transformations of a life dedicated to self-discovery. [31]

Galvanizing that transformation for Campbell, and for Ricketts and Steinbeck as well, was the poetry of Robinson Jeffers and specifically "Roan Stallion," Jeffers' best-known narrative poem. For Ed, Joe, and John, the marine biologist, the mythologist, and the novelist, "Roan Stallion" crystallized a vision of the god in nature, and the way toward him; ironically, some have suggested, by seeing through the tragic side of life. One evening at Ed's lab, Carol Steinbeck said that "Roan Stallion" was the key to it all, and she went on to read from the poem. Ed digested it all and later wrote, "In Jeffers' poems, the thing [breaking through] is stated clearly, with full conscious recognition, and with that exact economy of words which we associate with scientific statements: 'Humanity is the mold to break away from.'" Ricketts goes on: "This . . . quality may be an essential of modern soul movements . . . not dirt for dirt's sake, or grief merely for the sake of grief, but dirt and grief wholly accepted necessary as struggle vehicles of an emergent joy—achieving things which are not transient by means of things which are."[32]

"Breaking through" became a passion for Ricketts; he wrote an essay on achieving transcendence that he shared with Campbell and shopped around to upscale journals. He worked on the essay for the better part of a decade, telling Campbell in July of 1940 that it was still under revision (it was finally published in the Hedgpeth volume thirty years after his death). Ricketts first shared his interest in breaking through with Campbell in 1932, during the days when Campbell was becoming involved with Ed's science and his collecting expeditions in the Central California intertidal zones. Here are Campbell's notes about a 1932 collecting trip to Santa Cruz:

> We went through Santa Cruz to a stretch of beach a bit to the north. There we parked the car on a cliff, got out the burlap bags, two pairs of boots, an adze, and a few iron gadgets for prying starfish loose from the rocks. Ed and Rich put on the boots. And then we filed down to the beach . . . and began prying off the starfish, stepping on sea-anemones. . . . Ed went into a gulch—and into a great cave in the cliff wall—where he found a lot of fantastic things to put into glass jars. Carol lay down on the rocks and went to sleep. Rich was working hard. Tal, in sailor trousers, was working with the adze, chopping off mussels and collecting funny worms. She found a flat worm and brought it to Ed on her fingers, to put it in a jar. I went about with one of those iron gadgets questing for helpless starfish. I collected about two hundred and tossed them all into bags. Then about nine, we started away.[33]

A half century later, in the July 1, 1980, edition of the *Alta Vista Magazine*, Campbell told interviewer Winston Elstob that, above all, "Ricketts was the workman, knee-deep in the tidal waters of Monterey Bay, trying to discover the universe. They [Ritch, Carol, and Tal] would often assist at his work, and you couldn't help but be impressed with the way he went about his tasks, always the thorough and complete scientist."[34]

Campbell wrote about one evening when he accompanied Ed, Ritch, and Tal for a walk through the Corral de Tierra (the site for *The Pastures of Heaven*, Steinbeck's second published novel). Commenting on how the group felt when they stumbled on a mysterious house that stood alone like "a lighthouse on a promontory," where the "gaunt windows and door seemed actually the desolate lineaments of death itself," something happened that Campbell struggled to describe for years afterward. Stephen and Robin Larsen describe this moment as "a mystical union of the companions with themselves, with the great world, the starry sky. It was one of those mystical moments of 'breaking through' that Ed Ricketts was seeking, and that Campbell would later describe as the 'transparent to the transcendent.'"[35]

According to multiple sources, it was Ritch and Tal Lovejoy who first asked Joe if he would be interested in going to Alaska on the Calvins' boat (the *Grampus*) with Ed, Tal's sister Sasha, and Jack, to help the group collect marine specimens. Initially uneasy, Campbell pondered it for a time. Once he felt sure that Jack was qualified to captain the *Grampus* through the Inside Passage (after all, he had made the canoe trip with Sasha from Puget Sound to Sitka three years earlier), he agreed to go. After a raucous farewell party at the lab, Joe and Ed drove to Tacoma where they met the Calvins and began their ten-week trip. In his conversations with Campbell in *The Way of the Myth* (1994), Fraser Boa comments about how Joe laughed when Boa asked him, "You remember the party in Cannery Row?" Campbell responded, "'That was my birthday party. Even the flagpole sitter was there, they used to do that sort of thing back then.' 'And Doc Ricketts,' I [Boa] asked. Joe paused and then answered: 'Ed Ricketts was the heart of it all.'"[36]

As for the trip itself, Campbell recalls,

> Ed made an arrangement to go to Alaska on a small boat. Great! What else is there to do? So we cruised up the Inside Passage from Seattle to Juneau. . . . Well, the inside passage was gorgeous. We sat on the stern as that little launch went out into the waters of Puget Sound, off for six weeks, much of which we'd spend at an absolutely uninhabited island gathering animals while Ed made notes. The cost: twenty-five cents a day for the whole crew. We would pull into port, all the canneries were closed, the fishing fleets immobilized—they'd throw salmon at us. Put your hand in the water and pull fish out. Just an idyll. And the towns were supposed to be dead and they were the most living things. There's nothing like living when you're not living with a direction but just enjoying the glory of the moment. That's what we were doing.[37]

The Grampus, Ed Ricketts bottling collected specimens, 1932. Photograph courtesy of San Jose State University, Martha Heasley Cox Center for Steinbeck Studies.

The voyage of the *Grampus* (the name of the boat derives either from a ubiquitous species of dolphin or, perhaps, from the name of a whaling vessel in Melville's *Moby Dick* or Edgar Allan Poe's *The Narrative of Arthur Gordon Pym of Nantucket*) lasted ten weeks during the summer of 1932, and the information Ricketts gleaned about marine life in the intertidal zones during the trip forms a major portion of the content of *Between Pacific Tides*. Ed, Joe, Jack, and Sasha observed and collected animals. They talked about the animals and how each species seemed to function in their various habitats. Ed and Joe talked about books—the Bible, Tolstoy, Dostoevsky, and James Joyce, and from their talking, they fused science and myth in ways that occasioned understanding and even transcendent meaning. For both men, it was another instance of "breaking through." For Ed, it was all about what he called "participation." It is the nature writer's personal response— the pleasure of looking closely, the sense of revelation in all things attended to that takes an equal or an almost equal place with the facts themselves.

At thirty-three feet, the *Grampus* was not a large vessel, and although most of the waterways it traversed were sheltered from the open ocean, there were difficult crossings with tricky currents and hidden shoals. Jack and Sasha's familiarity with the Inside Passage was a big help, and for Ed, and particularly for Joe, that was reassuring.

As they moved through different waters and did their collecting, Ed was struck by the fact that wave shock had a dramatic effect on the distribution of life in the intertidal zones. Shortly after the end of the *Grampus* expedition, he wrote that "we had collected for weeks in an environment from ground swell and surf. Then suddenly, within a few miles, both appeared, we were again on open coast. And more than coincidentally, the whole nature of the animal communities changed radically, more than it had in a thousand miles of inland waterways. The species were different, their proportions were different, they even occurred differently."[38]

Read any part of *Between Pacific Tides* that deals with animals who live exposed to rocky shores on the open ocean and find striking similarities between Ricketts's observations of wave shock during his trip on the *Grampus* and statements about the same subject in *Between Pacific Tides*. It was the subject of the essay he later wrote titled "Notes and Observations, Mostly Ecological, resulting from Northern Pacific Collecting Trips Chiefly in Southeastern Alaska, with Special Reference to Wave Shock as a Factor in Littoral Ecology." Ed arranged the facts of marine biology in such a way that the interplay of forces pointed inescapably toward an ecological, a holistic, understanding of the natural world.

During their time on the *Grampus*, Ricketts and Calvin considered the design of *Between Pacific Tides*. Ed was determined to craft a book that appealed to both lay readers and working biologists, a book for beachcombers and academics. In the preface to *Tides*, he later wrote that "the enormous wealth of life that occurs between the upper and the lower limits of the tide is a phenomenon of intense interest to the biologist and to the layman alike. Here strange plants and bizarre, brilliantly colored animals grow in such abundance that the most casual visitor to the seashore cannot fail to notice some of them. Almost invariably his curiosity is aroused: Is that gorgeous flower-like thing in the tide pool a plant or an animal? What is it called? What does it eat? How does it defend itself and reproduce its kind? Will it hurt me if I touch it?"[39] Campbell read the *Tides* manuscript during the *Grampus* expedition and offered editing suggestions that the collaborators readily accepted. In their continuing conversations, he took Ed and Jack beyond empirical considerations, working to broaden their perceptions of science by turning to poets, prophets, and philosophers. Thanks in part to Campbell, *Between Pacific Tides* is a magical read as well as sound science.

In his wave shock essay, Ed acknowledged the help he received from Campbell and from Jack and Sasha Calvin during the *Grampus* expedition.

> Grateful acknowledgements are due to a number of interested and interesting individuals along the way, by whose aid a fine cruise was made finer; foremost of course, to Jack and Sasha Calvin, skipper and mate of the dry decked (but not really too dry) good and congenial motor launch *Grampus*; to Father Kashevaroff, Curator of the Alaska Historical Museum for really exceptional hospitality and assistance at Juneau; to the Thompson family and especially to Kit Thompson for a pleasant stay and interesting collecting at Refuge Cove; to the Bolshanins at Sitka, and to George Sumption, master of a shrimp nettcr at Wrangell. I have specially to thank Joseph Campbell of New York, a constant and interested companion, for clarifying and outlining in some detail certain conclusions attained en route."[40]

Ricketts also acknowledges "Dr. W. K. Fisher, Director of the Hopkins Marine Station, who was good enough to read over the manuscript carefully and to make several significant suggestions," and he thanks "G. E. MacGinitie, director of the Kerckhoff Marine Station, and . . . Dr. Waldo Schmitt of the United States National Museum for similar kind offices."[41] Each of these and other expressions of gratitude appear in the acknowledgements section of Ricketts's wave shock paper.

Ricketts's days in Alaska were filled with collecting. Joe Campbell often awoke to find that Ed had been in the tide pools since before dawn; he would return before noon with bags of little animals. Calvin was similarly engaged. He took the *Grampus* to the best coves and fjords and with Ed collected specimens. For his part, Campbell combined days collecting specimens with Ricketts and lounging in the sun on Sitka's shoreline. On one such afternoon he chanced to find a topless Xenia Kashevaroff on the beach as he emerged from a swim, completely naked. They spent days together while the *Grampus* remained in Sitka, though from all accounts their friendship remained platonic.

In the evenings, Sasha and the three men read Spengler and Goethe; Eckermann's *Gespräche mit Goethe*; *The Signature of All Things* by the seventeenth-century philosopher and mystic Jacob Boehme; a German edition of Novalis's poetry; Jan Christiaan Smuts's *Holism and Evolution*; John Elof Boodin's *A Realistic Universe*; Robert Briffault's *The Mothers*; Dostoevsky's *The Idiot*; and Goddard's translation of the Tao Te Ching. These books took up as much space in the little library on the *Grampus* as the navigation maps, the tidal charts, and the handful of books about marine invertebrates (including Allee's *Animal Aggregations*) to help the crew identify and study the animals they collected.

For Joe Campbell, the *Grampus* trip was eye-opening. He learned a great deal from Ed, who was, as always, a gifted teacher. According to the Larsens, "Ed brought him back to his early love of biology, and initiated him into the mysteries of the tide pools, where there were always new revelations lurking under a rock or an anemone."[42] In 1985, a half century after his trip on the *Grampus*, Campbell recalled, "It was Ed who was especially important to me, because he re-enforced the interest in biology that I had had as a prep school student. And from our long talks about biology, I eventually came up with one of my basic viewpoints: that myth is a function of biology. It's a manifestation of the human imagination which is stirred by the energies of the organs of the body operating against one another. In other words, myth is as fundamental to us as our capacity to speak and think and dream."[43]

In *The Professor with a Thousand Faces*, Campbell recalls visiting Juneau, "a very exciting border town, a goldmine there and a lot of men working the goldmine, every other storefront was a bar and the alternate one's pool parlors. Alaska was first Russian, which I now spoke, and many Russians had married Indian women and were hangovers. They loved food, parties, no end of food!"[44] While in Juneau, sometime near the end of August, Sasha took Ed, Joe, and Jack to see Father Kashevaroff and two of her sisters, Xenia and Legia. It was a wonderful conclusion to a grand trip.

Finally, Ed and Joe turned for home. Aboard the *Princess Louise* en route to Seattle, carrying the cases of specimens they had collected, there was plenty of time to talk. They agreed on the towering transcendence of Bach, the greatness of Goethe and Novalis, and the profundity of Spengler. (Ed was brushing up on his high school German so he could read Goethe and Novalis in the original.) The insights they had previously gleaned from Jeffers's "Roan Stallion" were working on each man in similar ways, and as they talked, they strove for synthesis—positing the combination of myth and science as a unifying principle for breaking through. When the *Princess Louise* docked in Seattle, Ed and Joe loaded the specimens they had collected into Ed's Packard and drove south. Ed dropped Joe in Berkeley and completed the drive to Monterey alone.

Ricketts and Campbell saw each other infrequently after their trip to Alaska; their longest time together was when Joe returned to the Monterey Peninsula in 1939, the year *Between Pacific Tides* was published. But they corresponded regularly by mail, continuing conversations that had begun in Alaska. After the publication of *Sea of Cortez* in December 1941, Campbell, whose career as a mythologist was just beginning, wrote to Ed, telling him of his admiration for that book: "the marvelous form of living which we met during those weeks on deck, namely, a form directly in touch with the mother zone between the tides."[45] For Joe Campbell, Ed's belief that "everything is inherently related to everything else," and that to understand nature means above all to understand relationships between its constituent parts, was eye-opening. It affirmed and enhanced Campbell's understanding that human myths are by definition biological and that the hero's journey is universal across space and throughout time.

The weeks Campbell and Ricketts spent together on the *Grampus* and in Alaska made a lasting impression on both men; the spirit of their conversations is what in part makes *Between Pacific Tides* so special. In a review of *Tides* that appeared in the May 1939 issue of the *American Midland Naturalist*, George MacGinitie wrote that "when a scientific book is written so that it is useful and understandable both to the scientist and the layman, without detracting from its scientific value, the authors have accomplished a highly commendable work. In their '*Between Pacific Tides*,' Ricketts and Calvin have achieved this difficult and valuable combination."[46] This "difficult and valuable combination" owes much to the conversations among Ed, Jack, Sasha, and particularly Joe Campbell, on the *Grampus*. The result is a book designed, as Ricketts writes, for "our visitor to a rocky shore at low tide [who] has entered possibly the most prolific life zone in the world—a belt so thickly populated that often not only is every square inch of the area utilized by some plant or animal but the competition for attachment sites is so keen that animals settle upon each other—plants grow upon animals, and animals upon each other."[47]

We have spent a significant amount of time talking about Joseph Campbell, Jack Calvin, and Ritch Lovejoy—three remarkable people who were in Ed Ricketts's orbit during the years when he was working on *Between Pacific Tides*. *Tides* is Ed Ricketts's book, but one cannot dismiss the influence that friends and associates—scientists, as well as mythologists and novelists—had on his work. Ricketts's most important friendships were symbiotic—from Campbell and the crew of the *Grampus* to Steinbeck and everyone with whom he was close. He got a great deal and he gave even more than he got. *Between Pacific Tides* owes much to metaphysics, mythology, and poetry, as well as to good science. That is what makes it and its principal author so very special.

It is clear that as Ricketts sought to understand life in the intertidal zones, he drew on concepts from many sources and disciplines: the science of W. C. Allee, the landscapes of George Inness, Otto Spengler's model of history, Robinson Jeffers's "Roan Stallion," and the Tao Te Ching. Integrating them all into a coherent whole was no small feat. This is not to say that Ricketts tossed it all into a single pot. He grasped the differences between art and science, and he was careful not to mix and match in a way that would undercut an understanding of either. He knew that the scientist develops theories to explain recurring and orderly relationships in the natural world, whereas a work of art is not an object for theoretical generalization, that it exists for aesthetic appreciation and response. He understood that the scientist pursues hypotheses that exhibit and explain relationships between verifiable facts, while the artist neither formulates nor explains. The artist creates and those creations are equivalent, not to general propositions about phenomena, but to the phenomena themselves.

It is the oceans and the seashore in all their richness and variety that for Ed unlocked the meaning of art and science. The sea has always been a source of awe and wonder, as well as a subject of scientific inquiry. Our perception of it is as much influenced by the paintings of William Turner and the novels of Herman Melville as it is by the expedition of the HMS *Challenger*. For the artist the sea can be a wondrous and magical place, while for the scientist it both lures and frustrates, because it simultaneously demands and defies definition in precise propositional form. Ed Ricketts moved toward truth, but nowhere in *Between Pacific Tides* or in his other writings does he affirm that the answers to his questions are complete and final.

John Isaacs of the Scripps Institution and the director of California's Institute of Marine Resources said that the sea challenges the science, which, in turn, provides "opportunities to guide ourselves out of the present age and into a new and future world."[48] Remember Ricketts's disdain for the dry ball scientist, the pickler of the field whose science is compartmentalized, overly specialized, and devoted to trivia. Unlike Ed, they are "Prufrockian." They dare not disturb the universe. Ed studied the sea and he studied Bach and Boehme, Joyce and Jeffers. Fascinated by both art and science, he lived the creative and the re-creative processes, often speculating into the sun. Knowledge and understanding for Ed were stones in a developing cathedral that he sought to build with creativity and with style.

In the years immediately following the *Grampus* expedition, Ricketts returned to Puget Sound to collect more *Gonionemus* (jellyfish) for his supply business. In 1934 and 1935, he and Nan took the children there for much of the summer. Ed and Nan worked the low tides, collecting specimens for Pacific Biological Laboratories while Ricketts filled his notebooks with descriptions of the shorelines surrounding the entrance to the sound. There is no specific mention of these trips in *Between Pacific Tides;* but elsewhere Ricketts talks about visiting the Hood Canal and observing colonies of hydrozoans. "In late July 1935, the colonies of *Clytia* in southeastern Hood Canal were producing round, four-tentacled medusae."[49] In *Between Pacific Tides*, Ricketts writes about surveying the Saanich Inlet of Vancouver Island. "In lower Saanich Inlet, about Deep Cove, for instance, in the summer of 1935, almost every suitable stone upturned revealed one of these brilliant worms in an apparently fabricated mild depression."[50]

As a sidebar to his interest in the intertidal zones, Ricketts was curiously and uncharacteristically interested in automobiles, probably because having one in working order was critical for travel to all but the closest collecting sites. As early as 1924, Nan mentions trips with Albert and Doris in the "Old Mitchell," presumably the car the Galighers had driven from Chicago in 1922. "We had only one car, and when there were collecting trips to be made, we made it a picnic day too. We packed food if we had to go far. If not then we just packed food for the babies and put the babies in a wash basket in the back of the 'Big Mitchell,' our car. It was an oldie but was very good to us, taking us on many beautiful trips and adventures."[31]

Ed replaced "Big Mitchell" with a second-hand Packard sedan in good condition which allowed him to extend his collecting trips well beyond the Monterey Peninsula. He traveled to Southern California and Mexico during the winter months, and to northern Washington State and British Columbia in the summers. The Packard quickly tallied over 100,000 miles so that, in 1933, Ricketts traded it in for another Packard, this one a 7-40 Sedan Limousine with only 28,000 miles on the odometer. Bruce Ariss, an artist and writer in Monterey and Ricketts's close friend, joined Ed on a collecting trip to Baja California. He described Ed's new vehicle in his *Inside Cannery Row*:

> The Packard was an enormous eight-cylinder-in-line automobile, chauffer driven style, with the front and back sections separated by a vertical crack-down window. The car was black, shiny, had lots of chrome, and sported two huge tires in the front fender wells. It had been a great luxury car in its day. Ed had bought it from a bankrupt Pebble Beach estate. It had fine black leather upholstery in the front and mohair in the back, with cut-glass vases for flowers and even a phone, with a buzzer, that Jean and I had to try out, of course.[52]

In a letter to Torsten Gislén, Ed wrote that he expected to own this car for five years and rack up 120,000 miles.

Back in Pacific Grove, with a car full of specimens, Ricketts needed help with taxonomic identifications. He worked first with Walter Fisher and then with the other Stanford faculty—Rolf Bolin, Frank Mace MacFarland, Arthur Russell Moore, and Tage Skogsberg.

They and several visiting scientists helped Ricketts identify the species he had collected. Some of these visitors were leaders in their fields: Henry B. Bigelow, founder and first director of the Woods Hole Oceanographic Institution; T. Wayland Vaughan, director of the Scripps Institution of Oceanography; Naohide Yatsu, director of Misaki Marine Biological Station of the University of Tokyo, and the aforementioned Deogracias D. Villadolid, from the Bureau of Fisheries in the Philippines. There were other scientists who knew Ricketts personally since they had been at Hopkins. Each held a curator position at a leading natural history museum. Ed sent specimens to Waldo L. Schmitt at the U.S National Museum of Natural History (the Smithsonian Institution), Elisabeth Deichmann at Harvard's Museum of Comparative Zoology, and Libbie H. Hyman of New York's American Museum of Natural History. They all liked Ed and were happy to help.

Ed was aware of the limitations of the ecologist who knows little taxonomy and whose dependence in the field is on the identification of species by museum experts far from the collecting zones. He worked to become taxonomically self-sufficient, perusing whatever sources he could find to help him become better acquainted with the animals he had collected. An important resource with which Ed became familiar was Elizabeth Johnson and Harry James Snook's pioneering study of Pacific Coast marine biology, *Seashore Animals of the Pacific Coast* (1927). Ed found the book helpful since its authors had studied some of the same geography that he was exploring; he used it as a reference guide for identifying many of the animals he collected on the California coast. Later, though, it would become the source of problems Ricketts would have with Stanford University Press, the publishers of *Between Pacific Tides*.

Myrtle Johnson was a lifelong educator, beginning as a teacher of biology at Pasadena High School (1912–1921), followed by twenty-five years as a professor of biology at what was then San Diego State Teachers College (1921–1946). In a 1967 memoir she wrote for *Science Education*, she reminisced about how she and Harry Snook organized *Seashore Animals of the Pacific Coast*:

> Work began on the book in 1915 while Mr. Snook and I were both teaching biology at Pasadena, where the policy was to give

as much laboratory and fieldwork as possible with as much living material as we could furnish for study. This meant many collecting trips to gardens, to the beaches, and to the mountains to supply the needed material in attractive condition. Available books on marine invertebrates dealt with Atlantic coast species almost entirely, so we felt the need for a book with scientific names for our species and information on their habits and distribution. Urged on by our efficient and beloved department head, Miss Mabel Pierson, Mr. Snook and I undertook the job of combing research papers, quizzing research workers, collecting by the "dawn's early light" and gathering material on the invertebrates most commonly found on the western beaches. We were given laboratory space at the Scripps Institution at La Jolla where we worked for about six weeks each summer until 1921 when we worked at the Friday Harbor Marine Laboratory. Meanwhile I had taken time off from teaching to make collections and photographs or sketches of living material at a number of points along the central coast and had met marine biologists who were eager to help speed the book on its way and were most helpful. We were aiming for a picture book of the animals with a minimum of word description and as much of life history and habits as we could learn. The era of color photography, fast film and handy sized cameras was far in the future but we managed to get a photograph, outline drawing or a color sketch of nearly every species common enough to be included. We were thinking of high school students as we wrote, and the book has been sought by high school and college students, at marine stations and by beach combers of all ages.[53]

Seashore Animals of the Pacific Coast was an expansive and comprehensive enterprise. The 1927 volume totaled 659 pages, with seven hundred black-and-white sketches and twelve tissue-guarded colored plates. The authors describe more than five hundred species and subspecies of eleven phyla, no small feat indeed. Generally referred to as "Johnson and Snook," this book was the first substantial publication that identified and described, in an organized phylogenic manner, invertebrate shore life along the Pacific Coast. When Ed began his work in the tide pools along Monterey Bay, many invertebrates had yet to be described in any systematic way. As we mentioned earlier,

Book cover of Myrtle E. Johnson and Harry L. Snook's
Seashore Animals of the Pacific Coast (New York: MacMillan,
1927)

he was thus confronted by a new and largely unstudied fauna that
required him to ship specimens to experts for identification and
description. The silver lining in all this was that it enabled Ed to
make important and lasting connections with some of the most
prominent and accomplished marine biologists in the country.
But it was an extremely time-consuming process. Corresponding
with people across the country and the globe in an age before
computers and email was no small matter. But as he received
reports from the scientists to whom he had sent specimens, and
with additional assistance from "Johnson and Snook," Ed was

ultimately able to finalize work on a first version of *Between Pacific Tides*.

As for a publisher of *Between Pacific Tides*, the choice was obvious: both Ricketts and Calvin were convinced that the Stanford University Press should publish their book. It made good sense since so many of the people who helped Ed were members of the Stanford faculty. In the end, he and Jack were right. But for more than a few years they had their doubts. Working with the Stanford press would be a long and sometimes painful process that tested their patience and that of the Stanford press staff. To understand how Stanford approached the subject, we need to talk a bit about the press's history, its beginnings, and its development during the first decades of the twentieth century up to the time when Ricketts and Calvin sent its editors their manuscript.

CHAPTER 4

the saga begins

Publishing is a business. Writing may be art, but publishing, when all is said and done, comes down to dollars.

—NICHOLAS SPARKS

THE STANFORD UNIVERSITY PRESS

On a Sunday morning in March 1891, Leland and Jane Stanford traveled to Bloomington Indiana, where they met with then president of the University of Indiana, David Starr Jordan, to discuss their planned university and offer him the presidency. The following day, Jordan presented the couple with a four-point memorandum outlining the primary conclusions of their discussions, with which he hoped the Stanfords would agree. Of importance here is the fourth and final point: "That provision be made for the publication of the results of any important research on the part of professors or advanced students. Such papers may be issued from time to time as 'Memoirs of the Leland Stanford Junior University.'"[1]

Leland and Jane Stanford agreed to Jordan's request that the university establish an independent publishing company. What neither they nor Jordan anticipated, however, was that, during the following year, a sophomore named Julius Andrew Quelle would set up a one-person printing shop inside the university's power house near the Main Quad. Quelle was a New Yorker who spent his pre-college years working for a printing and bookbinding company. Quite the entrepreneur, he borrowed $25 from each of the university's twelve professors (yes, all twelve of them) to purchase a small, secondhand press, which he used to print the first editions of the student-run newspaper. He called it the *Daily Palo Alto*; it was later renamed the *Stanford Daily*. In addition to the student newspaper, Quelle published articles for faculty members, and, in 1895, he published the first work to bear the imprint of the Stanford University Press. It was a series of sketches titled *The Story of the Innumerable Company* and was written by President Jordan. And so, in a one-story building next to boilers and generators, the Stanford University Press was born. "Were it not for Jordan's vision and Quelle's industry, there may never have been a Stanford University Press," wrote Kalie Ann Caetano, a digital media specialist at the press who years later compiled its detailed history. "Yet, 125 years later, the publishing house that got its start in the campus power house is still going strong, supporting and refining scholarship that both extends and challenges prevailing views and disseminates new knowledge of all types around the world."[2]

In 1917, Stanford bought Quelle's printing shop for $9,500 and opened a new press building, spending thousands of dollars on upgraded equipment. In 1920, William A. Friend was named the press superintendent and became manager of the press' publishing and manufacturing departments. At the start of his twenty-five-year tenure at the press, Friend designed and copy-edited books, set them in type, and then operated the printing equipment himself.

In 1925, Friend hired William Hawley Davis, a Stanford professor of English, as the press's first editor, and he and Friend hired a staff to market and sell its publications. By 1925, Friend and Davis had moved the press's publishing functions to the main Stanford campus, where it became a standing department of the university. It remained in the same building for the next eighty years. William Davis retained his tenure in the English Department, where he continued to teach, but his primary efforts were directed toward building the press. According to a Stanford memorial resolution honoring him, Davis's editorial responsibilities were described "as those of a pack-horse, midwife, and theme-corrector."[3] Before his retirement, he saw more than three hundred titles through to publication.

When Davis assumed his position, the press catalog listed a total of seventy-five titles, one of the more successful of which was the *Illustrated Flora of the Pacific States* (1923) by a Stanford botanist named Leroy Abrams. Between 1923 and 1960, Abrams wrote three additional volumes, the last of which was published posthumously. The *Illustrated Flora* is a well-laid-out and traditionally structured set of books listing species under each family classification. Plant species are tallied in an outline format by both their scientific and common names. Because the press staff were not scientists, and may have assumed that Abrams's taxonomic approach was the best way to handle an inventory of plant or animal species, the book might have negatively influenced those who reviewed *Between Pacific Tides*, given that Ricketts and Calvin eschewed taxonomy in favor of ecology and that they submitted their manuscript to Stanford only a few years after first volume of Abrams's series was published.

During Davis's twenty-five years as general editor, the press published in an array of fields and formats, from the natural sciences to the social sciences, from mathematics to literature and languages, from pamphlets to multivolume collections. By 1939, the year when *Between Pacific Tides* was finally published, the Stanford press, under Friend and Davis's leadership, had 392 active titles, twelve book series, and seventy employees. Arguably the most important title that Davis pack-horsed, midwifed, and theme-corrected through Stanford University Press was *Between Pacific Tides*. That volume remains among its most successful titles, having gone through five editions with sales in excess of one hundred thousand copies—not a small number for a science text.

During the winter of 2014, a senior press staffer who was asked about the genesis of *Between Pacific Tides* identified a group of manila file folders containing a sizable collection of internal press memos and correspondence between Ricketts, Calvin, and the press staff. Taken together, they provide a definitive record of the history of the publication of *Between Pacific Tides*. They also convey a great deal about the indefatigable Ed Ricketts, who knew where to go and how to get there. It was eight full years after Ed and Jack submitted a typescript of their manuscript to the Stanford University Press that *Between Pacific Tides* was finally published. During those years Ricketts and Calvin, but primarily Ricketts, persevered to bring their project to completion. He did it with a single-minded dedication that was genuinely remarkable.

For Ed and Jack, there was no option but to persevere, since so much was hanging in the balance. Though a series of papers on intertidal ecology appeared in the publications of the Puget Sound Biological Station (later the Friday Harbor Laboratories of the University of Washington) in the 1920s, at stake now was the first book presenting an ecological view of life in the intertidal zones of the west coast of North America. Ricketts and Calvin knew—given the quality of the writing, the photographs, and the illustrations, and that their identification and description of animals had been satisfactorily fact-checked—that their book would be transformative. In the end, it was that and more.

Between Pacific Tides was transformative for Fred Tarp, a native Californian who decided to become a marine biologist at age eleven after spending a month during a summer in Pacific Grove, and who was a graduate student at Hopkins in the mid-1940s. Tarp then became a professor in the Department of Biological Sciences at Contra Costa College, where he devoted a lifetime to studying the ecology of San Francisco Bay. He was introduced to marine biology by Myrtle Johnson and Harry Snook. In a talk he presented at a Steinbeck and the Sea conference at Oregon State University's Marine Science Center (now the Hatfield Marine Science Center) in 1974, Tarp acknowledged that *Seashore Animals of the Pacific Coast* was "an excellent text, and the only one readily available to the general public at the time. . . . It contained short analyses of the principal species of marine invertebrates one would expect to find along the seashore from Baja California to Alaska. The organisms were arranged in phyletic order, the style of the day, which made it difficult to use by amateurs and inexperienced biologists."[4]

Tarp confesses that he was at the time "a rank beginner" who "quickly learned from the new text by Ricketts and Calvin the ease with which a beginner could identify the common intertidal organisms using the methods they outlined."[5] Armed with the results of Ed and Jack's work, Fred Tarp found that identification "began with the observation of a few environmental variables readily discernible to anyone." They included the exposure of the animal to wave shock, to its distribution relative to the tidal level, and to the bottom type—whether rock, sand, or mud. "These organisms," noted Tarp, "are then ranked according to their relative commonness in such environments. . . . The text considered 500 of the most common organisms encountered in the intertidal regions of the Pacific Coast. Today such an organism-habitat inter-relationship is basic to an understanding of marine biology, even at the level of high school biology students."[6] At the time, Tarp concludes, echoing Joel Hedgpeth, "such an approach was a radical departure from the traditional and contrary to that practiced by the reigning priesthood of biology to such an extent, that the 1939 edition of *Tides* was almost dismissed arbitrarily because of the hostility shown to it by just one traditionally-minded pre-publication reviewer."[7]

We take issue with the idea that most scientists were overtly hostile toward the ecological approach Ricketts and Calvin took toward their study of the Pacific seashore. Rather, given their own predilections and their familiarity with the scientific literature at the time (remember Abrams's *Illustrated Flora*), they simply found it foreign. One possible reason for unease by traditional biologists is the idea that the Ricketts-Calvin approach is somehow imprecise, since relationships between animals and their habitats can be fluid depending on even slight changes in the makeup of those habitats. There are, after all, shifting degrees of wave shock depending on a variety of factors, which are influenced by the presence or lack of rocky shelters of various types and sizes. This is a legitimate concern, best mitigated by repeat investigations of the same environments at different times with different weather conditions. Ed understood the potential problem; he referenced it in the 1936 "Zoological Preface" he wrote for *Between Pacific Tides*.

Also at stake was Ricketts's belief that books of science generally, and natural history in particular, should be accessible to the general reader and not solely to the scientific elect. In their preface to *Between Pacific Tides*, Ed and Jack write that "our visitor to a rocky shore at low tide has entered possibly the most prolific life zone in the world. . . . To supply such a person with as much as possible of the information that he wants is the chief aim of this handbook." Again, Ed anticipates Rachel Carson, who insisted that science does not belong in a compartment of its own, that it is not the prerogative of isolated priest-like academics in their laboratories. For Ricketts and Calvin, the arrangement of their book would be "the one which we believe can be most readily grasped by the person who has little or no biological training."[8]

Fred Tarp was one such person. He is but one of as many as a hundred thousand "rank beginners" for whom *Between Pacific Tides* was their introduction to life on the Pacific seashore. In their approach to the study of marine ecology and their belief in how and to whom the results of their work should be disseminated, Ricketts and Calvin were pathfinders. But with the publication of *Between Pacific Tides* in almost constant jeopardy for the better part of a decade, it took uncommon efforts by both Ricketts and Calvin—principally by Ed— to make it happen.

The nine-year publication saga began on March 24, 1930, when Jack Calvin wrote to Dean Storey, then the press's advertising manager, detailing his and Ed's hope for a manual about marine life in the intertidal zones along the central Pacific Coast. It would be, Calvin wrote,

> a non-technical handbook for the casual seashore visitors (and for classes in nature study) illustrating and describing the common inter-tidal animals of the Pacific coast between Alaska and Lower California. The treatment will be ecological (i.e. by habitat), and inductive; stress being laid on forms with relation to their prominence and strikingness. Illustrations will be photographic when possible, otherwise by line drawings. There will also be included a minimum of perhaps a half dozen color plates showing animals noted particularly for their vivid or delicate coloring. Scientific names cannot be avoided, for many animals have no popular names, but popular names will used where they exist.[9]

If the press staff believed that good biology was grounded in a taxonomic approach to its subject, they seemed to suspend their disbelief after a first reading of Ricketts and Calvin's manuscript. But other matters did concern them. In Calvin's letter are some scribbled notes—by whose hand remains a matter of conjecture—that would raise red flags. Chief among them is, first, a reference to Johnson and Snook. A second handwritten scribble on Jack's letter reads

"Sea-Beach at Ebb-Tide" and refers to a different publication, this one by Augusta Foote Arnold, titled *Sea-Beach at Ebb-Tide: A Guide to the Study of the Seaweeds and the Lower Animal Life Found between Tide-Marks* (1901). Even though this book is about life on a different coastline—the Atlantic—by an author noted primarily for writing cookbooks, someone at the Stanford press thought it, as well as Johnson and Snook, might be comparable, in terms of pricing and sales, to what Ricketts and Calvin were proposing.

Finally, in the same handwritten scribble are the words "Consult Fisher and Skogsberg," by which whoever wrote the note was referring to Walter Fisher and Tage Skogsberg at Hopkins. The suggestion is that they should be asked to review the manuscript to evaluate its content and assess the competency of its authors. Although Friend and his group at the press were not opposed to an ecological study of marine invertebrates, they were evidently concerned that neither Jack nor Ed were traditionally trained scientists.

Besides questioning Ricketts and Calvin's scientific expertise to author a scientifically sound book-length study of marine invertebrates, the press staff wondered whether the book would sell. The proposed $7.50 price tag for *Between Pacific Tides* seemed risky but was necessary because of the book's many illustrations and photographs (112 figures and 45 full-page plates with pictures of 187 animals), which increased the cost of production. Without some sort of subsidy, the press staff was concerned that the book would not be profitable. An unsigned note in the press files reads that "they [the authors] should submit (virtual) copy for a typical section, illustrations included, and estimate of multiple of this which completed work will include. On this basis, Press will determine commercial practicability."[10] Within a couple of months after negotiations began, it was clear that the publishing of *Between Pacific Tides* would be neither a simple nor a speedy process.

In response to the request for some pages of text, Ricketts sent along the introductory chapter and provided William Davis with a detailed outline of the book, explaining that its ecological approach would distinguish *Tides* from other titles and would interest both lay readers and credentialed scientists. Ed also told Davis that he and Calvin would include, as part of the book's contents, the research findings of faculty and students from Stanford's Hopkins Marine

Station that would enhance its scientific credibility and also bring credit to the university. He insisted that the book would sell and even offered the resources of Pacific Biological Laboratories to help generate sales.

> We are submitting herewith the introductory chapter or section of our intertidal animal handbook, one section written up about as for final copy (with illustrations), and a tentative outline of the whole. Here are some general considerations in connection with the modus operandi, etc.:
>
> The ecological treatment will have the virtues of
>
> (a) novelty
>
> (b) ease of application by tourist and ordinary observer
>
> (c) enhanced quick value even to the scientist and serious student.
>
> We can make popularly available such work done since Johnson and Snook as Fisher's and MacGinitie's work on the natural history of Urechis, Fisher's starfish work, etc.
>
> The prime objective of this work is to familiarize the casual observer with the animals, not to make a specialist of him, as would have to be done if he wished to separate the allied hermit crabs or hydroids. At the same time, we can reach a numerically powerful field by making the account accurate enough (and with adequate bibliographical references) for the student, which opens up the zoological departments of all colleges, and the libraries of most high schools to our work. Assuming that the thing is well done, Stanford and U.C. will use many copies officially, and there should be several thousand copies in use in the secondary schools of the United States, even in the east. In this connection, Pacific Biological Laboratories can send out inserts of sample pages with our next mailing, covering all the large universities of the world, most of the colleges and many of the high schools and gymnasia.[11]

Contrary to what some press staff may have believed, Ricketts and Calvin were not the first to propose an ecological study of marine invertebrates. Although previous practitioners of the habitat approach may have been few in number, and none had written about life along the Pacific shoreline, the few who did employ an ecological approach were a distinguished group. We've already noted that Joel Hedgpeth, who years later managed two of the four revisions of *Between Pacific Tides*, recognized that Ricketts and Calvin's work was modeled in part on Allee's understanding of intertidal biology. It also owes to A. E. Verrill and Sidney Smith's 1874 classic work "Report upon the Invertebrate Animals of Vineyard Sound and Adjacent Waters Sound," in which the authors conducted their study of animals according to habitat. Ricketts confirmed this, writing in "Zoological Introduction" in *Between Pacific Tides* (1936), "Revising again this laborious and long-continued work, now after more than three years, the writers realize more keenly than ever how great a task has been undertaken. The ecological arrangement (in part after Verrill and Smith's pioneering 1872 Report—a natural history in every sense of the word) has entailed not only considerable clerical difficulty but has necessitated a great amount of field work, most of which could have been obviated if the traditional treatment had been used."[12] It was, however, the "traditional treatment" that Ed and Jack wanted to avoid.

Joel Hedgpeth provides evidence that Allee's published research about his habitat-focused work at Woods Hole was important to Ricketts as he surveyed marine life along the Pacific Coast. In an essay titled *Philosophy on Cannery Row* (1971) that was based on a talk he gave at the first Steinbeck-Ricketts conference that was held at Oregon State University, Hedgpeth explains how Ricketts's reliance on Allee's publication contributed to the book's structure: "The basic organization, the approach by the various seashore habitats, including exposed and protected shore, was modeled upon a paper by W. C. Allee which appeared in *Biological Bulletin* in two installments in 1923. This work was starred (*) in the bibliography of the first edition of *Between Pacific Tides*."[13]

Some years later, in his two-volume annotated collection of Ricketts's writings, *The Outer Shores* (1978), Hedgpeth reaffirmed the impact of Allee's thinking on Ricketts. "In the spring of 1923, Allee had published his '*Studies in Marine Ecology*,' which summarized observations and fieldwork over an eight-year period at Woods Hole. Ed studied these papers very carefully (undoubtedly, they were the material of some of Allee's lectures), and Ed used them as guides in his own observations on the Pacific coast, for he considered them to be 'applicable anywhere.'"[14]

Besides drawing on the classic work of Verrill and Smith and that of
W. C. Allee, Ricketts respected and, where appropriate, referenced
the work of many of his contemporaries. In his communications with
the press staff, he mentions corresponding with many accomplished
invertebrate biologists, attempting to put to rest concerns about his
own scientific bona fides. All were acknowledged experts on various
species of marine invertebrates whose ability to identify those species and, on occasion, name new species, was critically important to
Ricketts and Calvin. Highlighting his list were Walter Fisher and
George MacGinitie, but there were others, including spongiologist
Max Walker de Laubenfels, an interesting character who published
upward of four dozen articles about his beloved sponges, many of
them punctuated with a wonderful sense of humor.

De Laubenfels came to Hopkins as a graduate student after finishing his undergraduate degree at Oberlin College. Like so many
new Hopkins graduate students, he met Ed shortly after he arrived.
In early 1931, Ricketts gave him several sponges he had collected. De
Laubenfels was extremely grateful, writing, "I have had the benefit of a small collection which I found at Stanford University, and I
have received some very interesting forms from Mr. E. F. Ricketts of
the Pacific Biological Laboratory."[15] Beyond this recognition, in his
1932 publication, *The Marine and Fresh-Water Sponges of California*, de
Laubenfels credits Ricketts fourteen times, and names a species of
sponge after Ed: *Poecillastra rickettsi.*[16]

After finishing his doctoral work at Stanford, de Laubenfels taught
at Pasadena Junior College, a job he was lucky to get, given the woes
in higher education caused by the Great Depression. When jobs in
universities finally opened, he went to the University of Hawai'i and,
in 1940, relocated to the Department of Zoology at what was then
Oregon State College. Once established in Corvallis, his meetings
with Ricketts were infrequent, but the two communicated often by
mail. De Laubenfels remained a good friend and offered to help Ed
in any way he could. When, in the mid-1930s, he learned of problems
with the publication of *Between Pacific Tides*, there was little he could
do except offer moral support.

Actually, moral support helped. Ricketts and de Laubenfels were
kindred spirits. Take, for example, de Laubenfels 1956 essay in the
Journal of Paleontology in which he suggests that "the extinction of

dinosaurs was the result of a large asteroid striking Earth. . . . It is not fantastic to consider the likelihood that an extra-large impact affected this planet some sixty million years ago. No human being was here to see it or study it with radar. But just such extinctions occurred, and just such survivals occurred, at the end of the Cretaceous, as would be expected to occur as the result of impact from a planetesimal or an extra-large shower of meteorites."[17] Ricketts enjoyed scientists like de Laubenfels who took their work but not themselves too seriously.

In the narrative portion of *Sea of Cortez*, Steinbeck and Ricketts talk about the "little men" of science, noting that "it has seemed sometimes that the little men in scientific work assume the awe-fullness of a priesthood to hide their deficiencies, as a witch-doctor does with stilts and high masks"[18] "The true biologist," Steinbeck and Ricketts write , "deals with life, with teeming boisterous life, and learns something from it, learns that the first rule of life is living."[19] De Laubenfels, and those other scientists to whom Ricketts was attracted and with whom he worked, was such a biologist. *Between Pacific Tides* is animated by "teeming boisterous life."

Ricketts took his own scientific work very seriously. In fact, if there was anyone guilty of avoiding hard work on the project, it was Calvin. In late 1930, John Steinbeck wrote to his friend Carl Wilhelmson about a conversation he had with Jack. "Says Jack Calvin, 'I long ago ceased to take anything I write seriously.' I retorted 'I take everything I write seriously; unless one does take his work seriously there is very little chance of its ever being good work.'"[20] Ricketts agreed with Steinbeck, which is why, shortly after he and Jack submitted their manuscript to Stanford, Ed assumed responsibility for dealing with all of the authorial issues concerning its publication.

Meanwhile, back at the press, discussions about the possible publication of *Between Pacific Tides* continued. Unbeknownst to Ed and Jack, advertising manager Storey was a strong believer in the project, telling William Davis that Ricketts and Calvin were continuing to work on portions of the text that would expand and enhance its content and improve its overall readability. He urged Davis to review the introductory chapter Ricketts had provided and to pinpoint any issues in the manuscript that needed to be addressed or problems that required attention. Dean Storey was likely not a newcomer to the world of Ed Ricketts. He had been a classmate of John Steinbeck and

Webster (Toby) Street at Stanford and, with them, a member of the school's English Club. Given his early enthusiasm for *Between Pacific Tides*, one could surmise that either Steinbeck or Street (or both) had briefed him about the manuscript before he ever saw it.

In October of 1930, Davis heard from Jack Calvin, who indicated that he and Ricketts were working to secure an artist to sketch color drawings for their book. Before committing to anyone, he and Ed wanted assurance that the press staff would support top-quality work, including color drawings they believed needed to be included. Calvin told Davis, "Two local artists have tried their hands at color drawings for our marine handbook, and the results are enclosed herewith. Other things being equal the job will go to Ethel Call [a local illustrator], who made the two mounted drawings, but we should like to know your opinion first, or the opinion of your color plateman, as to which of the two styles of work will reproduce better. . . . We don't like to ask the artist to go ahead without some assurance that the work is likely to be satisfactory from the reproduction point of view."[21]

Jack then tells Davis that work on the manuscript "is progressing . . . and we have hopes of seeing it about complete by spring. As was to be expected, it's a bigger job than it looked at the start, but the farther along we get the more convinced we are that it is going to be a worthwhile piece of work from every angle." With more than a touch of bravado, he closes by telling Davis, "We see no reason (although we may be naively optimistic) why it shouldn't be chosen by the Scientific Book of the Month Club, which ought to mean a send-off of something like 5000 copies. It's a pleasant thing to think about, anyhow."[22] As we know, Ethel Call was not chosen as the illustrator; the job went to Ritchie Lovejoy, who had been Jack's student at Mountain View High School and had followed him to Carmel. Calvin may well have felt responsible for Ritch. But Lovejoy was a talented artist, and Ricketts concurred that Ritchie was well suited for the job.

THINGS GET COMPLICATED

By contrast with his work in the field and in his lab, which he thoroughly enjoyed, Ricketts found his discussions and negotiations with the Stanford University Press tedious. Still, he persevered, rarely if ever venting his frustrations. On August 18, 1931, more than a year after discussions with the press staff began, he wrote William Davis, who by that time had become Ed's chief contact at the press, requesting that Davis get the necessary permissions to use photographs in *Between Pacific Tides*. Beyond requesting these permissions, Ricketts told Davis that "we will have the illustration situation pretty well in hand," writing that Ritch Lovejoy was making good progress with the line drawings.[23]

Davis and Storey were pleased that Ricketts and Calvin appeared to be progressing toward a final draft of the manuscript, with the authors awaiting reviews by Walter Fisher and George MacGinitie. Storey remained enthusiastic about *Between Pacific Tides*, even more so than Davis, writing to his editor that "books of that nature, sufficiently untechnical to be read by the lay collector and library patron, seem to have a considerable market."[24] He was also pleased with Ricketts's willingness to help publicize the book. In a lengthy memo written on September 17, 1931, Storey told Davis,

> Jack Calvin was on campus today doing some work in Mrs. Oldroyd's laboratory in connection with his manuscript "Intertidal Fauna of the Pacific Coast." He says the thing is virtually completed and is now waiting to be read by Fisher and MacGinitie, of the Hopkins Marine Station before final touching up and submitting to us. There is a point in which he is interested concerning the possibility of getting out a preliminary announcement in time for mailing to Ricketts's (his co-author) prospect list. Ricketts, who operates a marine biological laboratory supply house in Pacific Grove, has a mailing list of ten thousand museums, zoologists, large high schools, and laboratories throughout the world. These people are sent announcements of his specimen stock twice yearly, and Calvin feels that a notice sent to these people immediately (in case of acceptance of the manuscript, of course) would not only stimulate interest among their prospects, but might give some indication of what would be a sufficient first printing.
>
> The reason for this last paragraph is that Rickett's [*sic*] is about to make his fall mailing and is willing to hold it up a few weeks if we can get an announcement ready to go with it. So when the MSS is in, a quick decision will help both them and the press,

inasmuch as we could never assemble any such list ourselves, and if we could, postage to mail it out would be prohibitive to us.

He said further that Macmillan's man spent the evening with them the other night and wanted very much to get hold of it for submitting to his own house. I am not trying to push this thing myself. But it does occur to me that with this information at hand a rapid decision would work beneficially to all parties.

Having seen a bit of the mss, including the unusually excellent illustrative material, I am enthusiastic.[25]

The reader will note a reference to a "Mrs. Oldroyd" in Storey's memo and might wonder who she is. It is an interesting story. Originally from Indiana, a young woman named Ida Shepard and her parents moved to Long Beach, California, sometime in 1888. Ida became a lover of beaches and the ocean and, in time, an avid shell collector. Along the way, she met Tom Oldroyd, who shared her passion for shells. They married in 1895, and nearly two decades later, Ida, by this time quite an expert on shells, traveled to Oakland to prepare a portion of a large collection belonging to the famous shell collector, Henry Hemphill, that was to be transferred to the California Academy of Sciences. In 1916, Stanford's Geology Department acquired the rest of the Hemphill collection and recruited Mrs. Oldroyd to organize it. The following year Stanford purchased Ida and Tom's private shell collection, and the couple was hired by the university as curators of the collections, positions they held for the rest of their lives. They did their jobs well, and the Stanford shell collection became the largest in any university in the United States, second in this country only to the collection at the Smithsonian.[26] Ida Shepard Oldroyd published numerous scientific papers on marine mollusks. Ricketts and Calvin, always on the lookout for anyone with a passion for the seashore, were struck by Ida's work and later referenced her contributions to *Between Pacific Tides.*

At some point in the late summer or early fall of 1931, Ricketts, who was unaware of Storey's enthusiasm for his manuscript, became uneasy. He felt the decision-makers at the Stanford press were dragging their feet and probably losing interest. And so, in November 1931, he decided it was time to approach Walter Fisher directly; he needed Fisher's review. In a carefully penned and solicitous letter, Ed asked Fisher for help. Of interest are Ricketts's comments about Johnson and Snook. Although never critical of their book, he makes it clear that *Between Pacific Tides* will be more interesting. He also suggests that he would be pleased if Fisher would write a foreword. This was not simple flattery—well, not entirely. Ed genuinely welcomed Fisher's advice even as he sought his support. After some introductory questions and comments on matters of lesser importance—copies of anemone papers, de Laubenfels' sponge thesis, some spelling issues in the index of his manuscript, and a question about "a rare and curious worm," Ed gets to the point:

25 Nov. 1931

Dear Dr. Fisher:

There are several things I had purposed asking you—to which end I have been haunting H. M. S. [Hopkins Marine Station] unsuccessfully for the past few days on the chance that you might have driven in. The typewriter will have to suffice again. I will push under your office door the anemone papers concerning the Cribrina-Bunodactis-Evactis mixup. We will turn in copy "as is" so far as this situation is concerned, making only the one change when you have determined which genus name is correct, and what the species had best be called. Is your Dendrostoma spelled petraeum, as I have been using it, or petroeum? MacGinitie questioned my spelling. As the name appears in italics in the Ann. Mag. article it could be either. I am using this name instead of Chamberlain's pyroides unless you advise differently.

Sometime soon I should like to look over deLaubenfels sponge thesis again. Want to get title, describer of Axinella sinapeos, check spelling, and substitute correct name for what I call Stelletta, the stinging sponge. Also if you would let me look over Verrill's west coast polyp papers, I'd like to see if he says anything about our Corynactis-species name etc. These papers are hard to locate elsewhere.

I have been checking thru the spelling in the zoological index as you suggested, with distinctly positive results. I slew about 15 or 20 inaccuracies; on some of them however authorities disagree. Constructing a key would be decidedly useful; might still be wise to do, but it would take a very long time and would add to the length of the book.

I am calling the green "rare and curious worm" at the Slough Phoronopsis harmeri Pixell in conformity with what I take to be HMS usage, Hilton seems to think this is the same as his Ph. [Phoronopsis] viridis. Let me know if you think it should be changed.

We have about decided to see this thru with Stanford Press, if they are still interested. They already have some of the drawings (2 color plates); it was largely through their encouragement that most of the work has been done; and I think they will provide better than average press work and illustrations, PBL caring for a share of the advertising.

Before we drive up there with the M/S, within the next few days, we need your written opinion. You are apparently generally favorable and approve of publication and I could probably tell them this acceptably, but a written statement from you would be more effective. If you could mail this to me or stop by at the lab (on Ocean View Ave between Wu's Hotel and Hovden's Cannery) or advise when you will be at your office so I can stop over there—any of these will suit our purpose; everything else being equal with you, the most expeditious way will suit us.

Of course it wouldn't be hard to take if you would care to go so far as to write a foreword to the book; no other recommendation would be required, none could be greater. It may even be presumptuous for me to mention this; but it's done; and I'd be pretty well tickled if you had the idea of writing this foreword even before I suggested it. . . .

So here is another letter I hated to bother you with; but unless I had written you, the Press would surely do so.

Sincerely,

EF Ricketts [Signature][27]

Ricketts's strategy worked—sort of. Fisher read Ed and Jack's manuscript as Ed had asked, and he did so within a week. But the results of that reading were not quite what Ed had hoped or perhaps expected. Fisher applauds Ricketts, recognizing him as a "collector of considerable experience." But he equivocates on Ricketts's "method of taking up the animals from the standpoint of station and exposure on the seashore," since the first thing the reader wants to know is, "What is it?" He then states that "the method of taking up the animals from the standpoint of station and exposure on the seashore seems at first sight very logical but from the practical standpoint it seems to me not particularly happy. Both Professor MacGinitie and I were quite frank with Mr. Ricketts on this score." He does suggest that "certain zoological keys could be inserted which might overcome to a large extent this difficulty," and he offers a backhanded compliment about Ed and Jack's writing, "barring a certain vulgarity in places." (Ed and Fisher were not exactly late-night drinking buddies!) But then, and rather suddenly, he tells Davis, "I am rather averse to setting down on paper my view of its quality and desirability of publishing it," writing that he would be glad to come to Palo Alto to discuss all this with Davis in person. He is explicit on this point, writing, "I think that it would be much more useful to you if we could discuss the book with manuscript in hand. After that, if my opinion is important, you can make different decisions if you care to." Fisher closes his letter by stating, "In any event I think the manuscript should be carefully read by a professional zoologist." After all, he writes, "It must be remembered that neither of the authors can be classified in this category, although Mr. Ricketts is a collector of considerable experience."[28]

Fisher's review of the manuscript, often interpreted as extremely negative, is really quite mixed; it is not a categorical rejection of Ed and Jack's work. Although obviously disappointed, Ed accepted many of Fisher's suggestions, some of which were later adopted as requirements by the press for publication. The overarching point, however, is that *Between Pacific Tides* is a different sort of book than those with which Fisher was generally comfortable. Fisher was a classic academic whose publications were written in conventional scientific and technical prose, and he was discomfited by Ricketts and Calvin's free-flowing writing style and their more than occasional digressions. For Walter Fisher, the best science was pure science. In an article he wrote about the Hopkins Marine Station for the *Stanford Illustrated*

Review a decade before he read Ricketts and Calvin's manuscript, Fisher discusses the matter in some detail in regard to Hopkins' scientific mission:

> Although its final object is to ascertain something of benefit to man, yet its beginnings are always in pure science and distant from the goal. Usually the solving of the problem, however simple it may seem, is the result of the effort of many, carried on through a series of years until the story is pieced together bit by bit. It is our hope that each one who works at the station may add his definite contribution to the solution of some one of Nature's riddles. If in the years to come Stanford men and women find insight and training in this cooperation, certainly the Hopkins Marine Station will be justified.[29]

Fisher does not completely reject applied science, but he is clear about what he most admires: "We are interested in pure science, and this is one place we carry on pure science without having any responsibility to make it immediately useful." Eschewing the notion that he is a "know-it-all" whose scientific achievements set him apart from lesser members of the species, Fisher writes that, "on the contrary, we are flabbergasted by what we don't know."[30] At the same time, he was critical of Ricketts and Calvin's sometimes minimal descriptions of species, which explains what for Fisher was so critically important: "What is it?"

Fisher avoids this strain of his thinking in his review of *Between Pacific Tides*, but the fact is that, at the time, he was no fan of science popularizers. Consider his remarks about the work of William Beebe in another letter written to William Davis, this one in February 1936: "I have found few, very few, who can 'travel the knife-edge' which the author mentions on the first page. Wm Beebe thinks he does it, but although a master of 'Atlantic' style he is anathema to most biologists."[31] At times, Fisher bordered on the caustic when discussing popularizers—particularly those whose orientation is ecological rather than taxonomic: "The material will not impress the stereotyped ecologist, anyway, for he must have his salt and mustard in the guise of hydrogen ion activity tables and temperature graphs!"[32]

Walter Fisher was not a constipated stuffed shirt, although, as we've already noted, his shirts were always well starched. He had a broad range of interests—from marine critters and birds to upside-down rivers. Ed knew and understood this, which is why he genuinely respected the Hopkins director. Consider, for example, the fact that Ricketts and Calvin devote a good deal of space in their discussion of octopods and decapods to a lengthy and lively discussion about the fertilization activities of an octopus who had been captured near Hopkins. It was kept in an aquarium at the station, where Fisher oversaw the business of keeping the critter he named Mephisto well fed with a nightly diet of fish and abalone. When it was discovered that Mephisto was a female, Fisher quickly renamed her Mephista.

Ricketts and Calvin quote Fisher, who writes that Mephista "had a little shelter of stones in the front corner of the aquarium. A moveable board was so arranged as to exclude all but dim light, since in the language of animal behaviorists an octopus is negatively photostatic (unless, perchance, it is too hungry to care)." Fisher goes on to discuss what happens after "two or three festoons of eggs were deposited on the sloping underside of the granite roof of Mephista's retreat." She cared for the eggs unstintingly for nearly two months until, as Fisher writes, "they hatched during my absence from the laboratory near the middle of September. On my return, October 1, Mephista was still covering the remains of her brood—the dilapidated clusters of empty egg-capsules. She refused to eat either fish or abalone, and had become noticeably smaller. On October 11, she was found dead at her post. . . . I find it hard to believe that . . . death is a normal sequel to egg-laying."[33] In this and in other parts of *Between Pacific Tides*, we see a Walter Fisher who isn't "one of the boys," but who is a scientist the boys admire and are loath to criticize.

By contrast with much of his own work, in which he wrote with a great deal of interest in and feeling for the animals under his watch, Fisher was not impressed when he believed that scientists veered off-subject, often in an effort to popularize their work. Perhaps he viewed it as a form of sensationalism or something approaching it. A good example of what Fisher would have disparaged is when Ricketts and Calvin describe the process by which the octopus is readied for human consumption. Writing that "delicious as the flesh is," Ed and Jack affirm that "it is decidedly tough and rubbery, and the meat-grinder treatment is recommended."[34] Elsewhere in *Between Pacific Tides,* Ricketts and Calvin end their discussion of the gastropod known as the giant owl limpet, *Lottia gigantea,* with the comment that "Mexicans justly prize the owl limpet as food, for when properly prepared it is delicious, having finer meat and a more delicate flavor than abalone." Each limpet, they write, "provides one steak the size of a silver dollar which must be pounded between two blocks of wood before it is rolled in egg and flour and fried."[35] This was not Walter Fisher's idea of science.

Neither was Ricketts and Calvin's definition of the "pleasant and absurd hermit crabs," who, we will remember, are "the clowns of the tide pools."[36] Nor was their portrait of a sea slug who escapes the advances of "voracious tide-pool animals" by "taking up the gauntlet" and eating a vividly colored one alive. There is the spiny lobster that "so often meets the fate of the innocent oysters that accompanied the Walrus and the Carpenter."[37] There is that species of mussel that can, at times, be poisonous, which Calvin documented in translating the accounts of a certain "Father Veniaminoff and other Russian explorers [in Alaska]. Baranoff lost a hundred or more Aleuts all at once in Peril Strait"; write Ed and Jack, "the stench arising from the stricken made even the others ill. One of Vancouver's men is said to have died thus, and others nearly lost their lives similarly."[38] Finally, there is the lengthy discussion of the wave-swept, rocky shore goose barnacle, which "comes to us from the middle-seventeenth-century writings of that amiable liar, Gerard, who ended his large volume on plants '. . . with this wonder of England,' 'the Goose-tree, Barnakle tree, or the tree bearing Geese.'"[39]

Ricketts was aware of Fisher's dislike for the popularization of science, and he walked a fine line when discussing it with the Hopkins director. In the letter quoted above, Ed had argued for a writing style that would appeal to the lay public. "Actually there isn't much to be said against the mild popularizing of science, so long as it's done decently. We set out only to write an account as accurate as Johnson and Snook, but more interestingly told; there should be some sober and dignified excuse for this."[40]

Nine years later, Steinbeck and Ricketts wrote, in the narrative portion of *Sea of Cortez,* "It is usually found that only the little stuffy men object to what is called 'popularization,' by which they mean writing with a clarity understandable to one not familiar with the tricks and codes of the cult."[41] The person of Ed Ricketts was really very different from how many "Ed Heads" picture him. He was kind and was usually gentle, but he was unforgiving about the things that mattered most. Those things were about his science. He was deadly serious about it, and he was determined to bring his work to publication.

Walter Fisher was not alone in his criticism of *Between Pacific Tides*. Ralph Buchsbaum, a well-regarded invertebrate zoologist at the University of Chicago and a frequent visitor to Hopkins, wrote, in his review of the published volume, "The style [of *Between Pacific Tides*] is clear and interesting, though it frequently lapses into statements that might irritate the biologist and mislead the untrained reader." He may well have been thinking about hermit crabs and goose barnacles. However, Buchsbaum recognizes that Ricketts and Calvin's approach to identifying species eliminated the need for detailed morphological descriptions. "There is little or no morphological description of the animals and identification must be made chiefly on the basis of habitat and reference to the line drawings and photographs, almost all of which were made especially for this book."[42] George MacGinitie, Ed's good friend and collecting companion, noted in an otherwise positive review of *Tides* that, while the animals "are described to some extent, often the descriptions are inadequate."[43]

Compounding concerns raised by Ricketts about the publishing of *Between Pacific Tides* were the continuing worries about the matter of cost. Big books with large numbers of illustrations and color plates are expensive. It was, after all, two years into the Great Depression, and concerns about money were paramount. In February 1932, press director Friend told Davis that publishing the book in its current format would be a financial disaster. Friend focuses on (1) the sheer length of the manuscript; (2) whether the work was significantly better than Johnson and Snook; and (3) the cost of production. He suggests that it would be good if the authors would subsidize or secure a subsidy for the book, thus reducing the press' financial liability. In an internal memo, Friend describes the substance of the manuscript: "372 pages of text paper, 44 leaves full-page halftone inserts, printed one side, 4 leaves process halftones, printed one side."[44] We see, then, that by 1932 much of the book had been completed, though Ricketts would add to, subtract from, update, and refine the manuscript for the next seven years.

Adding to the press staff's worries was the 1931 publication of a book about the seashore animals on the Atlantic Coast by marine biologist William Crowder that, unfortunately for Ricketts and Calvin, was titled *Between the Tides*. Given the similarity of the two titles, the press staff suggested that Ricketts and Calvin's book be retitled. They suggested the less attractive title of *A Natural History of Pacific Shore Invertebrates*. Crowder's book was billed by its publisher (Dodd and Mead) as a detailed guide to representative species of nearly all types of invertebrate animals of the North American Atlantic coast, and included 571 species. The guidebook was an expert reference manual—perfect for beginners and even advanced readers, who could go to the seashore and identify animals about which they had previously known nothing. Fortunately for Ed and Jack, Crowder was writing about marine invertebrates in a different ocean.

While Ed was in frequent communication with Friend, Davis, and others on the press staff, Jack was in Sitka, where he became engaged in a myriad of new activities. He was writing again, but now about Alaska rather than marine invertebrates. He continued to provide Ed with advice and consent, but his time and interest were limited. By the mid-1930s, he had become more of a cheerleader than an active collaborator.

By early 1932, William Davis was besieged with concerns about and, in some quarters, objections to the Ricketts-Calvin project. But he remained steadfast in his belief that the press should consider *Between Pacific Tides* for publication. Still, he told Ricketts about the Crowder book and expressed his fear that it and a pending revision of Johnson and Snook's *Seashore Animals of the Pacific Coast* would compete for sales. In February 1932, he told Ed and Jack, "We think very highly of your illustrations and would like, alas, to include them all. Your text seems excellent. However, the total unit cost so far seems impossibly high for a list price under $7.50 and we observe that Johnson and Snook is a subsidized work."[45] It is not clear whether Ed reacted in any way to Davis's comment about a Johnson and Snook subsidy. As developments proceeded at Stanford however, it was a harbinger of things to come.

Ricketts was sensitive to Davis's concerns and, in an uncharacteristically defensive posture, wrote to Davis, stating that he was willing to do some strategic cutting to reduce costs. He indicated that he "was able to eliminate tentatively some sixty-three out of the four hundred and ninety animals considered. These omissions total about thirteen thousand words, and would cover fifty-four pages of double-spaced type."[46] He went on to include a detailed list of what could be cut, though he insisted that *Between Pacific Tides* would be a commercial success, since it contained material that Johnson and Snook had overlooked and covered intertidal regions with which they were unfamiliar.

Ed's efforts were to no avail. Two weeks after reviewing Ricketts's correspondence about cost-cutting, William Davis received an internal memorandum from director Friend terminating Stanford's interest in the project. Friend's veto was based strictly on financial considerations, and contrary to what some believe, it had nothing to do with direct or implied criticism of Ricketts and Calvin's science by Fisher or anyone else. It was the early 1930s, and Stanford was feeling the impact of the Great Depression. Director Friend had to be extremely judicious about what the press could afford to publish. Though he was unwilling to gamble, Friend did leave the door open a crack by suggesting that a $1,000 cash subsidy or a guaranty of more than five hundred copies in sales might change his mind. After all, Johnson and Snook had raised a subsidy for their book, why shouldn't Ricketts and Calvin raise one for *Between Pacific Tides*—or whatever the book would be titled? On April 25, Davis received a memo from Friend:

> Have gone over this affair carefully, considering the suggested cut in material as outlined in letter of March 17 from Ricketts, and I do not see how we can afford to gamble on this as present. My memo on February 2 gives two extremes, neither of which would give us a book, which could compete with the subsidized "Seashore Animals." The reduction as suggested by Ricketts would land somewhere between the two extremes which I outlined. Some library and scientist sales are going to be lost by these omissions.
>
> Until book-buying comes out of this present acute slump, I do not think we can take this on unless accompanied by a

substantial subsidy or large guaranty of sales. It would require
from $1000 up in cash or a guaranty of from 500 copies up to
make it safe. The minimum amounts would not be sufficient
for the reduced book as outlined in Ricketts' letter, and the "up"
figures would mean at least doubling these minimums to go
ahead with an "Unabridged" book.[47]

It was days later that William Davis wrote Ricketts terminating
Stanford's interest in the project—at least for the present. It's interesting that the required subsidy of $1,000 stated by Friend was dou-
bled in the rejection letter that Ricketts and Calvin received on April
11, 1932.

Dear Mr. Ricketts:

It is with great regret that I inform you of the Press's inability to
accept for publication "Between Pacific Tides" by Mr. Calvin
and yourself. The scope of the work, owing clearly to the amount
and interestingness of the subject-matter it had to include, is far
greater than we had contemplated that it would be, and the cuts
which seem possible still leave an impractically large work to
be produced and marketed. We have the greatest confidence in
the high quality of the work you have produced, including both
text and illustrations; but in these depressed times it would be
folly to expect any large number of buyers among those already
equipped with Johnson and Snook, and the work you have
prepared, unless accompanied by a really large subsidy, would
remain in the same price class as Johnson and Snook.

You may find an Eastern publisher who will be interested in
the venture, and if so of course I wish you all good fortune with
it. If you should happen to find a two-thousand dollar subsidy
available somewhere, by all means come back to us; we are not
in a position to seek aid for the book.

I propose to hold the valuable manuscript and illustrations
here until either you call for them or direct me to send them.

Cordially yours WHD, Editor[48]

Ricketts was crushed. In 1971, Jack Calvin said that he had never
seen Ed so "down," far more so than he had been after his recent

separation from Nan—the first of several that would culminate in their divorce.[49] Still, despite his distress, which was tinged with anger, he remained resolute, and his response to Davis was tempered. In a letter typed by Carol Steinbeck, who was working at Ed's lab at the time, Ed told Davis, "I am sorry you found it necessary to reject our manuscript, but finances being what they are, I suppose there is no way of getting around it. We have already spent so much time, and there is so much cash tied up in the thing that I believe we will put the finishing touches on it and try to market it elsewhere."[50]

Undeterred, Ricketts continued collecting specimens and sending those he could not identify to experts for review. The timing of all this is interesting: even before Ed left on his 1932 trip, he knew that Stanford had rejected the manuscript. One would never have known it from the enthusiasm with which he did his work in the tide pools of Vancouver Island and Southeast Alaska, and in his animated conversations with the Calvins and Campbell on the *Grampus*. In May 1932, just days before leaving for Alaska, he wrote a letter to Torsten Gislén, about a collecting trip he had taken with George MacGinitie to Ensenada, in which he talked about everything from American whiskey ships selling liquor offshore for $2 a quart (the Eighteenth Amendment was still in effect) to his recent separation from Nan; he writes that "Nana and the children are at Santa Barbara, whence she has probably written Mrs. Gislén. We decided to try living apart at least for a while on the chance that distance would settle some of the difficulties that certainly weren't being worked out by proximity. The kids are all in the best of health, brown as Indians, and are going to school down there. Nan plans lots of handiwork and has discussed taking up some general orientation courses in the Santa Barbara High School, which is, by the way, one of the fine secondary educational institutions in the west."[51] Ed did not so much as hint that Stanford had rejected *Between Pacific Tides*. Carol Steinbeck typed this letter as well.

Immediately after completing the trip aboard the *Grampus*, Ricketts wrote again to his friend Torsten Gislén from Sitka (August 8, 1932). In yet another long and newsy letter, Ricketts talked about their journey to Alaska, about reading Whitman and Joyce, listening to Brahms, Stravinsky, and Scarlatti, and reflecting on the current state of his aging Packard. Midway through this letter, he does talk

about the status of *Between Pacific Tides* and his plan to raise the subsidy requested by Stanford:

> Publication of the book—the merits of which, by now espe-
> cially, I very much believe in—is being held up by subsidy
> requirement on the part of Stanford Press. Certainly the result
> of an over-chary attitude incident to the depression. Originally
> I thought I would let the thing ride a while until conditions
> straightened out; but it seems to me now that this is sufficiently
> worthwhile and useful to justify my attempt to raise the subsidy
> needed. I plan on writing the professors of zoology at a number
> of the Pacific universities and colleges—the ones likely to be
> most benefited—in an attempt to have them requisition a cou-
> ple of copies each, thru their purchasing offices at figure high
> enough to cover subsidy needs if a sufficient number of the local
> schools will cooperate.[52]

Shortly thereafter, Ricketts approached his Swedish friend, hop-
ing that some support might come from the University of Lund. In
this letter, however, Ed moves on to issues about his car and his wife,
in that order, telling Gislén, "The Packard is still perking right along,
with something like 84,000 miles. We drove from San Francisco to
Seattle, almost a thousand miles, in one single stretch. Nan is still in
Santa Barbara, getting along I gather fairly well, and I hope working
out some of the difficulties that have beset us mutually. I plan on
driving down there immediately after I return to California. I had
a letter from Nancy Jane, and later another from Junior, enclosed in
communications from Nan."[53]

Ten days later, Ricketts wrote to Walter Fisher about the rich collecting regions in Alaska generally and particularly about the Sitka
shoreline. The tone of this letter is unlike that in his epistle to Gislén,
since Ed's intent in writing Fisher was to provide reassurance that he
was still working on the book and to keep him interested in seeing
it published should Ricketts be able to raise the required subsidy. Ed
tells Fisher that

> the extraordinary richness of the Sitka region seems to me to
> arise at least in part from the variety in conditions of topogra-
> phy and shelter. Most of the open coast animals found at PG

occur here also; there is in addition the rich but rather delimited Puget Sound-B.C. quiet inlet fauna; and of course the bay and estuary forms. The similarity of the Sitka outer coast fauna with that of Monterey Bay (or even with that of such vertical shores as occur at Boca de la Playa) seems to me just another example of the relative unimportance of temperature barriers (unless sudden), and the significance of such factors as wave shock and type of bottom.[54]

In this and in other letters he wrote at the time, Ricketts again displays a great deal of interest in the determining factors of wave shock, degree of tidal exposure, and bottom types in different kinds of intertidal regions. Taking these physical factors into consideration broadened his understanding of the relationships between habitats and the animals that populate specific regions. Ed was again enthused; he clearly had not given up after his disappointing discussions with the Stanford press; in fact, he was more energized than ever.

As soon as he returned from Alaska, Ed wrote a brief note to William Davis asking for confirmation of the Stanford press' willingness to publish *Between Pacific Tides* should he be able to raise the required subsidy: "If it so happens that I am successful in raising the $2000 subsidy mentioned in connection with our seashore book, will it be safe for us to count on Stanford Press going ahead with the project? I don't actually anticipate having much luck in doing this, but wanted to make certain of your angle before going ahead with the attempt."[55]

Davis read Ed's note and went directly to Friend, seeking clarity on the press's current stand on *Between Pacific Tides*. Friend's answer was incisive: "I am positive," he tells his editor, that "the venture is safe financially with a $2000 subsidy, provided the copy and illustrations are approximately as when we last considered the book. Am in favor of acceptance with that subsidy, and suggest a prompt meeting of committee, or informal approval (or rejection) by Roth and others, as individuals, if committee meeting cannot be arranged."[56]

Ricketts knew nothing of any renewed interested at the press and so continued working on Fisher, telling the Hopkins director that while the "Stanford Press finally turned down our book m/s for lack of subsidy," "this summer's trip convinced me more than ever of the value of such a work. I'm going to continue trying to get it published; will soon attempt to raise the needed amount by subscriptions from interested schools. A form letter is being sent out which outlines the scheme I have in mind; you will receive a copy."[37] He then moves on to a discussion about reading Spengler's *Decline of the West* while on the *Grampus,* followed by a mention of some fish he brought back for Hopkins ichthyologist Rolf Bolin. One can only wonder how Fisher reacted to Ricketts's digression about "the supposedly metaphysical and pessimistic Spengler." Ed also included with this letter "a data-sheet covering localities etc. on the hydrocoral, actinian and sipunculid material,"[38] which he had collected specifically for Fisher.

On the one hand, Ricketts knew that Fisher was likely to be a major player if there was any chance that Stanford would reconsider publishing *Between Pacific Tides.* His letters to Fisher, while not patronizing, suggest as much. But they also demonstrate Ed's admiration for Fisher's science and his desire for the Hopkins director to consider him a valued colleague. He had no illusions about Fisher joining him for long evenings of drink and conversation at his lab. But the fact is that he not only sought (and needed) Fisher's support—he also genuinely respected the man.

While Ricketts was decompressing from his Alaska trip and reconnecting with friends and with his colleagues at Hopkins, press director Friend continued dealing with financial concerns about the book, which included matters relating to the required subsidy, a royalty scale, and a proposed sales price. In October 1932 he told Davis, in a memo,

> A check of estimates, correspondence, etc., convinces me that the book is perfectly safe with a $2000 subsidy, provided the authors and/or subsidizing source are satisfied with a low starting royalty scale. This should be made specific in our acceptance letter
>
> No royalty first 500 copies
>
> 5% second 500 copies
>
> 8% next 1000 copies
>
> 12% thereafter

List price $3.50 unless radical change in the market between now and publication make a change of price advisable.[59]

Davis was pleased that Friend had reopened the door on *Between Pacific Tides*. Shortly after getting Friend's memo about subsidies and royalties, he told Ricketts, "We have examined the "Between Pacific Tides" project and its financial side again and can state that if accompanied by $2,000 the manuscript can be accepted and published here, on royalty terms which I believe will be satisfactory to you."[60] Interestingly, he said nothing to Ed about royalties or the proposed sales price.

Ricketts was pleased to hear from Davis, and despite previous disappointments, he became cautiously optimistic that the press would publish *Between Pacific Tides* should he secure the requisite financial backing. He wrote to Torsten Gislén on October 21 about the subsidy, stating that the reason it was required was because of the substantial cost of the illustrative material. He spoke about the number of illustrations, "some 45 full page plates and more than 100 drawings," which suggests that Calvin's photographs and Lovejoy's line drawings had been completed. The tone of this letter is formal, particularly compared with his previous correspondence with Gislén. He tells his Swedish friend that "the writer and a collaborator, out of considerable experience during the past ten years collecting and observing from Lower California to Sitka, Alaska, have compiled a handbook of the marine invertebrates. Rather exceptional illustrative material has been provided in the way of photos and drawings. The approach is by way of the Johnson and Snook data, our project being supplementary to that fine work."[61] Ricketts asks Gislén to try to get his university to pony up $100 and tells him that he'll get a complimentary copy "if the thing is ever published."[62]

In May 1933, Ricketts again wrote to Gislén, this time about the possibility of obtaining some scientific papers pertinent to his own research. He mentions the work of several invertebrate specialists and ecologists who have been helpful (Theodor Mortensen, William Ritter, John Colman, Harold Mestre, Willis G. Hewatt, Max W de Laubenfels)—the last three with direct connections to Hopkins. He tells Gislén, "I have lots of interesting ecological and natural history dope as a result of last year's northern trip," by which he means that he has

> finally, after several years work, definitely solved the question of tidal factors with reference to the vertical zoning of shore animals on this coast. At least I've worked out the probable critical horizons from the physical evidence, and it seems to tie in well with work on plant associations (Mestre) and animal counts per square meter (Hewatt) being done here at the station. Something along the line of Coleman's (Plymouth) 1933 paper, but my physical work on tides is more comprehensive and considers more factors than his, but I can't tie it indefinitely with the animals, not having the background of quantitative work there.[63]

It would come to pass, of course, that Ricketts's work on tides was among his most important contributions to intertidal ecology. The scientific findings outlined in his two unpublished essays—"The Tide as an Environmental Factor Chiefly with Reference to Ecological Zonation on the California Coast" and "Notes and Observations, Mostly Ecological, resulting from Northern Pacific Collecting Trips Chiefly in Southeastern Alaska, with Special Reference to Wave Shock as a Factor in Littoral Ecology"—form a good portion of the science in *Between Pacific Tides*.

Ricketts had been concerned with tides since the beginning of the early 1930s (and probably before). He writes in "Tide as an Environmental Factor" that "the most obvious regulatory factor in the vertical distribution of littoral life is the tide."[64] He knew at the time that this was a somewhat radical departure from existing norms, that "there have been no serious attempts to evaluate or analyze this factor, despite the fact that tides are particularly susceptible to rigid analysis, and that the new science of oceanography is intimately concerned with the consideration of environmental factors in their biological significance."[65] His extensive study of the tides led Ricketts to divide the rocky intertidal into "zones," which he used to delineate different habitats along the shorelines of the Pacific. As we read in *The Light and Smith Manual: Intertidal Invertebrates from Central California to Oregon*, this delineation was done "relative to the MLLW (mean lower low water, the zero point of the tide tables), from where Ricketts delineates the high, upper, middle and lower intertidal zone."[66]

By including the influence of tides in his ecological view of the littoral, Ricketts demonstrated a more complete understanding of Pacific intertidal habitats than any work done by other west coast marine biologists. His in-depth knowledge, which grew during a decade of collecting, research, and extensive reading, differentiates *Between Pacific Tides* from all other guides available at the time. Ricketts and Calvin write that the "shore topography of the Pacific coast differs considerably from that of the Atlantic coast. . . . More obviously on the Pacific coast than on the Atlantic coast, the three interlocking factors that determine the distribution of shore invertebrates are: (a) the degree of wave shock, (b) the type of bottom (whether rock, sand, mud, or some combination of these), and (c) the tidal exposure."[67] They note that tidal exposure, which has to do with "the zoning of animals according to the relative lengths of exposure to air and water," lends weight to "an understanding of the extreme variations that exist between the uppermost region at and above the line of high spring tides, where the animals are wetted only a few times in each month to waves and spray, and a line of low spring tides, where the animals are uncovered only a few hours in each month."[68] Ed and Jack conclude by noting that "many animals adhere closely to one particular level, and all have their preferences."[69] Sensitive to the environmental variables, they note that there are temperature differences, but that within such provisions, the system of zonation "is equally applicable to San Quintin Bay [Baja California], where the extreme range of tides is less than eight feet, and to Juneau, where it is more than twenty-three feet."[70]

Above all, what makes *Between Pacific Tides* a pioneering book is the manner in which Ricketts and Calvin combine the various factors that determine which animals live in which habitat (wave shock, tides, and bottom type) in a way that is immediately accessible to the "most unscientific shore visitor." They write that the "visitor" will know "whether he is observing a surf-swept or a protected shore, and whether the substratum is predominantly rock or sand or mud. . . . He will further know, or he can easily find out, whether the tide at a given time is high or low" and thus "be able to identify most of the animals that he is likely to find and thus to acquire considerable information about each."[71] This is in marked contrast to taxonomic shore guides about marine invertebrates, since the visitor "probably will not know the classification by which zoologists arrange the animals in which he is interested."[72] Without a doubt, Ricketts's desire to make his understanding of the Pacific shoreline accessible to even the least initiated observer is what drives the narrative in *Between Pacific Tides.*

With the publication of his manuscript at a standstill, Ricketts went about the business of adding to his scientific library and corresponding further with experts around the world who were helping with the identification and classification of species and to whom he was sending specimens. In June 1933, he wrote Theodor Mortensen, professor at the University of Copenhagen, thanking Mortensen for a collection of his scientific papers. As a leading authority on sea urchins, Mortensen published widely on these animals; he was also an expert field naturalist who later provided an enormous collection of marine animals to the Zoological Museum of Denmark.[73] Reading Ed's letter to a man he hardly knew, one is struck by his untiring efforts to acquire important scientific literature about marine invertebrates from elsewhere that were also common to the Pacific Coast. He tells Mortensen,

> The papers which you so kindly forwarded came to hand promptly; I am very glad indeed to get them. There seem to be three Dolichoglossus on the California coast, and none of them had been described heretofore. And this in spite of the fact that certainly dozens, possibly hundreds of zoologists have turned them up, and much incidental work had been done on D. pusillus. I hadn't even heard of the new Beroë; believe it hasn't been turned up here, even in the oceanographical work at Hopkins Marine Station. The Straits of Georgia region is apparently unique in several ways; it would be interesting if it were shown to have a characteristic abyssal sub-fauna.[74]

In September 1933, Ricketts again wrote to Fisher, this time about the naming of a new species of ascidians (*Clavelina*), one among many in the genus of tunicates common in Monterey Bay. In his letter, he mentions Willard G. Van Name, curator of marine invertebrates at the American Museum of Natural History, who Fisher had recommended to Ricketts as a source of help in identifying some of the invertebrates he had collected. Van Name helped Ricketts with the taxonomy of several species of tunicates. Ricketts was forever seeking out biologists who could confirm the identity of species about which he was less than completely certain. Some, like Mortensen and Van Name, helped him only occasionally. He communicated with others a good deal more often. Among the latter category was Elisabeth Deichmann, an expert on Pacific Coast alcyonarians (soft corals, sea pens), gorgonians (sea fans and sea whips), and holothurians (sea cucumbers). Given her expertise on so many different animals, she was able to provide Ed with a great deal of help. She knew Ed personally and held him in high regard.

During the 1930s, Deichmann visited Hopkins regularly, doing her own research and, on occasion, contributing to Fisher's invertebrate zoology course. As he did with so many visiting specialists, Ricketts sought her out, and the two became fast friends. For more than fifteen years, she identified numerous alcyonarians and holothurians that Ricketts had collected, first from the shores of the Pacific Coast and, later, in the Gulf of California. In October 1933, by which time Deichmann had become the curator of invertebrates at Harvard University's Museum of Comparative Zoology, Ricketts wrote her about a recent collecting trip to Puget Sound. He apologizes for being unable to collect specimens that might have been of interest to her. "I was so excited about *Gonionemus* and other pelagic animals that I didn't get to make a single rocky shore collection. And at that I didn't get sufficient *Gonionemus* to take care of orders at hand [for PBL]. They are difficult little beasties to get at."[75]

A month or so later, Ricketts wrote a newsy letter to Torsten Gislén in which he updates the Swedish zoologist about everything from the state of his Packard (he had just acquired the newer one) to news of Jack and Sasha Calvin in Sitka and, even, to FDR's efforts to combat the painful effects of the Great Depression. Of tangential interest are Ricketts's comments about the writing Steinbeck was doing at the time. Interestingly, Ed notes his preference for *To a God Unknown* over *The Pastures of Heaven* (both had recently been published), and he singles out Steinbeck's interest in the "phalanx," which is the subject of a short essay Steinbeck wrote in 1933 and which would later underpin the thematic design of *The Grapes of Wrath*. Ricketts also tells Gislén about writers on his reading list: Swiss psychiatrist and psychoanalyst Carl Jung; the first female writer to win the Nobel Prize in Literature, Selma Lagerlöf; German writer and novelist Jacob Wassermann; the outspoken critic of American Jewish assimilation, novelist and translator Ludwig Lewisohn; and the British philosopher, novelist, literary critic, and poet, John Cowper Powys. Finally, Ed mentions "The Tide as an Environmental Factor Chiefly with Reference to Ecological Zonation on the California Coast," the essay he hoped to submit to the journal *Ecology*. This, of course, is the essay that wasn't published until Joel Hedgpeth edited a collection of Ricketts essays, *The Outer Shores* (1978). Ricketts ends by telling Gislén that while publication by Stanford is still on hold, he is hopeful that the requirement that he raise the $2,000 subsidy may become less important, since the American economy is finally improving. This letter illustrates Ricketts's state of mind at the time.

Dear Gislén:

Your most welcome letter, order and check came to hand some while back, and it is planned to dispatch shipment of what is at hand and is being collected early in January.

I have since made another trip into Southern California. Saw MacGinitie, who is now director of the CIT marine station at Newport Bay, and collected there several days, staying with them.

Picked up alot of amphioxus, and got some fairly definite dope on growth groups; thru measurements.

Since you left, we havn't [*sic*] made the trip up to Chews Ridge and Tassajara Springs, so there was no opportunity to get your Santa Lucia pine seeds. However, you will be glad to know that on the last trip south, I stopped near Paso Robles and picked up some good cones and seeds of the similar pine that occurs there; I imagine it is actually the Santa Lucia also. In addition, after examining trees unsuccessfully, I got you some Torrey pine cones and seeds. Those cones are rare as hens teeth; and the seeds are still rarer. The life history of that race is presumably in a pretty dopy and decadent stage.

Anyway, this stuff is finally at hand and can be sent.

Also, if you want any of the Pacific toads, we have lots of them. Welcome. The animals seem to be coming back. I have been unbelievably up to my ears in work, without much productivity showing. This NRA thing pretty nearly had me down. PBL is the smallest of a group of nearly a hundred scientific supply houses, such as Bausch and Lomb, Central Scientific, Arthur H. Thomas, etc, that have formed an association now devoted to dealing collectively with the government. A great deal of data is required of the member houses, and each must file, before Dec. 27th, a complete pricelist and statement of policy, with the presidents committee. In a large company, that work is simply delegated to one of the officers, some clerks and stenographers; but here, in this small firm, I must do it all myself, plus my own work. A m/s of 40 to 60 typed pages will be required, in 6 or 8 manifolded copies.

The whole thing (I mean as it effects the economics of the country in general) is pretty fine. Moreover it seems to be working—practically enough in the blundering way inherent to new thing—but with a drive of idealism behind it that must later give way to desultory. The result however will probably be a step forward. Roosevelt most certainly saved the day (or, as the growing group of Carmel communists say, staved it off a bit) but whether or not some other leader would otherwise have come forward, I suppose no one can say. The correct attitude may be to regard him as a product of the times, or rather as an expression of a need generally felt. Perhaps it was in the destiny of the country and of the times that some new quanta should suddenly be expressed out of the plateau of the arithmetic curve of progress past the inertial threshold into another plateau. Where everyone can catch his breath for a while. I hope so.

I guess I told you we left our PG house last year. Gave it up; couldn't make the payments on it. As so many others have given up equities and contracts, helping to precipitate still more remote financial crises. We had a hard hard time. I practically got all the wood we burned for cooking and heating for nearly a year, and even the pantry wasn't as full as it might be. But it's certainly looking up now. The debts arn't [*sic*] all paid yet, and nothing is set by, but there seems to be enough to pick up a little of this good legal wine and beer now. Prohibition was an atrocity. All except a few die-hards were glad to see it go. I have seen little drunkenness, but everyone seems to be buying liquor. Don't know where the money comes from.

The Packard piled up more than 100,000 miles. I finally broke the oil pump one night down the coast. Put in 1 1/2 gallons of extra that I carry and came on in anyway, cold and tired. But the bearings were pretty scored, and I just turned it in on another. A bigger and better one; the 7-40 Packard 1930 Limousine-Sedan. Got a good buy, chauffeur-driven, only 28,000 miles, and by one man only. I expect to keep this 5 years, and pile up 120,000 miles.

We wish you folks were here. Nan and I have found no one even remotely taking your place, and I suspect we never will.

Did you meet John Steinbeck while you were here? He's writing exceedingly well. "The Pastures of Heaven" 1931 NY, Ballou, is good. The 1933 "To a God Unknown" also Ballou NY, much better. And his fine opus magnus, for which he is trying for a Guggenheim fellowship, projects treatment in novel form of the group motivating force, the race unconscious, the holism that he calls Phalanx. Sort of a literary summation of some of the ideas of Allee, Spengler, C G Jung and Whitman-DH Lawrence-Robinson Jeffers.

I have been reading Jung's "Two Essays," especially the last, which I think goes very well. Exceedingly difficult, for me at least. He seems to pioneer a new realm; very much needed. Hard to see why some one hadn't discovered it before. Nan finished with Lagerlof; now is into Wasserman's [*sic*] "Doctor Kerkhoven." I am thinking of dangling Lewisohn and Powys before her next. We are having some moments, but alot of difficulty.

Sasha has a baby. They are homesteading in Sitka. You possibly saw his article and photographs in this summer's National Geographic. I forget which number. Xenia, having got already to the point in her painting and drawing where she exhibited at the Palace of the Legion of Honor in SF, has left Henrietta

Shore in Carmel, and is studying with Jean Charlot in Los Angeles. I just had a box of cigars from her. Maybe she will go far there. Very interested in Mexico, and the work of the two very famous painters and fresco-ists, Diego Rivera and the other duffer. We had a winy party at the house Saturday. Edward Weston (supposed to be one of the foremost photographers, maybe you hear of him over there or maybe he doesn't rate more than regional recognition) held forth with one of his parodied dances. Skogsberg is still at the Station, Fisher, Van Neil; other wise it's awfully dead over there. Stanford has just barely been keeping the place running. One of Mac's pupils, a Texan by the name of Hewatt, did some quite decent ecological work there and will return to finish it next summer.

I have fine, most satisfying dope on the tides. Working up a comprehensive and possibly even significant paper which I don't suppose will find a publisher acct length and because it lies in a little frequented field. Will try Ecology and then some of the oceanographical bulletins.

No more dope on the book m/s. It is still unofficially holding fire at Stanford, and the assumption has been given me tacitly than after the depression the subsidy requirements may not be so pressing.

There isn't enough time for all one wants to do; and so much of what is available is frittered away in lost motion and frustration.

We'll be glad to hear from you. Happy holidays to you[76]

Ed's friendship with Torsten Gislén had become very special and was quite different than that with Deichmann, Mortensen, and the other scientists whom he met and with whom he corresponded over the years. He and Gislén were the closest of friends, though separated by thousands of miles.

There was no progress on *Between Pacific Tides* during the winter and spring of 1934, and so Ricketts spent much of the summer collecting along the Oregon coast and on Washington's Olympic Peninsula, this time with Nan, with whom he had reunited, and their three children. Upon returning to Monterey, he provided Walter Fisher with a lengthy summary of his most recent scientific findings.

He titles his epistle "Highlights of The PBL Summer 1934 Northern Collecting Trip Summary For Dr. Fisher" and begins by telling the Hopkins director, "Recently a road has been completed almost clear through to Cape Flattery, and on this trip I was interested in walking up from the south nearly to the Cape itself, and in collecting both inside and outside that possible line of demarcation. Just inside the Straits at Neah Bay, and clear through to Clallam Bay and Pysht, there is some of the finest collecting I have seen short of Sitka and Carmel. This fairly completes for me the examination of the coast line of western US."[77]

At about the same time that he filed his report with Fisher, Ricketts again wrote to Elisabeth Deichmann, this time about several specimens he collected during his visit to the Cape Flattery region of Puget Sound, which he sent her for identification. The summer collecting trips to the Pacific Northwest continued as annual excursions, providing Ricketts with the opportunity to gather large quantities of *Gonionemus* for his biological supply business. In a letter dated August 31, 1934, he tells Deichmann, "Some while back you asked me to save you some representatives of the Puget Sound ophiurians, especially Amphiodia. Last year I failed to run across any of these, not collecting in any suitable region. This summer however, I made a couple of trips out toward Cape Flattery, where there is magnificent rocky shore collecting, and I am forwarding the desired material under separate cover."[78]

Progress on *Between Pacific Tides* may have stalled, but Ricketts had not lost any of his enthusiasm for studying the habits and habitats of marine invertebrates along the Pacific shoreline. Even though he had at most vague hints that there was renewed interest in his book by the Stanford press, he was more determined than ever to do whatever it took to make sure that *Between Pacific Tides* would be published.

CHAPTER 5

ed undaunted

In the depth of winter I finally learned that there was in me an invincible summer.

—ALBERT CAMUS

A ONE-MAN ADVERTISING CAMPAIGN

In April 1935, Ed wrote another long letter to Gislén in response to correspondence he had received from the Swedish scientist. Like most of his letters to Gislén, it is full of news about numerous subjects, with some interesting comments that we have not seen in any of his earlier letters. The letter includes some uncharacteristically personal comments about the strong personal feelings he and Nan have about Torsten and his wife; Ed regrets that distance make it impossible for them to see one another. There are also encouraging comments about a possible end to the logjam with the Stanford press, the most positive Ed has been since he received the rejection notice three years earlier: "Have started work again on plans for publishing the tide pool book, and a printed and illustrated announcement will appear probably within a month or so. That may put it across. From the unofficial Stanford grapevine I gather that when that school's finances ease up a bit, the subsidy requirement won't be so pressing. But when do one's finances really ease up?"[1]

Despite the qualifier at the end of this comment, Ricketts believed that things with Stanford were improving. In the same letter, Ricketts talks about his problems with taxonomy—the first time we've seen his concern about the problems he was having identifying the animals he collected. He writes,

> Taxonomy is the obstacle. I haven't yet carefully examined any single group without turning out some new species, with, in most cases, no one to describe them, or, as a final hurdle, any place to publish work already done. I tried to construct a careful and honest key (most of the general keys by non-specialists are superficial, and based on literature rather than on examination of typical specimens of all the species) of a group so well known as the Idotheidae, based on all iterative characters in graded series. This mostly for my own use; and it would have been a nice piece of work and fairly definitive. But in examining even these specimens in our own stock of unidentified forms, I turned up 2 new species; and these are at the U S National Museum awaiting description.[2]

The real issue for Ricketts was the impact of taxonomy on ecology. He concludes by writing that "careful ecological work I imagine is based on careful taxonomy made available for the competent non-specialist. But many of the groups most common on the Pacific coast have no systematic champions, and even the obvious and large anemones constitute a hodge-podge."[3] Ed may not have enjoyed doing taxonomic work, but he recognized its importance.

Though the source of Ricketts's optimism about a possible breakthrough on *Between Pacific Tides* is not clear, it was well founded. In May 1935, he and Jack received a letter from Stanley Croonquist, the press' sales manager—the first official correspondence between the Stanford press and Ricketts in three years. Croonquist indicated that, some time ago, the press had received orders for a book it had not published. He tells Ricketts that "a notice of 'A Natural History of Pacific Shore Invertebrates' by E. F. Rickets and Jack Calvin has just come to our attention." The last paragraph carries a notice that "orders can be sent with the understanding that the purchaser will incur no obligation until the date of issue, to Stanford University Press, Stanford University, California, or to Pacific Biological Laboratories." The notice also contained "three specimen pages which the recipient of the circular would naturally suppose were taken from the book being published by our press." "As a matter of fact," Croonquist writes, "we know nothing about the publication."[4]

Croonquist may have known little about all this, but Ed knew everything. In his April 1935 letter to Gislén, Ricketts mentioned that he had generated an illustrated and printed announcement for *Between Pacific Tides*. Specifically, he wrote that "a printed and illustrated announcement will appear probably within a month or so." He then suggested, "That may put it across,"[5] by which he meant that his advertising scheme might help get the book published. Of course, Ricketts never informed the press staff about his one-man advertising campaign. But after reading Croonquist's letter, which ends with its author writing that "we feel that you should have consulted us before using our name and ask that you furnish us with further information concerning the project,"[6] Ed came clean. Croonquist and his colleagues were not amused.

In the Brubaker Collection at the Center for Steinbeck Studies at San Jose State University is the original of a four-page advertisement for *A Natural History of Pacific Shore Invertebrates* by E. F. Ricketts and Jack Calvin. The advertisement has for years puzzled scholars as to its connection, if any, to *Between Pacific Tides*. We now know the source of this document: it was Ricketts's own advertising campaign. He advertised the book for $7.50, the price originally suggested by Davis in his February 1932 letter, and so was obviously unaware that Friend had indicated that the price should be half that amount. The business reply card from Pacific Biological Laboratories for *A Natural History of Pacific Shore Invertebrates* is shown here. Note that the reply card encourages recipients to place a pre-publication order for the book. Ricketts likely wanted to prove to Friend that five hundred copies of the book could be sold, a requirement by the press for publishing *Between Pacific Tides*.

CHANGES

Despite Stanley Croonquist's chagrin about Ricketts's end run, Ed's prepublication notice about the forthcoming *A Natural History of Pacific Shore Invertebrates* helped reopen discussions between Ed and the Stanford press. According to Tom Mangelsdorf, in *A History of*

Business reply card from Pacific Biological Laboratories allowed one to place a prepublication order for the book. Photograph courtesy of Harold A. Miller Library, Stanford University Libraries.

Steinbeck's Cannery Row (1991), *Between Pacific Tides* was accepted for publication by the Stanford University Press in August 1935. On August 14, the *Monterey Peninsula Herald* published a short column titled "Local Scientists Announce Volume," indicating that a book of said title authored by Ed Ricketts and Jack Calvin was soon to be published. Then, in October 1935, Ricketts sent sections of the annotated systematic index to invertebrate specialists, requesting their review of material in the typescript.

One such letter went to Steve Glassell, a research associate in the Department of Marine Invertebrates at the San Diego Natural History Museum, requesting his review of the decapods (crayfish, crabs, lobsters, prawns, and shrimp) section of the index. Another went to Elisabeth Deichmann requesting her assessment of the alcyonarian (soft shell coral and sea pens) and holothurian (sea cucumbers) sections. A third went to Frank Mace MacFarland, a professor of histology at Stanford who, for fourteen years, served as president of the California Academy of Sciences, requesting his review of the nudibranch (sea slugs) and tectibranch (sea hares) portions of the index; and a fourth to Henry Augustus Pilsbry of the Academy of Natural Sciences in Philadelphia, requesting his comments on the cirriped (barnacle) entries.

Henry Augustus Pilsbry was a dominant figure in various fields of invertebrate taxonomy. He was a malacologist (i.e., expert on mollusks), and a leading authority on Cirripedia (barnacles). During his tenure at the academy, which lasted upward of seventy years, he served as its curator, its conservator, and the head of the Department of Shells. He founded and edited the *Nautilus*, a highly regarded scientific journal publishing research in malacology. As a leading authority on the classification of several species of invertebrates, Pilsbry published on the biology of barnacles and mollusks.[7] An endorsement from him was no small recognition. Beyond an acknowledgment by Ricketts for Pilsbry's contributions to *Between Pacific Tides*, four of his scientific papers are referenced in the volume's appendix. Held in the archives of the Academy of Natural Sciences of Philadelphia, Ewell Sale Stewart Library Archives and Manuscript Collection, are two letters from Ricketts to Pilsbry, dated between 1928 and 1935. Pilsbry thought well of Ed. His two letters of reply are addressed to "Dr. Edward F. Ricketts."

Contrary to the belief that Ricketts was insulted by Walter Fisher's recommendation that a "professional zoologist" review the science in *Between Pacific Tides*, Ricketts welcomed the opportunity to get as many reviews as possible. Engaging nationally known and respected figures such as Glassell, Deichmann, MacFarland, and Pilsbry, Ed more than satisfied Fisher and anyone at the Stanford press who may once have doubted his scientific acumen.

Sadly, as Ed's scientific career blossomed, his domestic life deteriorated. He and Nan were very different personalities, and it was probably inevitable that they would eventually go their separate ways. They had first separated in 1932, and their marriage was on and off for the next three years, during which time Nan grew increasingly frustrated by Ricketts's nonstop work during the day, his evening drinking affairs with Steinbeck, Campbell, and others, and his more than occasional romantic dalliances. Finally, in 1935, she gave up and took Nancy and Cornelia to Bremerton, Washington. Ed Jr. remained with his father. With Nan and the girls gone, father and son moved into the lab, where Ed Sr. lived for the rest of his life.

Meanwhile, at the Stanford University Press, plans to publish *Between Pacific Tides* were moving forward. In early January 1936, William Davis asked Fisher to review the manuscript again to determine whether Ricketts had addressed his previous criticisms. Despite suffering from some medical problems, Fisher offered what help he could, telling Davis that, "owing to depleted eye energy I cannot undertake to read the MS of Ricketts and Calvin. I am willing to do random sampling if that will be of service to you. I went over the MS pretty carefully some years ago, as Ricketts indicates; consequently, I think I can find by sample method whether certain general criticisms have been heeded."[8]

A little more than a month later, Fisher provided Davis with his findings. He remained ambivalent about certain aspects of the manuscript but, conceding that books about science need not be only for scientists, he realized its value for the casual reader. This was something of an about-face for Fisher, who had heretofore been unenthusiastic about popularizing science. Fisher criticizes some of Ricketts prose (he was neither the first nor the last to do so), insisting that the text needs editing. Overall, Walter Fisher liked the book. His letter represents a marked departure from his earlier statements of Ricketts's work, though he pays Ed something of a backhanded compliment, suggesting that he is less than a trained biologist.

Hopkins Marine Station
Pacific Grove California

Feb 29, 1936

Dear Prof. Davis:

Many apologies are due herewith tendered for keeping the Ricketts MS so long. Our Dr. Skogsberg to whom I wanted to read some samples took a nervous header and will not be able to contribute what is always good advice. I read some portions to Dr. Heath; and Dr. Bolin has read a good deal of the MS.

The MS needs vigorous editing but not by the author, who will be hampered by unfortunate limitations in the use of English. There is some good ecology scattered through the work but I hardly see the need of a "Zoological Introduction." This particular 4 1/2 pages is a classic for words which reveal an attempt to reach a clientele which will not be impressed but only puzzled by it. I have found few, very few, who can "travel the knife-edge" which the author mentions on the first page. Wm Beebe thinks he does it, but although a master of "Atlantic" style he is anathema to most biologists.

Why not frankly write this book for the lay reader? Whatever is new of technical value will not suffer in being recorded in non-technical manner. The material will not impress the stereo-typed ecologist, anyway, for he must have his salt and mustard in the guise of hydrogen ion activity tables and temperature graphs

In other words, I think the book will make the grade if aimed at high-school teachers and students and if edited to take out in some places stylistic stiffness, and in others, soft-clay spots. (A terrible mixture of metaphors I realize.) The book will be useful for a well educated lay-man at the sea-shore (but not in his "arm-chair"). Presumably only such, of the non-zoological laity, will have patience with Latin names which are a necessity. The book should also prove useful as a collateral text for sea-shore classes in college biology.

Of course I realize that the MS loses in the absence of the very essential illustrations, and is written with the idea that these are handy for reference. From what I have said you may perhaps infer that I do not think particularly well of the MS. As a matter of fact I think Ricketts (a collector rather than a trained biologist) has done very well indeed. Only he doesn't realize his limitations and that he has undertaken a very diffi-cult job.

Probably the above leaves you rather mystified as regards the main purpose which you had in mind when submitting it. But I may be a little foggy in my own mind

I wish to add a long delayed personal message: That of hav-ing spent a very pleasant and profitable morning with your brother in looking over William and Mary, October 1933.

With best wishes

Sincerely

W. K. Fisher[9]

Aware that Fisher was again reviewing his manuscript, and want-ing to leave nothing to chance, Ricketts provided the Stanford press with the names of the scientists who had assisted him with the iden-tification of species and the compilation of scientific data. Reviewing this cast of notables, it is clear that Ricketts enjoyed the support of a good many genuine experts. In the Stanford press folder for *Between Pacific Tides* are several sheets of data from Ricketts, titled "List of specialists who have collaborated in portions of EFR-JC book." Though the lab fire of 1936 (discussed later) destroyed copies of many of his letters to and from these experts, some have been retrieved from other sources. For example, taken together, Ed's list is a who's who of invertebrate biology:

List of specialists who have collaborated in OKing portions of EFR-JC book.

Dr. M. W. DeLaubenfels, Altadena, Calif. Pasadena Junior College.

Sponges

Dr. C. McL. Fraser, Univ. of British Columbia, Vancouver.

Hydroids

Dr. Elisabeth Deichmann, Museum of Comparative Zoology, Harvard Univ. Alcyonaria. Holothurians.

Prof. J. Hickson, Cambridge, England. Alcyonaria (previously)

(identifications)

In connection with the Anthozoa, the United States National Museum has forwarded manuscript sheets and date for correction to Dr. Oskar Carlgren of Copenhagen, and to Dr. Stephensen of London, but both are away on field trips in the wilderness and contact has not been established.

Prof. Daniel Freeman, Albany College, Albany, Oregon.

Polyclads

Prof. W. R. Coe, Osborn Zoological Laboratory, Yale University.

Nemerteans

Prof. C. H. O' Donohue, Univ. of Edinburgh, Edinburgh, Scotland.

Bryozoa

Olga Hartman, Dept. of Zoology, Univ. of Calif., Berkeley. Annelid worms

W. K. Fisher, Hopkins Marine Station, Pacific Grove.

Sipunculids. Echiuroids. Asteroids.

Dr. Austin T. Clark, Curator, Division of Echinoderms, U.S. National Museum, Washington. Ophiuroids. Echinoids

Dr. H. A. Pilsbry. Academy of Natural Sciences, Philadelphia, Pa.

Cirripedes

Dr. C. R. Shoemaker, Division of Marine Invertebrates, U.S. National Museum, Washington.

Amphipods

James O. Maloney. Division of Marine Invertebrates, U.S. National Museum, Washington. Isopods

Dr. W. L. Schmitt, Curator, Division of Marine Invertebrates, U.S. National Museum, Washington.

Schizopoda, Nebaliacea, Stomatopoda, Cumacea, Picnogonida.

Steve A. Glassell, Beverly Hills, Calif. Decapoda

Mrs. A. R. Grant, Dept. of Zoology, Univ. of Calif., Berkeley.

Complete revision of Docolossa. Correction & OK on all Mollusca, except Tecti.

Dr. F. M. MacFarland, Calif. Academy of Sciences, San Francisco.

Tectibranchiata

Dr. V. G. Van Name, American Museum of Natural History, New York City

Tunicates

Dr. Rolf Bolin, Hopkins Marine Station, Pacific Grove, Calif.

Fishes

All of the above (excepting Dr. Hickson, whose branch was more recently considered by Dr. Deichmann), have looked over MS relating to their fields, and have made factual, spelling, citation, etc. corrections. A number of other specialists have cooperated in the matter of identifications, literature and suggestions (but have not corrected MS) as follows:

Dr. T. Wayland Vaughan, Director, Scripps Inst., La Jolla

(corals)

Dr. Jeanette S. Carter, Miller School of Biology, Univ. of Va.

(Rhabdocoels)

Dr. J. L. Lynch, School of Fisheries, Univ. of Wash.

(Syndesmis)

Dr. C. Berkeley, Pacific Biol. Station, Nanaimo, B.C., Canada

(annelids)

Dr. C. B. Wilson, Dept. of Biology, State Normal School, Westfield, Mass.

(copepods)

Dr. H. Boschma, Leiden, Holland

(Rhizocephala)

Mr. & Mrs. MacGinitie, Kerckhoff Marine Station (Calif. Inst. Tech.) Corona del Mar, Calif. (Crustacea)

J. W. Hedgpeth, 1015 Hollywood, Ave., Oakland, Calif.

(pycnogonids)

Mrs. Oldroyd, Geological Museum, Stanford University

(Molluscs)

Dr. W. A. Clemens, Director, Pacific Biological Station, Nanaimo, B.C. (literature, specimens, date on collecting locale)

Dr. T. Gislén, The University, Lund, Sweden (literature, personal coop.)

Dr. W. C. Allee, Dept. Zoology, Univ. of Chicago, (Literature)

Dr. V. E. Shelford, Dept. Zoology, University of Illinois (literature)

Both Dr. Fisher (Hopkins Marine Station) and G. E. MacGinitie (Kerckhoff Marine Station), have read critically more or less through the entire manuscript, but in its original form before revision. Their suggestions were incorporated in the revision. Dr. Light and others at University of California, and the various specialists at the United States National Museum but especially Dr. W. L. Schmitt have cooperated very widely.[10]

REAL PROGRESS

By early 1936, the book's publication appeared imminent. In the advertisement section of the February 7, 1936, issue of *Science*, one finds mention of *A Natural History of Pacific Coast Invertebrates*, by E. F. Ricketts and Jack Calvin, among the list of books available from the Stanford University Press with a late spring publication date. The printed advertisement reads

A NATURAL HISTORY OF PACIFIC COAST INVERTEBRATES

BY E. F. RICKETTS AND JACK CALVIN

A profusely illustrated consideration of some five hundred common marine invertebrates of the Pacific littoral from Mexico to Alaska. The classification is ecological, by habitat, tidal zone and station. A phylogenetic index is provided and a bibliography which concentrates most of the scattered important references to Pacific coast invertebrates. Late Spring. $7.50

In March 1936, Ricketts received a letter from Davis informing him that the press would publish *Between Pacific Tides*, and, happily for Ed and Jack, there was no mention of the $2,000 subsidy. Davis wrote his letter to Ed just two weeks after Fisher had reviewed the manuscript. He was very pleased that things were back on track, since he liked the manuscript when he first read it and he enjoyed working with Ricketts.

March 13, 1936
Mr. E. F. Ricketts
Pacific Biological Laboratories
Pacific Grove, California

Dear Mr. Ricketts,

Our mature consideration of your "A Natural History of Pacific Shore Invertebrates" has been favorable, and you will shortly receive from Mr. Friend our formal agreement to publish it. I propose to begin the editing as soon as possible. I believe you will welcome such changes in expression or presentation as I care to make, and in a few weeks I shall be glad to have you inspect what I may then have completed. I expect to be in Carmel with my family week after next.

Congratulations.
Cordially yours
William Hawley Davis, Editor"

Sometime during late March or early April, Ricketts wrote to the press suggesting ways the manuscript could be shortened by as much as 18 percent. Ricketts appears to have written this letter without being asked to do so (Davis had indicated that he was personally editing the manuscript) and not in response to any request from Stanford that he pare down the text. There was no ostensible reason that Ricketts should have suggested cutting the manuscript. One can only guess that he may have been concerned about Stanford later balking about the cost of publication. He may have feared that a big book would cost more and that too high a purchase price would limit sales. He may also have thought that selective cutting would improve the manuscript. Whatever his thinking, Stanford did not deem Ricketts's proposed cuts necessary or even desirable.

In June, Croonquist wrote to Ricketts, enclosing three copies of a formal agreement for the publishing of *Between Pacific Tides*. He told

Ed that Stanford hoped to have the book available in time for use in college classes in the fall of 1936.

Uncharacteristically, Stanford seemed to be moving quickly. In the advertisement section of the July 4, 1936, issue of the *Collecting Net*, a list of available books by Stanford University Press includes *Between Pacific Tides*. Note that the title had reverted to the original.

BETWEEN PACIFIC TIDES

BY EDWARD F. RICKETTS AND JACK CALVIN

An account of the habits and habitats of some five hundred of the common, conspicuous seashore invertebrates of the Pacific Coast between Sitka, Alaska, and Northern Mexico. The classification is ecological, by habitat, tidal zone and station. A phylogenetic index is provided and a bibliography which concentrates most of the scattered important reference to Pacific Coast invertebrates. Fall $7.50[12]

This advertisement pre-dates a signed formal agreement between Ricketts, Calvin, and the Stanford University Press, and there appears to have been no communication among the parties about the book's title. Not until mid-July 1936 did Ricketts suggest to Davis that the title of the book be changed, from *A Natural History of Pacific Shore Invertebrates* back to the original; clearly, he didn't know that it had already happened. Ricketts told Davis that he had not yet received the contract with Jack Calvin's signature, but that he was certain it would arrive soon.

The formal agreement generated by the Stanford University Press is titled "Articles of Agreement" and dated June 11, 1936. It displays the handwritten title *Between Pacific Tides* above the crossed out ~~A Natural History of Pacific Coast Invertebrates~~, with required signatures by the authors and William A. Friend. The agreement was mailed to both authors on June 12, but as of early July it had still not been returned by Calvin. An advertisement for the book was printed in the *Stanford Daily* on July 30, 1936, announcing that *Between Pacific Tides* was scheduled for publication in the fall of that year: "'Between Pacific Tides' is the title of a popular account of invertebrates of the Pacific Coast which will also be published in the fall. It will add another volume to the list of outdoor books which includes, among others, Dickey's 'Familiar Birds of the Pacific Southwest,' and Keep and Bailey's 'West Coast Shells.'"[13] With signatures or without, the presses seemed ready to roll.

SETBACK: THE FIRE AND ITS AFTERMATH

On the evening of November 25, 1936, a fire started in the Del Mar Cannery on Ocean View Avenue, adjacent to Ed's lab. It spread rapidly toward Pacific Biological Laboratories and destroyed Ed's supply business and almost all of his belongings. Ricketts was a collector—the lab contained a voluminous collection of his professional and personal correspondence, manuscripts, and research notes, as well as his extensive personal library of book and records. Ricketts escaped, saving only his car, the clothes he was wearing, his typewriter, and a portrait of him by artist James Fitzgerald. Homeless for a time, he and Ed Jr. moved in with his sister and brother-in-law, Frances and Fred Strong, in Pacific Grove, while the lab was being rebuilt. Ricketts had never been obsessive about anything; things per se were relatively unimportant to him. But when the lab burned down, he was devastated. He lamented his losses in conversations with and letters to friends and colleagues locally and all over the world. In 1972, Fred Strong told Richard Astro that Ricketts was utterly distraught—not by the fire itself, but by the loss of his notebooks, records, papers, and books.[14] Ed estimated his financial loss at $12,000; he recovered only a quarter of that amount from insurance. At some point, he joined with the Del Mar Cannery in a lawsuit against Pacific Gas and Electric for "criminal carelessness," but he was no match for PG&E, with its army of savvy lawyers. Among the losses that troubled Ricketts most were the originals of the two scientific manuscripts he had in preparation and hoped to have published: "The Tide as an Environmental Factor Chiefly with Reference to Ecological Zonation on the California Coast" and "Wave Shock as a Factor in Littoral Ecology." Fortunately, a newly edited copy of the manuscript of *Between Pacific Tides* had just been sent to the Stanford press and so was secure.

Among his letters at the time is a December 16, 1936, note to V. E. Bogard and Austin Flanders in Berkeley, to whom Ed writes, "You will be interested to hear what's been happening." Turning almost

Photograph of Pacific Biological Laboratories engulfed in flames, result of the fire that began in the Del Mar Cannery on November 25, 1936. Photograph taken by Wm. L. Morgan. Photograph courtesy of San Jose State University, Martha Heasley Cox Center for Steinbeck Studies.

immediately to the fire and the impact it has had on the business at the lab, he tells them that it "looks not impossible now, altho still terribly difficult. Very hard to pack orders, without any decent facilities, out in the rain."[15]

Meanwhile, in Alaska, Jack Calvin knew little about the fire (he heard about it from Ritch Lovejoy) or about the ongoing negotiations between Ed and the Stanford press. Increasingly distanced from life in Monterey, Jack had, for all intents and purposes, checked out. In late December 1936, though, he wrote to Ricketts about the loss of Pacific Biological Laboratories, commiserating and offering to print new letterhead and envelopes for the lab. Referring to the fire, he tells Ed,

> Tough, fella, tough. Hope you can find a tent in which to start business anew. Would that I could enclose check for fifty thousand with a blessing . . . No news hereabouts to top a first rate fire, except maybe the bloke that got himself buried in a snowslide in Silver Bay. A rescue party gave up hope after thirty

hours and came to town to drown their grief. His lodge went
into mourning and cancelled a party; radio announcers shed a
few tears; another party went out to hunt for the corpse. Six feet
down they met the silly ass coming up, grinning, fifty hours
after the slide dumped twenty-one feet of snow on top of him.
He'd had lunch for three men on his back, and had eaten during
his rests in his up upward-digging operations. Fancy that.

The enclosed are to help you start a new rogues' gallery.[16]

In a more positive mood, in February 1937, Ricketts wrote a long
letter to Lucille Lannestock who, with her husband Gustav, hosted a
December 1936 Christmas party during which Ricketts friends presented him with gifts of his favorite books to replace those that had
been lost in the fire. Ed begins by lamenting that so many scholars
are pedants, telling Lucille that "most are more interested in scrupulous accuracy of small details than in the more difficult honesty
of large pictures." He then moves on to matters relating to the lab,
writing,

> I am gradually getting work done; putting in lots of hours; don't
> know whether I'm keeping ahead or not. To rebuild 15 years in
> one is anyway impossible. The new lab tho is quite nice. I had
> no idea anyone could do so well on three thousand. Library is
> chief difficulty. But so far as the personal end extends, I got a
> fine start thru that Christmas surprise. I have been studying the
> 2nd hand book stores assiduously, too, with some good invest-
> ments of dimes and quarters. A complete Goethe for $2.00.
> Such things tickle me. Ideal method is to have a list of what
> you absolutely must have, classified and arranged secondarily by
> urgency. Then to search until as many as possible of those items
> are found; then not ever to hesitate if anything under 50 cents
> is involved, to think a long time about a dollar, weep violently
> about anything over that.[17]

Several days later, Ricketts responded to Calvin, thanking Jack
for a collection of pictures and for helping him with finances relative
to the previous summer's *Gonionemus* collecting. He also mentions
that Steinbeck was helping him rebuild his library, and that a group

of family and friends (Lucille Lannestock, et al.) surprised him with gifts for his library on Christmas Eve. He chastised the Stanford press for moving so slowly and told Calvin to hold on to his copy of the contract, since he had lost his in the fire.

At roughly the same time, Ricketts wrote to George MacGinitie, talking about his efforts to get Pacific Biological Laboratories up and running again despite a serious shortage of funds. In response to something MacGinitie must have said to him, Ricketts talks about his thyroid condition—the first reference to it or to any physical ailments we find in his notes or correspondence: "That thyroid thing might make a lot of difference; can make a person pretty jumpy. Several years back I went thru with a situation of that sort where readings were up to plus 18 and 20—probably not nearly as bad as yours—but it seemed to me then in my own case, a temporary thing; I got by without operation, took some lugol, and seem to be fairly normal now."[18] Lugol is a medication containing a mixture of iodine and potassium iodide.

Despite spending so much of his time rebuilding PBL, replacing as many of its lost contents as he could find and as his funds permitted, Ricketts was back at work in his lab by March of 1937. On March 19, he wrote to Willis G. Hewatt, discussing the mean exposure interval associated with the intertidal zone that he'd outlined in "The Tide as an Environmental Factor." Ricketts tells Hewatt that he discussed the subject with Harold Mestre, a professor of biophysics at Stanford whom he met when Mestre was teaching at Hopkins. Once again, Ricketts mentions the fire and the devastating impact it had on his work, including the loss of his research materials: "My tide records, graphs, charts, all went."[19] He ends with a request to Hewatt for reprints as part of his effort to rebuild his scientific library.

Willis Hewatt was among the first scientists to investigate the community ecology of the rocky shoreline of Monterey Bay, which he did when he was preparing his doctoral thesis at Hopkins between 1930 and 1934. Hewatt's work involved a qualitative and quantitative survey of a 1-yard-wide by 108-yard-long transect (a path along which one counts and records occurrences of objects of study), located in the intertidal zone adjacent to the seaside laboratory. He appears to have discussed with Ricketts matters relating to the distribution of invertebrate populations in the transect and the physical forces responsible for intertidal zonation. In his dissertation, Hewatt provides insight about the absence of research on the ecology of the littoral communities along the Pacific shore:

> A survey of the literature published on the littoral faunas of the California coast reveals that, until the present time, practically all of the work, has been of a taxonomic, morphological and embryological nature. The ecological aspect has been greatly neglected. It is true that scattered facts concerning the specific ecology of some of the animals are to be found in these papers and that the ecology of a few species has been dealt with in quite an exhaustive manner, but not a single paper dealing primarily with the sociological aspect of the littoral communities has been published.[20]

Hewatt writes that a systematic classification of the intertidal animals needs to be completed to a degree that allows for ecological research at a community level, writing,

> This state of affairs is, of course, the natural consequence of the fact that the California coast was not available to biologists until, comparatively speaking, very recently. Sociological research must necessarily be preceded by a fairly complete taxonomic survey, in order that the ecologist be provided with the means of correctly identifying the forms with which he works. With the exception of a few groups, the systematic classification of the intertidal animals of the central California coast has reached a degree of perfection which permits effective ecological work to be conducted.[21]

Only one communication between Hewatt and Ricketts has been located, but this single document provides insight to the similar thinking by both men about marine ecology. Ricketts mentions having received Hewatt's recent paper, "Ecological Studies on Selected Marine Intertidal Communities of Monterey Bay, California," published in March 1937, in which Hewatt presented a figure he'd obtained (with permission) from Ricketts's unpublished essay on tides.[22] The figure presented the varying number of hours of exposure for organisms positioned at different levels in the intertidal zone over a six-month period. As this letter demonstrates, tidal variations and their impact on periods of animal exposure had become very important to Ricketts. Note that Ricketts ends his letter with a lament about the losses he sustained in the fire.

March 19, 1937

Dear Hewatt:

Your paper arrived this morning, and altho I had a good many other uses for my time, I was tempted to look it over at once.

Since last discussing the situation with you, I think that in the analyses of the factors "Extreme Exposure Intervals" and "Mean Exposure Intervals" of "Duration," there is the explanation of the sudden zonation at 3.5'. Mester thought the significance of the 3.5' horizon was due to frequency; I doubt its effectiveness. However, I evaluated the exposure intervals, both mean and extreme, for every six inches, and discovered the most sudden change of all at about this height. I haven't now the figure, so I can't quote exactly, but it's as tho an animal at 3.0 might be exposed during a 6 months period, to a singled period of air as long as 20 hours; at 3.5 the possibility would be 120 hours. The mean exposure interval curve showed also a sudden jump about here. I treated that subject fairly exhaustively in my MS, one copy of which Gislén has in Sweden. John Steinbeck has another copy, and I'm mighty thankful these copies were out. Don't suppose you heard; on the night of Nov. 25th, there was a waterfront fire that burnt PBL to the ground. Everything was destroyed, and the insurance was only $3000. Worst of all, I had been living here off and on, my complete library, both personal as well as scientific, was burnt, clothes, furniture. I had even stored some old fine pieces of furniture that had been in the family for a hundred years—Mother gave me when Father died and she broke up their home. Those went too. I have it fairly well put back together now, but wotta blow Library can never be replaced; all those ecological and old exploration reports of Pacific invertebrates that I laboriously dug up went out like a light.

In this connection, if you have another copy of your previous paper I'll be glad to have it.

My tide records, graphs, charts, all went. The long paper was all written, but I never finished the drawing because I didn't see the use of spending the time on something that probably never could be published. But now I can never finish them unless I reconstruct the figures. Stanford Press fortunately had the books MS and I wish they'd get the darn thing out; our contract reads "within a reasonable time" and I suppose that means anytime.

By the way, any other duplicates you have of ecolog. papers, I can certainly use.

Sincerely[23]

On March 31, 1937, Ricketts wrote his first letter to Torsten Gislén since the fire. He begins by telling Gislén that Steinbeck was traveling to Sweden and suggests that the two men meet. It never happened. He also tells Gislén that Steinbeck had been classified by the critics as something of a mystic, but Ricketts objects, identifying his friend as a bohemian, a strange appellation since we know of no one else who ever applied such a term to the novelist. Ricketts also writes about the fire, and, as in his letter to Hewatt, he requests copies of scientific papers to help him rebuild his library. But the most interesting lines in this letter are those in which he describes for Gislén the quality of his library. An exaggeration? Considering the amount of material held at Stanford University's Harold A. Miller Library, a good bit of which came from Ed's lab and which he gathered from diverse sources after the fire in 1936 until 1948, Ricketts's comment to Gislén is probably accurate.

March 31, 1937

Dear Gislén,

Chief purpose—hasty note—is to say that John Steinbeck is enroute to NY, Sweden and Russia; may have a chance to see you, and I have urged him to look you up. I am taking care of his dog during the six months. He figured on being in north Europe, probably Denmark, for mid-summer night. He has read some of your papers "Tendencies toward death and renewal"[24] He is a good man, now a famous author. I hope he likes you and you him. His "Of Mice and Men" which followed "In Dubious Battle" I considered a fine piece of work. Classed often more or less as a mystic; I think not, except in the finer sense of the word. Certainly unconventional, formality would surely call him bohemian.

Many things have happened since I last wrote. On Nov. 25th I had the champion of all strokes of bad luck. During the Monterey water-front fire, the lab was completely destroyed. For sometime now completely separated from Nan, I was living here. Sleeping at the time. Got out with my life and that's about all; had time to put on pair of pants and shirt. Succeeded in getting the car out, and a painting of which I was fond—James Fitzgerald's portrait of me. My library, general and scientific, all my personal belongings, clothes, furniture, including a few pieces that had been in the family for more than a hundred years and which came to me at Father's death last year, all destroyed. Most of the records, except for some in the safe, are gone, and with them records of distribution and methods. Worst of all, my library had been assuming good proportions, possibly the best on the Pacific coast with reference to local marine ecology. In this connection, if you have still available any copies of your Misaki, Gulmar Fjord and "Tendencies towards death and renewal" papers, I'll be exceedingly glad to have them. I suppose too late now. I had amassed really a good library on Pacific coast invertebrates, including the Carlgren anemone papers, and several on polyclads and enteropneusts. Many I can never replace. And only a little insurance, $3,000. Loss 4 or 5 times that. Not enough even to replace the buildings, but I am going ahead again with what little there is; if I can keep up the energy and interest, plus a little luck, I can get back again. Nothing recent from Stanford Press about the book. It has been scheduled for issuance a dozen times during the past few years, but they are slow. Our contract reads "Within a reasonable time." Best of regards to you and the family.[25]

Gislén responded, commiserating about the fire and Ed's marital troubles:

> It made me awfully sorry to hear your last letter. Poor boy, your whole lab gone, the library gone, and furniture and all. And more over, as I can understand, family troubles too. I hope anyway that you and Mrs. Nan will find the way back to each other. We have a proverb saying "If there are troubles between two it is never the fault of only one of them. When bad luck arises it is always better to share it with another, but to be worth it one has to be patient and sacrifice a little of one's own principles and dislikes or fancies, to be mild, and forgiving, to see the best intentions of the partner, and to learn from the mistakes one has done." I hope to God that you two will be humble enough and have sufficiently mild and loving hearts to begin anew on a better and durable basis. Life is short and it is not easy if we intend to develop something more than transient luck within us.[26]

In May 1937, Ricketts traveled to Mexico, collecting from the rocky tide flats north of Ensenada, the old Lighthouse, Ensenada, and the sand flats at Estero de Punta Banda. John and Xenia Cage joined Ricketts on the trip, with Ed noting their presence in the collecting reports he later typed up to document his survey. A month later, Xenia sent a letter to Ed, letting him know she'd enjoyed seeing him.[27]

1508 Georgina Ave
Santa Monica
June 6, 1937

Dear Ed—

It was nice to get your card—although I had planned on writing you first, before you had a chance to write me.

It was wonderful seeing you again—not like an old world, but a new world. And this trip was fine. I'm not usually much for roughing it, but with a bar not to far away—it all seems civilized enough. . . . We have a chance to go up to Vancouver this month and it would it be probable and possible to run into

you in some bar along the way
  Wouldn't surprise me a bit.

Love Xenia[28]

Ricketts responded to Xenia's letter, suggesting he may be visiting Vancouver in the summer.

Well just to make it come out even I'll write you first again. . . . I'll be in the Vanc. Island-Puget Sd region not before July. If then. But probably then. If we do meet, we'll establish for John's direction, a percussion orchestra on Gonionemus and Echiurus. You remember—the stomach worm. Tight stomach should percuss fine. . . . Maybe on the way you'll have a chance to stop over at Monterey. . . . If you do be sure to see Mr. PBL. First and last always. If you do I'll buy more enchiladas than we can possibly eat, more beer than we can drink, and Chinese poetry until out eyes are dim and we have long white whiskers. Love.[29]

Meanwhile, at the Stanford press, progress on *Between Pacific Tides* was moving forward. In early June 1937, William Davis received a letter from Sol Felty Light, the distinguished professor of zoology at the University of California, Berkeley. The author of the highly regarded *Light's Manual: Intertidal Invertebrates of the Central California Coast* (1941)—which has enjoyed a history nearly as long as *Between Pacific Tides* (the fourth edition, edited by marine ecologist Jim Carlton, was published in 2007)—emphasized to Davis the importance of the bibliography in the Ricketts and Calvin manuscript, which the editors at the press had considered omitting. Light told Davis, "I have found time to examine the Ricketts MS. I am heartily in favor of its publication. It contains an accumulation of information and reference to be found nowhere else which will be of the greatest value to students in this much-neglected field. It has been checked in many points by competent authorities and even if published alone would be a very distinct contribution. Among other things it presents as does nothing else in print the amazing gaps in our knowledge of the fauna of our shores."[30]

Sol Felty (S. F.) Light. Photograph courtesy of James Carlton. UARC PIC 13: 2541, The Bancroft Library, University of California, Berkeley.

Some marine scientists believe that *Light's Manual* corrects the one major shortcoming of *Between Pacific Tides*. The Ricketts-Calvin volume provides no keys to the species, nor any intent to provide the reader with a way to "identify" the species Ricketts wrote about. This may be, in fact, one of the main things that drove the writing and publication of *Light's Manual*, which is a book of keys for identifying intertidal invertebrates.

Sol Felty Light was an internationally known and respected zoologist who received his doctorate from the University of California, Berkeley, in 1926, with Charles A. Kofoid as his major adviser. His graduate research focused on termite systematics and the biology of symbiotic flagellates and freshwater copepods. Before beginning his work at Berkeley, Light spent two years teaching at a government school in Japan and two more at a high school in Manila. He joined the faculty of the University of the Philippines where, in short order, he advanced from instructor to full professor and department head. From 1922 to 1924 he led the Department of Zoölogy at the new University of Amoy in China. Light's scientific activity while in China consisted of a series of systematic studies of marine invertebrates from tropical waters as well as of Asian termites. He was then hired as a professor in the University of California, Berkeley, Department of Zoology, a position he held for more than twenty years.[31] Among his graduate students was Joel Hedgpeth who, as we know, became a friend of Ed's and who, after Ricketts's death, edited the third and fourth editions of *Between Pacific Tides.*

Although the primary focus of Light's handbook is taxonomic, he is sensitive to concerns that animals need to be considered in the context of their environments. He begins the introduction to his book by writing,

No picture of organisms which ignores their physical and organic environment can be even approximately complete. Studies of dead animals or their parts or even of living animals in the laboratory, valuable and indispensable as they are, give but partial pictures. In the studies here contemplated we seek a firsthand knowledge of living invertebrate animals in their natural setting, their behavior and interrelations, their distribution within the habitat, the influence of physical conditions on this distribution and the correlation between their structures and their behavior patterns on the one hand and the places they occupy in the environment on the other.[32]

Light's bibliography of indispensable readings includes *"Between Pacific Tides*, by Ricketts and Calvin, published by the Stanford University Press, [that] will be of great value to students of the invertebrates of the Pacific Coast and . . . is required of all students in this course. While it will not serve as a manual for the identification of animals it will give a valuable picture of faunas characteristic of the major environments of the seashore in this area, and its excellent

illustrations in conjunction with references to classification lists will
make possible the identification of many common animals."[33]

During the 1930s, Light offered a five-week summer invertebrate
zoology course, taking students to Dillon Beach near the mouth of
Tomales Bay, and then to Moss Beach just north of Half Moon Bay.
He authored a detailed manual for the course, complete with species
lists, keys for taxonomic identification, and field and laboratory exer-
cises. The syllabus for his 1937 summer course, a whopping 122 pages
in length, lists *Between Pacific Tides* as recommended reading even
though it had not yet been published.

So concerned was Light about the importance of Ricketts and
Calvin's index and bibliography that he wrote a follow-up letter to
Davis about three weeks after his letter of June 1937, reinforcing his
earlier comments. In it he writes, "I am returning under separate
cover the ANNOTATED SYSTEMATIC INDEX AND BIBLIOGRAPHY proposed by Mr. Ricketts for his BETWEEN PACIFIC TIDES. It has been
gone over by two of my advanced graduate students, Doctor Olga
Hartman, who is a thoroughly competent specialist in the Annelids,
and Mrs. Avery Grant who knows the Gastropods. They both agree
with me that it would be a very great misfortune if these were to
be omitted from the book, in that it presents a unique accumulation of very important information, which is not to be obtained from
any other source. I sincerely hope that it will be included."[34] Ricketts
knew and respected Light and his work, but it is not clear whether he
knew about the Berkeley zoologist's letters to William Davis. If he
did, he would surely have been pleased.

Increasingly optimistic, Ricketts wrote to Calvin with a status
update, noting that "Stanford has much of the book rolling; I really
think eventually we'll have that thing out. They've been after me for
two months to chase up there to look over what they've done, but
I haven't anymore time to fool around with them the way I did in
the past, acct. bread and butter still more urgent even than before.
Anyway, it's surely coming out soon. Even they can't possibly hold it
up more than another 6 or 8 months."[35] He would soon find out that
they could.

Jack Calvin did not share Ed's optimism. In an October 1937 letter to Ricketts, he laments the endless machinations of the Stanford
press, telling Ed,

Three months and one day ago you opined that Stanford couldn't hold up our opus more than another 6 or 8 months, so in another 3–5 months I'll begin looking for it—with tongue in cheek, fingers crossed, and a rainbow round my shoulder. The thing that hurts me the worst about the whole situation, is I think that my vocabulary—a vocabulary which I have always felt to be adequate where profanity was called for—fails me utterly. If I could just think of a series of words, with gestures, which would really do justice to Stanford Press, I would be happy in spite of no book.

At the end of his lament, he tells Ed, "As for you, who have borne the brunt of the interminable mess—have a whisky and soda."[36]

Just before Christmas, with still no word on a publication date and the rainbow on Calvin's shoulder having faded away, Ricketts wrote to Davis regarding some small corrections to the manuscript and told the Stanford editor that he would like to visit the press. If Davis responded, we have no record of it. The months continued to pass without any definitive word on a publication date. Ed's patience was running thin. Seeking a diversion, he wrote George MacGinitie in February 1938 commenting on one of MacGinitie's recent publications and, for some unknown reason, telling MacGinitie about the "Chinaman"[37]—his friend Chin Yip, who for years had collected specimens for Pacific Biological Laboratories.

Jeung Chin Yip and a number of other Chinese fishermen form an interesting backstory to the saga of *Between Pacific Tides*. Chief among the characters is Quock Tuck Lee, one of the more entrepreneurial members of the small Chinese fishing community once located on the property where Hopkins Marine Station stands today. Quock collected specimens for several Hopkins resident and visiting scientists. For help he taught his nephew, Chin Yip, how and what sorts of critters to collect. Chin Yip, in turn, collected for Ed. Jeung's home was at 774 Wave Street in New Monterey, just a block up from Pacific Biological Laboratories. Over time he and Ed became good friends.

Numerous Pacific Biological Laboratories (PBL) survey cards mention Chin Yip and identify the many specimens he collected for

NAME		Pterophysa grandis Fewkes							
DATE	REGION, STATION, POSITION, ETC.		BATHY-METRIC ZONE	DEPTH OR TIDAL HORIZON	EXPOSURE TO WAVE SHOCK	TYPE OF BOTTOM	NUMBER TAKEN OR OBSERVED	IDENT (OR "FIELD")
3.22.28A	Monterey Bay, ChinYip (probably a few days before 3.22.28)		Pelag	50 fms				Bigelow 3.30.28

IF ADDITIONAL SPACE IS NEEDED, USE UNPRINTED 4 X 6 WHITE CARDS

Pacific Biological Laboratories' Survey Card identifying Chin Yip as the collector and Henry Bryant Bigelow as the identifier. Photograph courtesy of Harold A. Miller Library, Stanford University Libraries.

Ricketts. In her "Recollections," Nan Ricketts tells us how indispensable Chin Yip was to Ed and how they befriended the Jeungs every Christmas: "One of our most dependable shark collectors was Chin Yip, a Chinese fisherman. He wanted to be paid once a year, and only the week of the Chinese New Year. We understood that according to their religion, all debts were to be paid before the New Year. On that day our family was invited to their house to partake of their specially prepared foods and drink their liquor, which was pretty potent."[38] John Steinbeck occasionally saw and talked with Chin Yip at Ed's lab and likely used him as the model for the "old Chinaman" in *Cannery Row*.

At the end of his letter to MacGinitie, Ed invited George and Nettie to Monterey for a visit, and then, almost as if he could no longer hold back, he complained that the "cursed SU Press still hasn't issued my book."[39] He concludes by telling MacGinitie that *Between Pacific Tides* may be out of date by the time it is finally published.

On May 27, 1938, a second article appeared in the *Stanford Daily*, announcing that *Between Pacific Tides* was scheduled for publication in the summer of that year: "Mr. Croonquist announced that several books are scheduled for publication during the summer months. Of special interests to those who live along the coast is Ricketts and Calvin's "Between Pacific Tides," a general book of the animal life found along the water's edge and in the tide pools."[40] This wasn't the first time the *Daily* had told readers that the publication of *Between Pacific Tides* was imminent when it wasn't. Neither would it be the last. One wonders what Friend, Davis, and their colleagues at the press thought when they read about the as-yet-unpublished book in the Stanford student newspaper.

A month or so later, Davis wrote to Ricketts, checking to make sure that Ed had survived a recent ordeal at the dentist. Ricketts's dental problems were a big deal; he'd spent countless hours in the dentist's chair and, by the late 1930s, had had many of his teeth extracted. For years a story circulated about his having met John Steinbeck in a dentist's office. It wasn't true, but he and Steinbeck maintained it as an inside joke. In fact, Steinbeck includes the joke as fact in the tribute to Ed he wrote for the stand-alone *Log from the Sea of Cortez*. In any event, Ed scribbled a handwritten response to Davis, affirming that he had survived his dental visit and was revising the index of *Tides*, a task he described as "a big job."[41]

The day after Ricketts's note reached Davis, Jessie Whittern, a technical editor at the Stanford press, penned a letter to Ricketts that offered insight into the issues associated with bringing the manuscript to completion. Since Whittern begins her letter noting that William Davis was away on vacation, it is unlikely that she had seen Ricketts's notes about his work on the index. Whittern had come to the Stanford press from the University of Chicago, where she was one of the original authors of the widely respected *Manual of Style*, published by that university's press in 1906, that now, more than a century later, is in its seventeenth edition. An authority on matters of style, Whittern was widely considered one of the outstanding technical editors in the country.[42] She was to become a key figure in bringing *Between Pacific Tides* to press.

My dear Mr. Ricketts:

Professor Davis is away on vacation. In his absence I shall try to answer your note to him.

First of all may I offer an apology for the omission of proof or some means of checking your illustrations when we sent you the page proofs. Since all your dealings with regard to illustrations had been with Mr. Light or Mr. Davis and I assumed, erroneously it seems, that revised illustrations had been sent you after they were corrected, I thought it would not be a great task to include the illustrations in indexing. It certainly would add greatly to the value of the book.

In lieu of such corrected copy, I am sending you a proof of the legends that were pasted up for plates and a duplicated proof of the list of figures in the List of Illustrations. I have marked the plate legend proofs with the section and page number which we are using as a key on the illustration pages.

The photolith sections are to be printed and inserted in binding thus:

Section I consists of 48 pages (keyed I.1–I.48) and contains Figures 3–56 and Plates I–XXIV. It will be inserted at or near the end of "Part I. "Protected Outer Coast," preferably after page 112.

Section II consists of 12 pages (keyed II.1–II.12) and contains Figures 57–69 and Plates XXV–XXIX, to be inserted at or page 144 (end of "Part II. Open Coasts").

Section III consists of 32 plates (keyed III.1–III.32) and contains 70–102 and Plates XXX–XLIV, to be inserted at or near page 230 (end of "Part III. Bay and Estuary").

Section IV consists of 8 pages (keyed IV.1–IV.8) and contains Figure 103–112 and Plates XLV–XLVI, to be inserted at or near p. 254 (end of "IV. Wharf Piling").

The list of plates has not been set yet to follow the list of figures because it must be planned to fit exact numbers of pages and the form may be condensed if you index the illustrations but should not be so condensed if you were not to include them, the list in that case being the only key to the illustrated items on the plates. However, with these proofs I believe you can complete the indexing.

If there is anything further I can do to help the cause, please let me know. I am sorry this information had not been given you earlier.

Yours very truly,
Jessie D. Whittern[43]

Ricketts was impressed with Whittern. He found her comments useful, and he appreciated her candor and her offer of assistance. What we do not know is whether Ricketts saw any of the "soon to be published" notices from the *Stanford Daily*. Neither do we know who was responsible for these premature and misleading notices. It is hard to imagine that an undergraduate journalism student would be lurking around the press exploring the publishing misadventures of a text about marine biology. Nevertheless, once again, this time on November 17, 1938, an article appeared with another notice, reading, "Sea Life to Be Subject: Soon to be published is 'Between Pacific Tides' by Edward F. Ricketts and Jack Calvin. The aim of the handbook is to supply the visitor to the shore a knowledge of the prolific life zone between the upper and lower limit of the tide."[44]

Walter Fisher was certainly correct when he stated that *Between Pacific Tides* was a big job. There were numerous corrections to be made in the body of the text as well as a large and complex index. Years later, Ritchie Lovejoy, in one of his Round and About columns, provided insight into some of what slowed the publication. "Things kept dragging along—the plates had to be as perfect as possible, the makeup was difficult, money was short."[45]

In early December 1938, Ricketts again wrote to Davis, this time providing corrections to the text and noting that work on the index was coming along well. He follows this letter with another the day after Christmas, telling Davis that he had finished the index. Specifically, he tells Davis that "the alphabetical index is completed, has been proof-read, checked and edited. I ended up making an entirely new one, as suggested. As arranged over the phone, I hadn't intended going over the entire account again, but in connection with a rigid rechecking of cross references in connection with the index, I found it necessary, and three of us—some friends fortunately jumped into the crisis—are putting through this considerable task."[46]

One of the "friends" to whom Ricketts refers to in the letter was Xenia Cage, who had been anxious to get back to Pacific Grove. She had graduated from high school in Monterey and then matriculated at Reed College in Portland, finishing her degree in 1935. Wanting to pursue a career in art, she returned to Monterey and then, after meeting and marrying John Cage, spent the next four or five years

John Cage. Photograph courtesy of Los Angeles Philharmonic Archives, Betty Freeman Papers.

with Cage attempting to cobble artistic careers together. She and Cage were together at the Cornish School in Seattle (where Cage met Merce Cunningham), writing music and painting. Cage was writing and organizing concerts of percussion music. One such piece was a four-movement *Quartet*. The score didn't specify instruments, and so the friends who performed it with him played on tire rims, brake drums, and kitchen utensils. Xenia sometimes played with Cage's percussion group at Cornish and, with John, worked at her bookbinding craft. The *Seattle Times* reported on her work, noting that, in addition to making cloth bindings, she and Cage wrapped "their favorites—mostly modern authors and poets—in leather of 'Nigerian goat-skin.'"[47]

In December 1938, Xenia traveled to Pacific Grove with Cage for Christmas to visit friends and her sister, Tal. During their visit, the couple was recruited by Ricketts to help him compile the index for *Between Pacific Tides*, a process that was likely punctuated by discussions about experimental music, the Chinese poetry of Tu Fu and Li Po, and goodly quantities of beer. Working well into the evenings, they got it done. How interesting that the most famous American experimental musician of the twentieth century spent his Christmas holiday compiling an index for a book about marine invertebrates.

Two days after Christmas, Ricketts wrote a long and newsy letter to Torsten Gislén, noting that the publication of *Between Pacific Tides* appeared likely. In this letter, which provides insight into Ricketts's state of mind at the time, he talks about the breakup of his marriage, his inability to rebuild his pre-fire scientific library, and finally, for what appears to be the first time, addresses the problem of overfishing in Monterey Bay. As time passed, Ricketts would become one of Monterey's leading critics of the area's sardine industry, joining faculty at Hopkins and staff from California Fish and Game who warned cannery owners that a collapse of the sardine fisheries was likely to occur. As we now know, it happened, and the collapse was total.

Ricketts also tells Gislén about his Christmas dinner at the home of Gustaf and Lucille Lannestock in Carmel, which was quite an event, attended by a whole host of friends, including members of the Kashevaroff outfit. Quite the socialites, Gustav and Lucille had come to Carmel in the mid-1930s and bought a home on Scenic Road from Richard Dix, a silent film star who survived the transition to the "talkies" and who starred in the 1931 Academy Award–winning film *Cimarron* (based on Edna Ferber's novel of the same name). He named his Carmel home, which was modeled on a Taos pueblo, "The Cimarron." The Lannestocks were interesting characters. Gustav, a Swede, was knighted by King Gustav IV Adolph for his many contributions to his homeland's culture, and his wife, Lucille, helped found the Carmel Bach Festival and the Carmel Music Society. Evening events with distinguished guests were a staple at the Cimarron. Henry Miller, John Cage, and Robinson Jeffers were frequent guests, as were Ed Ricketts and John Steinbeck. Gustav and Lucille hosted a cocktail party every evening at 5:30, open to one and all, whether old and new friends or strangers merely strolling by on the beach.

The Lannestock Christmas dinner guests included Steinbeck, Robinson Jeffers, and the Swedish writer Vilhelm Moberg, who was at work on a novel about Scandinavian immigration to the United States he would title *Emigrants.* Gustav Lannestock told Richard Astro that Moberg happened to walk by the Lannestock house sometime and Lucille, as was her habit when she saw someone outside who looked interesting, invited him in.[48] Over time, Moberg and the Lannestocks became friends, and Gustaf, himself a Swede, took on the onerous task of translating Moberg's four-book series, *Emigrants*, from Swedish to English. Some years later, that series was made into two moderately successful Warner Brothers movies: *The Emigrants* and *The New Land*.

Dear Gislén:

It was good to hear from you. I know how you will be having fun with the increased family at the holiday time. Christmas is essentially a family time, and I think it's even more significant in the Scandinavian countries than it is here. Funny thing, Ed Jr. and I spent the afternoon and evening of the 25th at the home of some Swedish friends, a Gustav Lannestock who is living and writing in Carmel; we had goose and baked ham and imported pumpernickel and all the usual Swedish cheeses and meats and herrings and pickles. Before that we had spent Christmas eve at the home of Ritch and Natalia (don't recall if you knew them, part of the Kashevaroff outfit from Alaska), Xenia and John Cage drove down from Cornish School in Seattle, John Steinbeck and Carol came in and we had a good reunion. Then when we came back from there very late, I switched on the radio idly and heard some (apparently) Swedish station broadcasting "the favorite Christmas Hymn of Sweden" some sort of celebration, with announcements in Swedish and English. The business goes slowly, I have trouble picking it up since the fire, there is still insufficient money, the second depression is raging, I am getting along without any help and have to do all every thing myself. Which means that correspondence particularly suffers.

As unbelievable as it sounds, that shore book will soon be out. It cannot possibly be held up much longer. I never saw such a slow outfit as Stanford University Press, and of course lately, since the fire, I've had to budget my times so carefully that it left little opportunity for me to do the things they wanted me to do in the checking etc. Now for six months it has been already in page proof, with all the Illustrations in page proof also, and there only remained the revision and checking of the alphabetical index. I hadn't time for the considerable work required, but during these holidays friends have been helping me, and it will be done soon.

Nan and the girls are living in the Puget Sound country, I hear from them not often, and write infrequently. Ed Jr is living here with me, and it's a good thing for both of us. He's coming along fine, and I'm pleased to see that he shows no emotional marks for any troubles he has come through. He has become one of the most considerate people I know, I have now a sense of being a very competent parent; he will turn out pretty well, well balanced and self reliant; promises to be a fine mathematician. I shouldn't be surprised if we hear from him sometime in the field of mathematical physics. Good thing I got a geoduck for you, and will sometime devise an effective method of shipping it. I have had neither the morale, nor time, nor money to start rebuilding my scientific library, but in the fields of poetry and philosophy it has crept up to pre-fire status. Collecting has been going well, but many things havn't been replaced and I fear never will be; I made a trip south, covered pretty well the ground we went over on that fine trip. I have now a Ford 60, the small V-8, the cheapest car to run I have ever used. So I went from the largest to the smallest

Now it is warm and sunny; the canneries are going strong—they will extract every single sardine out of the ocean if legislation doesn't restrain them, already the signs of depletion are serious. Funny how americans can't learn the lesson that the north european countries have known for a century.

Say hello to Mrs. G. for me. I am remembering you folks very happily.

Ed[49]

Ricketts often wrote letters on holidays, and days later he penned a New Year's Eve note to William Davis, providing the editor with all the necessary edits for the book, except for the umlauts. The correspondence is interesting, since it shows that, by the end of 1938, the press had finally furnished Ed with a completed manuscript.

Dear Mr. Davis:

I start off the new year right, by sending not only the alphabetical index revised, checked and retyped (and needing still another retyping which I havn't time for), but the complete proof with all cross references checked.

This is the first time I have had all material to date complete at one time, and it seemed that, since the cross references would have to be checked some time, this time was as good as any, particularly since I had to refer constantly to the text anyway in making the new index. It's very fortunate that I did this, because many of the subsidiary references were incorrectly cited—to be expected, I suppose, with all the changes and all the years.

Only one thing I didn't attend to fully—the problem of umlauts over terminal e, etc. Originally I proposed to check this by a master index which derived from the opinions of the experts consulted in the matter of spelling and synonymies of their groups, but this original material was lost in a fire, so I went by what was in the systematic index in its present form. This means that there are some inconsistencies, even within a given group, as with the annelid worms, some of the pronounced final e-s havn't any amlaut, some have; I don't know the answer or which is correct.

So now the New Year starts, 6 PM Saturday, and some friends have already stopped by. The stuff I'm sending represents, as you can imagine, a very considerable amount of work, now I should be resting. Happy New Year to you all

Sincerely

Ed Ricketts [Signature][50]

By mid-January, the problem with the umlauts had been solved; Ed wrote to Davis in mid-January of 1939 about their proper usage. Eight years of discussions and negotiations with the Stanford University Press ended with an exchange about umlauts. Ricketts was certain that his book was on its way to press.

CHAPTER 6

finally

Genius looks forward: the eyes of man are set in his fore-
head, not in his hindhead: man hopes: genius creates.

—RALPH WALDO EMERSON

B y February of 1939, the editors at the Stanford University Press
were finalizing plans to publish *Between Pacific Tides*. On February
23, Stanley Croonquist wrote to Ricketts, updating him on matters
related to the book's publication. He told Ricketts that Stanford would
print one thousand copies. In addition, Croonquist mentioned that the
proposed price of $7.50 per copy would be reduced to $6.00 (not $3.50 as
Friend had indicated), allowing the book to compete successfully with
Johnson and Snook, which had recently been reprinted (1935). Had
Stanford moved more quickly, the price reduction might not have been
necessary. On the other hand, the improved state of the American
economy by 1939 provided impetus for sales.

February 23, 1939
Mr. Edward F. Ricketts
Pacific Biological Laboratories
Pacific Grove, California

Dear Mr. Ricketts

Everything seems to be moving ahead on your book and so I
am writing to all of the people who sent in orders in the past

(except those received within the past several months) asking
them to verify their orders. Our experience has been in the
past that when books are delayed too long in being published
addresses change, people change their interests, and it is almost
mandatory that we check up before shipping the books.

I am sure you will be pleased to know that Mr. Friend has
approved a reduction in the price of $7.50 to $6.00 per copy,
which will put it in the same price class as Johnson and Snook.
It all means that the lower price will have to sell a lot of extra
copies because even at $7.50 we would take a loss on the first
printing of 1,000 copies.

I think that our circular, which I want to get out within a
month, will bring in some additional orders. I'll let you see
copy for this before I send it out.

Cordially yours
STANFORD UNIVERSITY PRESS
S. M. Croonquist: g Sales Manager [1]

A day after Croonquist wrote Ricketts, Ed told Calvin he was
confident that *Between Pacific Tides* was going to press. He also spoke
openly about his clandestine advertising campaign. It is the first time
that he did so in so direct a fashion. Given the tone of his correspondence, it is unlikely that Ricketts received Croonquist's letter before
he wrote to Calvin.

Febr. 24, 1939

Dear Jack:

With characteristic meticulousness, I was going to reply at once
to your very welcome Christmas card and note. Well—it's something that I'm getting around to it now. As you may have heard
(my ways seem to have become infamous), I get something like
years behind in correspondence. Now it goes better, don't know
how I can keep up this preposterous pace of tending to things
but I can be thankful even for symptoms of budding discipline.
Too much work, you see, and I have to do it all soul alone.

Well if you saw John and Xen they probably told you about
the book. I honestly don't see how that procrastinating outfit

can possibly delay much longer; not even SU Press could do it. Everything is in page proof, all drawings, photos, text, systematic index and bibliography, even the alphabetical index. (Incidentally, the present index represents the third[;] I finally got so absolutely moraled-out that I doubt if I could touch the thing again. Imagine emending and finally completely re-doing that big job twice over. And you know how they did things. Changed around the numbering so that that all had to be done over—that was attended to up there—but the cross references were sometimes properly corrected, sometimes not. They were quite decent tho, and went along with my necessary slowness and even with my own procrastinations.

Practically all the illustrations are as good as the one you saw. I never saw such beautiful work. It may have taken ten years to blast the thing thru, but in some ways it was worth it.

I wish I'd had an opportunity to see you and to tell you of the finagling finally went thru in order to blast publication out of that funny outfit; too long even to sketch in a letter. Don't know if I ever told you—I finally got out that advertising campaign myself—they were a bit upset at first, but all OK now, relations are most friendly, and I have to acknowledge that I sense, and respond to, a general warm feeling there now again.

Sooo—lot's to write about, but other things to do. Hello to Sash. Don't ever try to forgive me for being such a poor correspondent. I'll forgive myself and then you won't have to![2]

At last, in late March of 1939, the first edition of *Between Pacific Tides* went to press, with a print run of one thousand copies. Ricketts was ebullient, telling Croonquist that Stanford had done a marvelous job. He also expressed regret that he had failed to adequately recognize Ritch Lovejoy's contribution to the project.

Pacific Biological Laboratories
Pacific Grove, California
March 29, 1939

Dear Stanley:

That's a beautiful job. I'm tremendously pleased. So is everyone else concerned with whom I've talked. After all that work
and time, errors should have been almost eliminated, but I have
already turned up one spectacularly my fault. Ritchie Lovejoy,
the very competent artist who did line drawings, originally
asked for what he called a "by-line" (he got cash only a dollar
apiece for all those fine drawings) and supposed that meant
merely a statement that that phase of the work was by him.
Well, I know better now. Sometimes my dumbness amazes me.[3]

Copies of *Between Pacific Tides* were in Ed's hands by the end of
March. Despite the long delays and the continuing frustrations, the
finished product was excellent.

SITKA ARTS AND CRAFTS CENTER SITKA, ALASKA

THE CALVIN STUDIO   THE ARROWHEAD PRESS   THE HANDICRAFT SHOP

April 19, 1939

Dear Ed:

Every morning after coffee and cigarette I tip-toe into the
library table, chanting softly, "You dreamed it, you sap. It can't
be, and things that can't be aren't." And I open my eyes and
look, and there is THE BOOK. It's been there for five mornings
now, and if I see it just one more morning I'm going to admit,
tentatively, that it is actually there. It's frightfully upsetting,
really, for if that can happen then anything can happen, and
I've got to that stage where I'm afraid to take a drink for fear it
will happen.

And what a swell job? Almost it softens my heart toward
Stanford Press. Ritch's drawings and my photos are beautifully
reproduced, and after looking at them I turned, without any
real hope, to Tethys, and blow me down if they hadn't left in
our description of that delightful creature's amatory escapades.
It is our cue to begin to love the Press just a tiny-bit, after all
these bitter years.

I have a new boat, a miniscule cruiser about a third the size
of the Grampus, so it's barely possible—though I make no
promises—that we'll be able to get you some Gonionemus this

summer. Time is the factor of which we wot not, but this year we have an assistant on call, so we have high hopes of getting in some photographic, biological and other cruises. Why don't you come up this summer? You could do it easily on the first royalty check from Stanford dear old Stanford Red. I'm not laughing; I'm crying.

                    Love and kisses and a shot of whisky.
                                    Jack [Signature][4]

"THE BOOK," wrote Paul Dayton, the Distinguished Professor of Marine Ecology at the Scripps Institution, "is nothing short of a masterpiece. Ed Ricketts completely changed the course of intertidal ecology in the eastern Pacific by focusing his questions on the most relevant natural history, and almost all productive scientists relied on *Between Pacific Tides* to define their research questions. For this reason, *Between Pacific Tides* may be the most important intertidal ecology publication ever written. . . . All coastal naturalists owe much of their understanding to Ricketts."[5]

"THE BOOK" was, then, and remains today, the richest account of the habits and habitats of the animals that live in one of the most prolific life zones of the world—the rocky shores and tide pools of the Pacific Coast from Sitka to northern Mexico. The captivating descriptions of the life processes of the animals are handled with the affectionate care that only Ed Ricketts could provide. His and Calvin's decision to group the seashore invertebrates according to their most characteristic habitats, whether rocky shore, sandy beach, mudflat, or wharf piling, was a grand success. Aided by Jack's photographs and his editing assistance, as well as by Ritch Lovejoy's illustrations, Ricketts provides a comprehensive and remarkably readable account of an animal's life history, its physiology, and its relationship with other animals and to the environmental factors of wave shock, bottom type, and tide levels. It is a masterful combination of good science and fine natural history. Even today, more than eighty years later, *Between Pacific Tides* is still talked about in intertidal ecology courses offered at colleges and universities along the Pacific Coast. Many factors—some more avoidable than others—contributed to the long delays in bringing the book to publication. At the same time, one must congratulate the Stanford University Press staff for understanding the manuscript's value and publishing such a fine and attractive book.

This is not to say that there haven't been some bumps in the road, as one edition of *Between Pacific Tides* morphed into another. Securing the services of John Steinbeck to write a foreword to the second edition was a master stroke. The plankton chapter authored by Ricketts in that same edition was, for most if not all readers, a welcome addition. And securing the services of Joel Hedgpeth to edit the third and fourth editions was a wise move, even if Hedgpeth proved to be a thorn in the side of more than a few people at the Stanford press. Replacing Hedgpeth with David Phillips for the fifth edition (1985) may have avoided the acrimony that had formed around Hedgpeth over the years, but the way Stanford handled the switch lacked tact and insulted the already disgruntled Hedgpeth.

In retrospect, Ed Ricketts was perhaps the easiest of the authors and editors of *Between Pacific Tides* with whom the Stanford press staff had to deal. Despite their mishaps and the delays, Ricketts never lost his temper. He was not only a gifted scientist; he was also an excellent strategist. He knew where he (and Jack Calvin) needed to go, and he wasn't about to lose everything because of momentary pique. He absorbed criticism by charming his critics and, in the end, he prevailed. The book was published and has been enjoyed for three-quarters of a century by professional biologists and by undergraduate and graduate students, as well as by casual readers who simply like the seashore. The authors of this volume encountered *Between Pacific Tides* as undergraduates. One of us was a biology major at the University of South Florida; the other was a student of English literature at Oregon State.

Jim Carlton, who, as we noted earlier, edited the fourth edition of *Light's Manual* and who has long been a fan of *Between Pacific Tides*, recently predicted that the fifth edition (2007) of Ricketts and Calvin's masterwork may be the last. Carlton believes that with the rapid pace of change in the natural world, *Between Pacific Tides* is in danger of becoming dated. Some Ed Heads would disagree. Carlton, who counts himself as an Ed Head—he has all six printed versions of *Tides*, including the 1939 edition, as well as some of Ed's original laboratory glassware; he also won, at the City of Monterey auction, the eight-foot-by-eight-foot painted mural called *Looking Back*, which depicts Ed looking down at Cannery Row and his lab—qualifies his concern, noting that even if *Tides* becomes dated, that "does not detract at all from its poetic and elegant descriptions and insights of intertidal life, making it still a vade mecum!"[6]

THE AFTERMATH

One cannot overstate Ricketts's euphoria when *Between Pacific Tides* was finally published. For Jack and Ritch, it was the end of a long journey. For Ed, it was validation of years of hard work and a belief that an ecological approach to the study of life in the intertidal zones was useful and important. In late April 1939, Ricketts told his friend Virginia Scardigli that it would be "nice if I'd make some money on the thing, but no royalties at all for first 500 copies, then 10%. So, if, in my lifetime, I get back 10¢ an hour for the time put into that job, I'll be lucky."[7] Richard Astro talked with Scardigli in 1971 and recalls her remarking that she doubted that Ed received even that much.[8] In fact, Ricketts received 75 percent of all royalties with the remaining 25 percent going to Calvin.

Shortly after the publication of *Between Pacific Tides*, Ed reconnected with Joe Campbell, who, in 1934, had accepted a position as professor of literature at Sarah Lawrence College in Yonkers, New York. After Joe married Jean Erdman, a dancer, choreographer, and avant-garde theater director, the couple moved into a Greenwich Village apartment, where they lived for most of their lives. Returning home from Hawai'i in 1939, where he and Jean visited Jean's parents, Campbell wrote Ed that "I expect to land in San Francisco, August 30, and should like to drop in on you before starting across the continent. As soon as I get my car out of storage I shall start for Pacific Grove-Carmel-Monterey & hunt you out." He concludes, "I am looking forward eagerly to the visit, old man. Every time I see a rocky coast I think of you in your boots. Jean has heard more about you than about any single experience of my wander-years."[9]

The Campbells visit with Ricketts, though brief, was uplifting. It was like old times. Ed, Joe, and Jean ate, drank, and talked late into the night about Spengler and Joyce, about Jeffers and Jung—their animated conversation reminded both men of their time together seven years earlier. Back in New York, Campbell wrote to Ricketts, "It was fine seeing you, if only for an evening, after all this time. Jean was smart enough to perceive that you and your life-way stand close to the source of her husband's enlightenment." Invigorated by even a short visit with Ricketts, he wrote that now "I shall do something to bring my ideas into cogent order. I always feel that I am on the brink of something like a unified field theory, and keep my pen waiting for the one root word but now I shall try to put things down; perhaps the effort of exposition will do the trick."[10]

Ed was energized after his evening with the Campbells. On October 7, 1939, he wrote Joe:

> I have started attempts toward publishing those three essays [non-teleological thinking that would eventually appear in the Log portion of *Sea of Cortez*, Breaking Through, and the poetry piece]. Sent them first to Harpers and they came back just a couple of days ago." Then, somewhat cynically, he writes, "Now I try *Atlantic Monthly*, then *Yale Review*, then *Southern Review*, then *Partisan Review*, but I think none will take them. So there I'll be. Guess I'll have to be well known before I can publish the darn things, and that may never be."[11] His self-mocking cynicism aside, life for Ed Ricketts was good. He tells Campbell, "I am to do another job for Stanford—a manual of the invertebrates of the SF Bay area. Won't take long, a year or so if I can get to it."[12]

Two days later, on October 9, 1939, Ed wrote Xenia Cage, "Stanford Press has a new job coming up for me, if ever I can get integrated to do it; a short manual of the important SF Bay area marine invertebrates." Ricketts says he is "just hammering in the lab, and tootings on the trumpet [Ed Jr. was quite the trumpeter], and the building shaking from the machinery next door (the canneries started up as soon as war was declared, the first of the profiteers), and drunks chasing each other up and down the street, and Flora's gals 'going and coming with hindrance . . . and the vermilioned girls getting drunk about sunset' and other times too."[13]

Ed's continuing financial struggle to keep Pacific Biological Laboratories afloat ended when Steinbeck stepped in and provided the needed funds for the lab in exchange for partial ownership. Then, in 1940, Ed met Toni Jackson, a remarkable young woman who had been one of Louis Terman's "gifted children" and who, with her daughter, Kay, moved in with Ed. As for Cannery Row, before and after Ed became famous as Steinbeck's Doc, it remained Ricketts's home.

Sometime late in 1939, Ricketts convinced Steinbeck to collaborate on the San Francisco Bay project. Shortly before Christmas he wrote Pat Covici, Steinbeck's editor at Viking Press, that "John and I start out today on some preliminary work, collecting here in the SF Bay area, but since the rain is coming down in a steady stream, I don't look forward to it very happily."[14] He also told Covici about a possible trip with Steinbeck to Mexico. Whether this was the germ of what would become the Sea of Cortez expedition is conjecture. But things became clear when, in early February, Ricketts wrote Peg Fitzgerald (the estranged wife of the artist, James Fitzgerald, who had painted Ed's portrait and that survived the lab fire) that "Jon and I are working up the first of two books together. It goes slowly but what we've done so far, I think is good. Planning a very extensive trip into the Gulf of California for next month; 6 weeks or two months."[15]

Perhaps Ricketts's most satisfying moment occurred when he read a copy of a January 31, 1940, letter from Walter Fisher that was to be provided to the Mexican authorities urging them to allow Ricketts to study marine life in the Gulf of California. Fisher's statement, that "Your book 'Between Pacific Tides' has put you in the front rank as an authority on the ecology of shore animals" was the perfect coda to a decade of successful hard work. It was, for Ed, the ultimate tribute.

January 31, 1940

Mr. E. F. Ricketts
Pacific Biological Laboratories
Pacific Grove, Calif.

Dear Mr. Ricketts:

I note by your letter of January 30, 1940, that you and Mr. Steinbeck are planning to explore the shores of the Gulf of California for intertidal invertebrate animals and to make a detailed study of their distribution and habits. This project meets with my enthusiastic approval. There is no coast of equal extent in North America which is so little known and which is so likely to produce valuable information if carefully and systematically explored. Your long experience as a collector makes you especially well fitted for this work, Your book "Between Pacific Tides" has put you in the front rank as an authority on the ecology of shore animals. So I see no reason why this expedition should not make a great contribution to knowledge. I feel sure that the Government of Mexico will take a similar view.

Very truly,
Walter K. Fisher
Director [16]

Over time Walter Fisher developed a high regard for Ricketts's work as a collector; he also came to understand and appreciate the contingent nature of Ed's science. In the laboratory, where all variables remain the same, so do the results. Of course, variables can be adjusted to determine effect, but in the field, things are always changing. As we've pointed out, what Ed Ricketts found in a particular intertidal location in 1932 might have been very different a year earlier or later. Given these kinds of changes, truths emerge slowly and are often conditional. Walter Fisher may not have fully appreciated this fact when he first reviewed the manuscript of *Between Pacific Tides*. He surely knew it a decade later when he told the Mexican authorities that there was no reason that Ricketts's "expedition should not make a great contribution to knowledge."

Ricketts scrapped the San Francisco Bay project when Steinbeck signed on for the Gulf of California expedition; for Ed it was to be a warm-water follow-on to *Between Pacific Tides*. The record of their trip, which included a phyletic catalog describing the animals they collected, was published as *Sea of Cortez* in December 1941, prefaced by a narrative (the Log portion) that most readers attributed to Steinbeck but that was the product of both men. Steinbeck drafted the narrative, which Toni Jackson edited and typed, with much of the material coming from a journal that Ed kept and a trip log by Tony Berry, who captained the seventy-seven-foot *Western Flyer* that Steinbeck and Ricketts contracted for their expedition.

The main body of *Sea of Cortez* is a descriptive inventory of the animals that Ricketts, John and Carol Steinbeck, and members of the crew of the *Western Flyer* collected in the Gulf of California. But the importance of Ricketts phyletic catalog would eventually be eclipsed by the narrative portion of the book; this despite the chagrin of many Steinbeck fans who, at the time, could not understand why the Pulitzer Prize–winning writer would follow *The Grapes of Wrath* with a book about marine invertebrates. Typical was the comment by critic Arthur Mizener, who said *Sea of Cortez* was plagued by "tenth-rate philosophizing." Equally damaging was Stanley Hyman's assertion that, in *Sea of Cortez*, Steinbeck "writes a final elegy to concepts of social progress," and that he "kills off all his remaining social compulsion and emerges into a perfect scientific vacuum."[17] Over the years scientists and literary scholars have unearthed a good deal of new information about the writing and publishing history of *Sea of Cortez*; it is a fine book with a history that's different but as interesting as that of *Between Pacific Tides*.

As for Steinbeck's role in writing the narrative section of the book, Ricketts told Joel Hedgpeth, in November 1941,

> However much it seems otherwise "Sea of Cortez" is truly a compilation. Jon worked at the collecting and sorting of animals, and looked over some [of] the literature, including the specialist literature, and I had a hand even in the narrative, altho the planning and architecture of the first part of course is entirely his, as the planning of the scientific section is entirely mine. But much of the detail of the narrative is based on a journal I kept during the trip, and some of the text derives from it and from unpublished essays of mine. I shall be interested to see what the critics have to say about the various parts of the job in connection with the oft repeated assumption on their part that they can spot a person's writings anywhere by characteristic tricks of style and thinking.[18]

As the dust was settling on the debate about the value of *Sea of Cortez*, Ricketts was drafted into the army. While stationed at the Monterey Presidio, a mile or so from his lab, his interests turned northward. After his discharge in 1945, Ed, Toni, and Ed Jr. surveyed marine life on the west coast of Vancouver Island and on Haida Gwaii (formerly the Queen Charlotte Islands). They made a second trip in 1946. Ricketts planned another collaboration with Steinbeck, this time on a book about his work in Canada and Haida Gwaii, to be titled *The Outer Shores*. Steinbeck was scheduled to join Ricketts on a third and final trip to Haida Gwaii in the summer of 1948. All the while, Ricketts was revising *Between Pacific Tides*, making minor corrections, adding citations to the reference section, and completing the plankton chapter.

A glimpse of the E. F. Ricketts notebook titled "Red Survey R-C-R. Specialists' reports: West Coast Vancouver Island-Queen Charlotte Islands," held in Stanford Libraries Special Collections, shows Ed in contact with some twenty-five taxonomists, requesting their help in identifying species he'd collected. The remarkable collection of correspondences are communications beginning in June 1945 through April 1948. Once again, we are left in awe at the number and prestige of taxonomists who corresponded with Ricketts. Ed had collaborated with many, if not all, of these specialists for more than twenty years. They include his longtime friends and colleagues Torsten Gislén, Walter Fisher, and Max W. de Laubenfels, as well as such distinguished scientists as C. McLean Fraser from the University of British Columbia, Frank M. MacFarland from Stanford, Waldo Schmitt of the United States National Museum, Elisabeth Deichmann from Harvard University, and Loren P. Woods from the Chicago Natural History Museum.

Also during this period, Ricketts designed an elaborate cross-referencing system to organize his scientific findings. In August of 1945 Ricketts wrote to Hedgpeth:

> Have been developing quite an efficient system of record keeping for my surveys. Standardized collecting reports, survey cards, species cards and bibliographic cards which sometime—if I can get all the forms printed and will keep the system posted—will form a coordinated mass of data backgrounding everything I do. Dall and Verill and certainly our friend Hilton try to keep all their records in their heads which makes their work a little bit hard to check 50 years later. Another 5 years collecting ought to build up good stockpile for the eventual manual.[19]

Ed's "eventual manual" was to be his capstone contribution to the literature of marine invertebrates on the Pacific Coast of North America. With *Between Pacific Tides* and *Sea of Cortez* already published, and with *The Outer Shores* under way, Ricketts was moving toward a larger goal, a comprehensive volume, combining the other three, titled "Marine Invertebrates of the Pacific Coast: A Checklist of the Common Littoral Species from Panama to the Bering Sea, with Keys and Bibliographies." Ed had been pondering this project as early as 1943, just two years after he and Steinbeck had finished work on *Sea of Cortez* and before his trips to the "outer shores." In December of that year, he told Xenia Cage that he would like to explore the intertidal zones in Alaska, the Aleutians, and even the Bering Sea, after which "I have covered the Pacific Coast pretty thoroly, and will be ready to take up in earnest the project of my definitive manual."[20] The manual would be "based on personal observations and analyses of the literature. Including all species to occur commonly or abundantly between the tides and to depths of 25 fathoms. Including also all commercially important animals and those taken abundantly with them (so that the student may identify the invertebrates taken by commercial fishermen, trawlers, shrimpers. etc., to depths of 75 or 100 fathoms)."[21] Little wonder that Ed enhanced his systems for record keeping and that he was working to standardize his collecting reports, and his survey, species, and bibliographic cards.

From Ricketts's "Permanent Expedition Notebook" we learn how Ed was planning to accomplish his required survey of shorelines, which would allow him to write his comprehensive manual. Ricketts crossed out each expedition as it was completed, with a line through the sentence mentioning the trip.

~~June 1-July 15-1945 Outer Coast of Vancouver Island~~

~~June & July 1946 Queen Charlotte Island, outer coast of Vancouver Island cleanup.~~

Summer 1947, perhaps a set of tides @ Hoodsport for Goniniums [*Gonionemus*], perhaps a set instead in Cape Blanco, otherwise during the year, all the missing parts of the Oregon/California coastline, San Felipe during the winter?

Summer 1948, another trip to Queen Charlotte and then write
up "the Outer Shores."

Summer 1949, visit to Gulf of Alaska.

Other required long trips:

Ecuador via plane.

Gulf of Alaska, possibly by car Alaskan Highway and then
return from Anchorage via boat. Bering Sea (Southern)
Aleutians—Kamchatka—preferably by small fishing boat . . .

Panama, Pearl Islands via freighter? and/or Gulf of Fonseca and
Cape Santa Elena, Nicaragua, Honduras, Costa Rica, Acapulco
Mexico via car or plane from Mexico City. Important mangrove
swamps Cedros Islands Complex, Magdalena Bay, chartered
boat, San Ignacio Lagoon—by car. Possibly by a Guggenheim
fellowship.[22]

It would be a massive undertaking, and Ed was steadfast in his
determination to make it all happen. But despite endorsements from
Steinbeck and others, Ricketts was not awarded the Guggenheim.
And then, just weeks before he was to join Steinbeck for the Vancouver
Island / Haida Gwaii expedition, Ed was killed in a car-train accident at the Drake Street railroad crossing, just blocks from his lab.
Why Ricketts's car stopped on the tracks is not clear. He'd been having issues with the old noisy 1936 Buick Sport Coupe he'd bought
a year or two earlier—a car in constant need of repair. Perhaps the
car simply stalled and Ed never heard the approaching Del Monte
Express. Sadly, there would be no "Outer Shores," no comprehensive
manual. Ed's legacy would be *Sea of Cortez* and *Between Pacific Tides*;
the latter is arguably the finest book ever written about marine life
along the shorelines of the central Pacific Coast of North America. It
is a volume to which the reader can return time and again, and with
each reading find more that both instructs and delights.

Ritch Lovejoy and his wife, Tal, spent several years in Alaska
where, as noted earlier, Ritch published a local Sitka newspaper, *The
Arrowhead*, and worked on *Taku Wind*. The Lovejoys returned to
Monterey later in the 1930s, but, having finished work on the illustrations for *Between Pacific Tides*, Ritch's friendship with Ed became
purely social. Ritchie bounced from job to job before finally landing

Ed Ricketts Memorial at Drake Avenue and Wave Street in Monterey. Photograph courtesy of Donald Kohrs.

a position best suited to his talents—as a reporter and staff writer for the *Monterey Peninsula Herald*. For many years, Lovejoy wrote his regular Round and About columns, which were always well received by the paper's local readership.

Ritchie Lovejoy died of a brain tumor in 1956. In an article in the *Herald* on July 11, 1956, the day after Ritchie's death, a *Herald* writer remembered Lovejoy as "a bulldog-type reporter, willing to spend hours and days digging out a story. . . . He had these two sides: he was an extremely honest reporter when dealing with serious functions of government or stories of a scientific nature and he had a deep and abiding interest in screwballs and the offbeat story."[23] Ritch's wife, Tal, died in Monterey twelve years later.

Jack Calvin's contributions to *Between Pacific Tides* were chiefly limited to work during the early 1930s in Pacific Grove, and with Ed and Joe Campbell on the *Grampus*. Calvin abandoned Monterey for Sitka in 1932 because he found it more congenial than a changing Ocean View Avenue. As John Straley notes, Calvin "was at home in the northern quality of light, this habit, this nostalgia. What's more he saw in abundance in southeastern Alaska what was quickly disappearing in northern California: wild country."[24] Calvin was prescient—Cannery Row no longer resembles the street onto which Ed Ricketts moved in the late 1920s and where he and Jack talked about writing their book. For the past three or four decades, the locals have fished for tourists rather than sardines.

Shortly after Ed's death, Floris Hartog from the Stanford press wrote to Calvin requesting help on the unfinished index for the 1948 revised edition of *Between Pacific Tides*. In his response, Jack demurs, writing, "I have been away from that kind of work for so long that I should be of scant help to you even if I were there. Ed kept me more or less informed of progress on the new edition, but I had no hand in the work."[25]

From the time Calvin first migrated north, paddling a canoe with his new Alaskan wife from Seattle to Sitka, he was hooked on Southeast Alaska. John Straley observes that "Sitka sits on the outside [Alaskan] coast, in the middle of the Tongass National Forest—the largest national forest in the United States," where "waves roll in from thousands of miles across the ocean to crash on the beaches." A place of natural beauty, Sitka is also a vibrant community of about ten thousand and sponsors an annual chamber music festival with musicians from all over the world. Calvin brought Ricketts and Joe Campbell on the *Grampus* to see and experience Sitka and Southeast Alaska. Ricketts and Campbell went home; Calvin stayed, becoming, as Straley writes, "a leader in the community. . . . Jack loved the Alaskan wilderness, and in it he saw the world and the wildness that his old partner Ricketts saw beyond the tide pool."[26] Jack's short history, titled simply *Sitka*, is above all a statement of his love for that community. The first edition of *Sitka* was published in 1936, as Ricketts was deeply engaged with the Stanford University Press. Jack Calvin died in Sitka in the spring of 1985. Joel Hedgpeth noted at the time that he was survived by "his 2nd wife, Margaret [Sasha died in 1971], and, I think, a very large son who answers to the name of Tiny."[27] After his death, Jack was honored in a proclamation by the Alaska legislature. Alaska's governor named Calvin the state's first Conservationist of the Year, in recognition of his "lifelong commitment to the wise use of Alaska's resources."[28]

In writing the history of *Between Pacific Tides*, we began with the proposition that the book is exceptional, as was its primary author.

Cannery Row resident Irene Longueira said that Ricketts "had room in his heart for everyone"[29] and, given his wide-ranging friendships with men and women as diverse as mythologist Joe Campbell, actor Burgess Meredith, Walter Fisher, novelist Henry Miller, Monterey lawyer "Toby" Street, Cannery Row vagabond Gabe Bicknell, whorehouse madam Flora Woods, and, of course, John Steinbeck, that certainly seems the case. In *Cannery Row,* Steinbeck writes that "Doc would listen to any kind of nonsense and change it for you to a kind of wisdom. . . . He lived in a world of wonders, of excitement."[30] Toby Street remembers Ed as "a good businessman, but not in the general sense of achieving monetary success; rather he was meticulous and very precise in everything. He had," says Street, "a profound influence on John."[31] Not just on John Steinbeck, Toby, but on so many people—during his lifetime and forever after.

Ed's work influenced serious marine scientists who have come to share his ecological approach to life in the tide pools. Paul Dayton, who praised *Between Pacific Tides* so heartily, is a perfect case in point. Marine biologist Rick Brusca affirms that "Dayton is one of the most famous marine ecologists of our time. . . . He's won virtually every big national ecology award there is, has been honored many times by scientific societies, etc."[32] In 2008, Dayton stated unequivocally that "there is no ecology, no understanding of the functions of ecosystems and communities, no restoration, or in fact, little useful environmental science without an understanding of the basic relationships between species and their environment, which is to be discovered in natural history."[33] Paul Dayton has as much respect for Ricketts's work in natural history as he does for Joe Connell and Bob Paine, his mentors who pioneered the idea of big experimental studies in the intertidal zones.

Complementing the acclaim Ricketts has received from accomplished research scientists like Dayton is the admiration he has generated from field biologists like Rafe Sagarin, a teacher and natural history popularizer who coined the phrase "observation ecology." Using a field approach inspired by Ricketts, Sagarin applied observations of nature to explain human issues of broad societal interest. Rick Brusca, his colleague at the University of Arizona, described Sagarin as an "outgoing and charismatic and enthusiastic teacher"[34] who motivated tremendous numbers of students to share his love of the natural world. He was the kind of college faculty member that Ricketts sought, but never found, at Illinois Normal and only rarely encountered at the University of Chicago. He was a man who believed in Emerson's claim, in his essay "The American Scholar," that "colleges can only serve us when their aim is not to drill, but to create; when they gather from afar every ray of various genius to their hospitable halls, and by their concentrated fires set the heart of their youth in flame."[35]

Sagarin's life was tragically cut short when he was killed by a drunk driver in a pickup truck just outside of Tucson in 2015. He was only forty-three years old. But while he was alive, he spent a great deal of time in the tide pools along the rocky coast of Monterey Bay. He loved working in the field, and in 2000 he and a group of colleagues retraced the Ricketts-Steinbeck expedition from Monterey through the Gulf of California. While in the Gulf, Rafe and his colleagues observed and collected marine life, then compared their findings with those of Ricketts and Steinbeck sixty-five years earlier. Sagarin was an undergraduate at Stanford and completed his doctoral studies at University of California, Santa Barbara. "Rafe impressed one as someone special," says retired Stanford professor Chuck Baxter, who became Sagarin's lifelong mentor and friend. "He has an incredible level of enthusiasm and motivation and commitment, and he was always the adventurer."[36] For that reason, he was the perfect person to take President Clinton and Vice President Gore to view the Hewatt Transect, which lies in the intertidal zone at the Hopkins Marine Station, when the president and vice president came to Monterey for a National Oceans Conference in late 1998.

In his address to those attending the conference, President Clinton acknowledged John Steinbeck and Ed Ricketts, who, he said, "summed up what for me is at the root of the work done at this conference—the understanding that man is related to the whole, inextricably related to all reality. Our abiding links to the world, to nature, and the oceans, our mystic and mysterious seas, has led us to this historic conference."[37] How ironic: In 1942, Ed tried several times to reach the secretary of the navy with information he had that would have been very useful to American naval vessels looking for landing places on the Japanese-held mandated islands. He learned about

President Bill Clinton and Vice President Al Gore visiting the intertidal zone with Rafe Sagarin and Nancy Euphemia. Photograph courtesy of Stanford News Service, Linda A. Cicero, photographer.

these islands in his extensive prewar communications with Japanese marine biologists. When he received no response from Washington, he asked Steinbeck, who was by that time a celebrity whose work was admired by Eleanor Roosevelt, to intervene directly with Mrs. Roosevelt on his behalf. Steinbeck did as Ricketts requested. Ed finally received a response: a draft notice ordering him to report to the medical inspection center at the Presidio. Fifty years after Ricketts death, another American president used the occasion of his own time in the tide pools with Al Gore and Rafe Sagarin to announce a series of major ocean protection measures, including a ban on offshore drilling on the US Pacific Coast.

Concluding his remarks, President Clinton stated that "during the marine expedition in the Gulf of Mexico, which I mentioned at the beginning of my remarks, John Steinbeck [and Ed Ricketts] called hope, the idea that tomorrow can be better than today, the defining human trait. Now, just about every American knows that I believe that. And I've been reading Steinbeck for most of my life. I didn't know about that [Ricketts and Steinbeck in the *Sea of Cortez*] until I began to prepare for this conference . . . [and] I agree with that, I think it's important to point out that we are also blessed as a species with two other crucial traits which make hope possible: creativity and imagination."[38] If Ed Ricketts's genius needed to be defined in just two words, they would be creativity and imagination. Remember that Ed's daughter, Nancy, once told an interviewer that her father was not really appreciated in his own time. Even she might have been surprised to learn that a half century after his death, he and his closest friend, John Steinbeck, were in part the inspiration for the most significant environmental protection measures for the Pacific Ocean ever implemented by the government of the United States.

Despite noting such lofty praise from so many diverse quarters for the primary author of *Between Pacific Tides,* the fact is that we did not set out to write a saint's life. Ed Ricketts was no saint. He loved and was loved, and sometimes his loving got him into trouble. He was an iconoclast of the first rank, a fact that irritated some of his contemporaries. Most Ed Heads revere Ricketts's environmentalism, citing his criticism of the fishermen and cannery operators who overfished for sardines in Monterey Bay and the shrimpers dredging the bottom of the Gulf of California. But Ed was not an environmentalist in the twenty-first-century sense of the term. He was no Barry Lopez, no Simon Ortiz. In fact, his environmentalism didn't even match that of William Hornaday or John Muir, whose writings inspired him as a young man. In fact, he took thousands of animals from the tide pools to maintain the business of Pacific Biological Laboratories. He also collected thousands of Pacific Grove's monarch butterflies, which he sold to schools. When Pacific Grove officials found that Ed had collected more than 34,000 of them during 1934, they enacted an ordinance to stop him from doing any further butterfly collecting.

These contradictions notwithstanding, Ed's intellect was remarkable; the range of his knowledge was vast, and his interests knew few boundaries. We're not suggesting that Ed Ricketts invented the science of marine ecology or the importance of field studies in the intertidal zones. Our brief discussion of the work done at the University of Chicago and at the Marine Biology Laboratory in Woods Hole presaged Ed's studies in classes taught by W. C. Allee and other marine scientists who shared Allee's passion for larger, more inclusive pictures. As we said at the beginning of this volume, no Newtonian apple hit Ed squarely on the head. What Ed Ricketts accomplished was to understand the science of intertidal ecology, employing it to study and report on the important relationships between animals, and between animals and their environments in the richest zones of animal life in North America. More than that, he brought that knowledge to science education, as it is taught today in the best marine stations in the country and as it is learned by laypersons who simply love the seashore. Sometime in 1911, former President Teddy Roosevelt wrote that "what the world needs is more men with scientific imagination . . . who can take the facts of science and write of them with fidelity, yet with interpretive and poetic spirit to make them into literature. . . . I mean such writers as John Muir and John Burroughs." Had he lived longer, Roosevelt might have added Ed Ricketts to that number.

Throughout this volume, we've talked about Ed's desire to bring the science of marine ecology to colleagues as well as to men and women who want to know more about life along the seashore. He had the gift of being able to connect with two very different kinds of audiences without losing one or insulting the other. His discussions of the lives of the critters he finds in the intertidal zones in *Between Pacific Tides* are both scientifically accurate (thanks in large measure to the expert help he sought and received from taxonomists) and full of earthy detail that makes them intriguing to the casual observer. More recently, his work has also found a ready audience among people who are engaged in what is called "citizen science," the practice of public participation and collaboration in scientific research.

Citizen scientists are not necessarily classroom trained, but they love nature and the natural world, and, working as volunteers, they contribute a great deal to conservation and environmental protection projects and programs. The US National Park Service sponsors a variety of citizen-science programs; in one, for example, volunteers collect water samples and other data to determine where and when harmful algae grow in bodies of water. This enables managers to understand and act on threats to the ecosystem and public safety. Many citizen scientists are voracious readers on subjects relating to the science they are engaged in; the more they know, the more effective they are in the field.

For those who work on projects in marine environments, particularly on the west coast of North America, Ed Ricketts and *Between*

Pacific Tides is a valued and valuable source of information. Consider, for example, Mary Ellen Hannibal, who works on citizen-science environmental programs in the intertidal zones along Half Moon Bay, just miles south of her home in San Francisco and north of Ed's lab in Pacific Grove. In 2017, she authored a book titled *Citizen Scientist: Searching for Heroes and Hope in an Age of Extinction*. Trying to understand just what she was looking for in the Pillar Point littoral, Hannibal turned to Ricketts's work, writing, "For those grappling with this profusion of life and its orderly disorder, the standard orienting text is *Between Pacific Tides* by Ed Ricketts and Jack Calvin. . . . Over the course of his life, Ricketts collected specimens from tide pools all along the coast, and many of these specimens provide a basis for comparison to help understand what we find in those places today."[39] His life was indeed an odyssey—a tidal odyssey—and that is how he viewed his work. His daughter Nancy recently told us that her father read Homer to her and her brother at bedtime. After the 1936 lab fire destroyed his library, she bought him a replacement copy of Homer's *Odyssey* that he treasured and that remains in the Ricketts family even until today.

One can only speculate how much more Ed Ricketts would have accomplished had his car not been hit by the Del Monte Express on that fateful day in 1948, just before his fifty-first birthday. Certainly, he and Steinbeck would have gone to Vancouver Island and Haida Gwaii; "The Outer Shores" would have been a cold-water follow-on to *Sea of Cortez*. The large manual, combining ideas and information from *Between Pacific Tides*, *Sea of Cortez*, and "The Outer Shores" would have been the coda to his studies of life in the Pacific intertidal zones. Early in 1948, he traveled through Death Valley in the northern Mojave Desert, writing later about "the need for future desert trips" that would lead to a study of the California deserts in the tradition of Mary Austin's *The Land of Little Rain*, a book he knew well. By 1948, Ed had rebuilt Pacific Biological Laboratories, he had replaced much of his record collection and the most important books in his vast library, he had moved through and beyond his separation from Toni, who had left Pacific Grove with a visiting Israeli biologist after the death of her young daughter; in fact, he had married again, and, to those who knew him well, he seemed more than content even until his death.

Ed Ricketts's person and his work live on in the work of others. Most prominently we find Ed's understanding of human and animal behavior in John Steinbeck's best fiction. We see him in the person of Steinbeck's Doc Burton, the sensitive doctor of *In Dubious Battle* who moves through and beyond the blind spots of the party organizers. We see him in Jim Casy, the ex-preacher in *The Grapes of Wrath* whose ideas about the human community fuel Tom Joad's commitment to a gospel of social action. Ed's animal aggregations live in Steinbeck's phalanx. We see Ed in Joe Campbell's monomyth, in his stories of the hero who crosses the threshold of adventure and returns transformed to the everyday world of daylight. And we see Ed Ricketts in the work of scientists today who are doing pathbreaking work to protect our endangered natural environment.

Early in our story we indicated that the practice of repeating surveys of the same littoral over successive years was not standard practice before the late 1960s. This was the case for Ricketts's collecting sites on the Pacific Coast, as it was for W. C. Allee's work in Vineyard Sound. But, starting in 1992, the Multi-Agency Rocky Intertidal Network (MARINe), a large consortium of marine research groups, began collecting compatible data from more than two hundred rocky Pacific intertidal monitoring sites. One of those locations is in Southeast Alaska, at sites visited by the crew of the *Grampus* in 1932. Pete Raimondi, who leads the University of California–Santa Cruz MARINe group, confirmed that his group is comparing data they gather with Ricketts and Calvin's findings to determine the long-term effects of environmental change on the intertidal zones near Sitka.

Above all, though, we see Ed Ricketts's person and ideas in *Between Pacific Tides*, a magnificent book that has reached wider audiences than the work of many of the most accomplished scientists in our time or in Ed's—some of whom have won Nobel prizes. Ed's appeal also emerges from the fictional portraits of him by John Steinbeck. But in the best and most authentic of them, we find a man, largely self-taught, expert in philosophy, music, art, and literature, combining an appreciation of different disciplines with an informed understanding of the natural world. It is little wonder that *Between Pacific Tides* is still in print. Fast-forward eighty years since its publication, and we find that understanding the relationships between living creatures and their environments is more crucial to the future of our planet now than at any time in human history. Ed Ricketts's voice is one we should hear and from which we can learn.

Sweet Thursday is among John Steinbeck's most maligned novels; sequels often are. As a follow-on to a book (*Cannery Row*) that critic Orville Prescott called "a sentimental glorification of weakness of mind and degeneration of character," it was at best a long shot to generate acclaim—and it didn't. Doc, who in *Cannery Row* was warm and likable, in *Sweet Thursday* seems lost, plagued by what Steinbeck calls a "leaking loneliness." At the end of the novel, Doc marries one of Dora Flood's loveable hookers and drives off into the California sunset. This portrait of Doc is unfortunate; his character barely resembles the original. But at the very end of *Sweet Thursday*, Steinbeck unexpectedly gets it right. As Doc and his new bride prepare to leave the Row, Mack and the boys—Steinbeck's "no-goods" and "blots-on-the-town"-his frog collectors and party planners—present him with the ideal wedding gift for a scientist, what they think is a shiny, new microscope. Mistakenly, they give him a telescope. Is this one last foul-up by the loveable misfits of the Palace Flophouse? Not at all. Driving off with Suzy, Doc now has microscopes and a telescope. Now, he will forever be able to look from the tide pool to the stars and back to the tide pool again. This is the unique genius of *Between Pacific Tides* and of its principal author, Edward Flanders Ricketts.

acknowledgments

I t's been a long journey since the day when Harry Burns, my graduate adviser at the University of Washington, suggested I write my doctoral dissertation on John Steinbeck and Ed Ricketts. By now, I've accumulated a lifetime of debts, too many to properly acknowledge. A few, though, require mention. At Oregon State University, Evan Gibson and Herb Childs helped me turn academic indifference into intellectual passion. At the University of Washington, Robert Heilman and, later, Bob Stevick taught me to convert passion into scholarship. And when I began teaching at Oregon State, Joel Hedgpeth introduced me to the real Ed Ricketts. It was life-changing.

After the Steinbeck-Ricketts world opened to me, so many people provided wisdom and direction. Jack Calvin shared memories, as did Toby Street, Carol Brown, Gwen Steinbeck, and Virginia Scardigli. Ed Ricketts Jr. gave me his father's letters and notebooks. Elaine Steinbeck reflected; she talked about how her husband revered Ricketts beyond anyone he ever knew. In Corvallis, the good people at Oregon State supported my research beyond normal limits. OSU President John Byrne had been my college instructor and became my mentor in all things oceanographic. English department chair Walter Foreman, Sea Grant Director Bill Wick, and Research Vice President Roy Young provided research funding and far more than usual amounts of encouragement. And my wife, Betty, was my constant helpmate and companion, becoming completely invested in the work I was doing.

Then, for reasons about which I confess some regret, I moved from teaching and writing into academic administration. We moved from Oregon to Boston, then on to Orlando and Philadelphia. So, a half century later, when Don Kohrs asked me to partner with him on a book about the writing and publishing history of Ricketts and Calvin's *Between Pacific Tides*, I was at once enthused and taken aback: enthused because *Tides* has been a treasured work of marine biology for nearly a century; taken aback because I hadn't written much about Ed Ricketts for many years and because, as an English teacher, I didn't know enough science to do the project justice.

Happily, my partner in this endeavor had the requisite scientific background, as well as a storehouse of information about Ricketts, Calvin, and Ritch Lovejoy (the oft-neglected third contributor to *Between Pacific Tides*). Don originally proposed the project and provided a goodly portion of its content.

As we worked, we realized that we needed assistance. Guidance from marine biologists Rick Brusca and Jim Carlton was very helpful. Rick and Jim provided useful suggestions as Don and I brought the project to conclusion. Keith Benson provided valuable insights about the history of marine ecology, for which he has my enduring gratitude. As does Will Ray, of *Steinbeck Now*, whose suggestions about the manuscript's organization and style were enormously helpful. John Chapman at Oregon State University, Tim Wootton from the University of Chicago, Pete Raimondi from UC Santa Cruz, and Bill Morrison from the Ucluelet Aquarium on Vancouver Island shared wonderful stories about how they were introduced to *Between Pacific Tides*. John Lovejoy provided a wealth of information about, as well as photographs of, his father. The good people at the Alaska State Museum and the Monterey (CA) Public Library furnished wonderful photographs of Ricketts and Calvin in California and in Southeast Alaska. Nancy Ricketts provided a wealth of information about her father, as did Ed's granddaughter, Lisa. Michael Hemp, founder of the Cannery Row Foundation, kept me in Ed Ricketts's orbit over the years—involving me in Steinbeck-Ricketts events and fueling my enthusiasm for all things Ricketts, even after I thought I had written my last words on the subject. Then, of course, there is the wonderful group at the Oregon State University Press: acquisitions editor Kim Hoagland, who provided early interest and plenty of encouragement; marketing manager Marty Brown and production manager Micki Reaman, who made the process of bringing our manuscript to life so very pleasant; and Susan Campbell, our copy editor, who cleaned, polished, and happily washed away our writing's many flaws. It's more than fitting that Oregon State publish this manuscript. After all, it's where this journey began. Closer to home was my cheerleader, Helen Lubinski, my mother-in-law who kept encouraging; my regret is that she's not here to see the finished product. At Drexel, Roger Kurtz, my department chair, provided financial as well as moral support. And Rick McCourt of the Academy of Natural Sciences helped immeasurably in and beyond Drexel classrooms.

Finally, thanks to my wife, Betty, and my daughter, Kelly. Betty has lived in Steinbeck-Ricketts world for decades. She typed my doctoral dissertation and my first book. She has traveled on and participated in Steinbeck-Ricketts journeys all over the continent and beyond. And, as I worked on this project, she and Kelly endured a sometimes grouchy husband and father who would slide off into soliloquies about people long dead and thoughts largely forgotten. Doing more than simply providing encouragement, Betty read and revised copy. She took on and completed my portion of the book's index. Before and during the difficult days of COVID, she and Kelly pushed when I needed pushing, criticized when I needed criticizing. Without their tolerance, their forbearance, and their love, this book— or rather, my part in it—would never have happened.

RICHARD ASTRO

ORLANDO, FLORIDA

&

I would first like to thank my wife, Leticia Rascon Medina-Kohrs, for allowing Ed Ricketts and the backstory about the publishing of *Between Pacific Tides* to take up a significant portion of my efforts. Thanks also to Richard Astro for agreeing to join me on the odyssey in the writing of this book. And thanks to staff at the Stanford University Libraries and their Department of Special Collections, the Stanford University Press, the Monterey Public Libraries California History Room, and numerous other academic archives for providing letters of correspondence. In addition, thanks to Geoffrey Dunn, who identified Ed Ricketts's connection to the Santa Cruz Wharf and provided valuable information about William J. Martin, Ed Ricketts's assistant at the Pacific Biological Laboratories; and Keith Benson, who located the Torsten Gislén letters held in the Manuscript and Archive Collection at Lund University, and willingly engaged in lengthy discussions about Ricketts, Calvin, and the making of *Between Pacific Tides*. Thanks to the Ricketts family, including Ed Ricketts Jr., Lisa Ricketts, and Nancy Ricketts for their many discussions, their sharing of letters, and their critical review of the manuscript. Thanks to John and Vicki Pearse for their endless encouragement and thought-provoking questions. Thanks to Steve Webster and Jim Watanabe for their early review of the manuscript. And finally, a big thanks to Robert Dees, George Baer, Jim Carlton, and Richard Brusca for their wealth of constructive criticism, editing suggestions, and endless words of encouragement. An extended thanks to Michael Hemp and Pat Hathaway for their continued support on many efforts related to Ed Ricketts. And finally, a gracious thank you to Chris Patton for his continuous support of my research related to Stanford University's Hopkins Marine Station and Ed Ricketts.

DON KOHRS
PACIFIC GROVE, CALIFORNIA

notes

NOTES TO CHAPTER 1

1. John Steinbeck, *The Log of the Sea of Cortez* (New York: Penguin Books, 1951), 228.

2. Edward F. Ricketts, "Zoological Preface to San Francisco Bay Guidebook," in *The Outer Shores*, vol. 1, ed. Joel W. Hedgpeth, 32–36 (Eureka, CA: Mad River Press, 1978).

3. John Steinbeck, "Foreword," in *Between Pacific Tides*, rev. ed., by Edward F. Ricketts and Jack Calvin (Stanford, CA: Stanford University Press, 1948), v–vi.

4. Henry Miller, *Big Sur and the Oranges of Hieronymus Bosch* (New York: New Directions, 1957), 25.

5. Susan Shillinglaw, *Portrait of a Marriage: John and Carol Steinbeck* (Reno: University of Nevada Press, 2013), 85.

6. Shillinglaw, *Portrait of a Marriage*, 85.

7. Edward F. Ricketts and Jack Calvin, *Between Pacific Tides* (Stanford, CA: Stanford University Press, 1939), 23.

8. John Steinbeck, *Cannery Row* (New York: Viking Press, 1945), 28.

9. A. L. Lundy, *Real Life on Cannery Row: Real People, Places and Events That Inspired John Steinbeck* (Santa Monica, CA: Angel City Press, 2008), 120.

10. Nancy Ricketts, telephone interview with Richard Astro, October 15, 2019.

11. Eric Enno Tamm, "Ed Ricketts' Death, 50 Years Ago Last

Week, Preceded That of Cannery Row by Only a Few Months,"
Monterey County Weekly, October 13, 2005, https://www.mon-
tereycountyweekly.com/news/local_news/ed-ricketts-death-5
o-years-ago-last-week-preceded-that-of-cannery-row-by-only/
image_16516a41-ac18-562e-934c-e4c9a63c39bb.html.

12.   Edward F. Ricketts, New Series Notebook Number 1 (February
1941, p. 47), Edward Flanders Ricketts papers, Department of
Special Collections, Stanford University Libraries.

13.   Katherine A. Rodger, ed., *Breaking Through: Essays, Journals
and Travelogues of Edward F. Ricketts* (Berkeley: University of
California Press, 2006), 95.

14.   John Steinbeck, "About Ed Ricketts," in *The Log of the Sea of
Cortez* (New York: Penguin Books, 1951), 225–274.

15.   Joel W. Hedgpeth, "Philosophy on Cannery Row," in *Steinbeck:
The Man and His Work*, ed. Richard Astro and Tetsumaro
Hayashi, 89–129 (Corvallis: Oregon State University Press, 1971).

16.   James G. Moulton and Robb Roy Ricketts, *Catalogue of the Loan
Exhibition of Important Works by George Inness, Alexander Wyant,
Ralph Blakelock* (Chicago: Moulton and Ricketts, 1913).

17.   Elliot Daingerfield, "George Inness, N. A., An Appreciation,"
in *Catalogue of the Loan Exhibition of Important Works by George
Inness, Alexander Wyant, Ralph Blakelock* (Chicago: Moulton and
Ricketts, 1913).

18.   Ben Joravsky, *Hoop Dreams: The True Story of Hardship and
Triumph* (Kansas City, MO: Turner Publishing, 1995).

19.   Jackson J. Benson, *The True Adventures of John Steinbeck, Writer:
A Biography* (New York: Viking Press, 1984), 187.

20.   William Temple Hornaday, *Campfires on Desert and Lava* (New
York: Charles Scribner's Sons, 1908), vii.

21.   Hornaday, *Campfires*, vii.

22.   Hornaday, *Campfires*, 240.

23.   Hornaday, *Campfires*, 354.

24.   "Local Men in Draft Drawing: Numbers Drawn in Washington
Call Young El Pasoans to War," *El Paso Herald* (Texas), June 27,
1918, p. 2.

25.   Steinbeck, "About Ed Ricketts," in *Log*, 225–274.

26.   Gregg Mitman, *The State of Nature: Ecology, Community and
American Social Thought, 1900–1950* (Chicago: University of

Chicago Press, 1992), 14.

27. Mitman, *State of Nature*, 14.

28. Edward F. Ricketts, "Vagabonding through Dixie," *Travel* 45, no. 2 (1925): 16–18, 44, 48.

29. Ricketts, "Vagabonding," 16–18, 44, 48.

30. Ricketts, "Vagabonding," 16–18, 44, 48.

31. Jack Antunovich, "'Doc' Gowanloch Is Gone," *Louisiana Conservation Review* 4, no. 8 (1952): 16.

32. Walter K. Fisher, "Hopkins Marine Station," in *Annual Report of the President of Stanford University for the Twenty-Ninth Academic Year Ending August 31, 1920* (Stanford, CA: Stanford University Press, 1921), 184.

33. Peter B. Waite, *Lives of Dalhousie University, Volume 2: 1925–1980, The Old College Transformed* (Montreal: McGill-Queen's University Press, 1997).

34. James Nelson Gowanloch, *Fishes and Fishing in Louisiana Including Recipes for the Preparation of Seafoods* (Baton Rouge, LA: Ramires-Jones Printing Company, 1933).

35. Antunovich, "'Doc' Gowanloch Is Gone," 16.

36. J. N. Gowanloch, "Contributions to the Study of Marine Gastropods II: The Intertidal Life of *Buccinum undatum*, A Study in Non-Adaption," *Contributions to Canadian Biology and Fisheries* 3 (1927): 167–178.

37. Mary Galigher Groesbeck, email message to the author, Donald G. Kohrs, June 7, 2014.

38. "Ten Years Progress," *Turtox News* 3, no. 4 (1925): 14.

39. Mary Galigher Groesbeck, email message to the author, Donald G. Kohrs, June 7, 2014.

40. Rodger, *Breaking Through*.

41. Warder C. Allee, "Concerning the Organization of Marine Coastal Communities," *Ecological Monographs* 4, no. 4 (1934): 541–554.

42. Hedgpeth, "Philosophy," in *Steinbeck*, 89–129.

43. Hedgpeth, "Philosophy," in *Steinbeck*, 94.

44. Hedgpeth, "Philosophy," in *Steinbeck*, 94.

45. Katherine A. Rodger, *Renaissance Man of Cannery Row: The Life and Letters of Edward F. Ricketts*, ed. Katherine A. Rodger, xix (Tuscaloosa: University of Alabama Press, 2002).

46. Eugene Odum, *Fundamentals of Ecology* (Philadelphia: W. B. Saunders Company, 1953).

47. Rodger, *Renaissance Man*, xx.

48. Ricketts, "Zoological Preface to San Francisco Bay Guidebook," in *The Outer Shores*, vol. 1, 32–36.

49. Jackson J. Benson, *The True Adventures of John Steinbeck, Writer: A Biography* (New York: Viking Press, 1984), 193.

50. Ricketts, "Zoological," in *The Outer Shores*, vol. 1, 32–36.

51. Hedgpeth, "Philosophy," in *Steinbeck*, 89–129.

52. Richard A. Astro, *John Steinbeck and Ed Ricketts: The Shaping of a Novelist* (Minneapolis: University of Minnesota Press, 1973), 28–29.

53. Rodger, *Breaking Through*.

54. Rodger, *Renaissance Man*.

55. Anna Maker Ricketts, *Recollections* (Ts. Stanford University Library, 1984), 1.

56. Joel W. Hedgpeth, "'Sea of Cortez' Revisited, or 'Cannery Row' Revised," *Pacific Discovery* 6, no. 1 (1953): 28–30.

57. Walter K. Fisher, "Discussion and Correspondence: Research in Marine Biology," *Science* 57, no. 1469 (1923): 233–234.

58. "Anco Biological Supply," *Transactions of the American Microscopical* 42, no. 2 (1923): 1.

59. Anna Maker Ricketts, *Recollections*, 1.

60. Anna Maker Ricketts, *Recollections*, 7.

61. "The Needs of the Physics Laboratory Met by a California Manufacturer," *Western Journal of Education* 14, no. 1 (1909): 652–653.

62. Rodger, *Renaissance Man*.

63. Edward F. Ricketts, *Pacific Biological Laboratories 1925 Catalogue* (Np: np, 1925), 2.

64. Anna Maker Ricketts, *Recollections*, 16.

65. Mary Galigher Groesbeck, email message to the author, Donald G. Kohrs, June 7, 2014.

66. Mary Galigher Groesbeck, email message to the author, Donald G. Kohrs, June 7, 2014.

67. "Microcosm & Macrocosm," *Contact Point* 62, no. 2 (1984): 20.

68. Anna Maker Ricketts, *Recollections*, 46.

69. Edward F. Ricketts, Pacific Biological Laboratories Survey

Cards, Monterey Bay (1945–1946), Edward Flanders Ricketts papers, Department of Special Collections, Stanford University Libraries.

70. Geoffrey Dunn, *Santa Cruz Wharf* (San Francisco, CA: Arcadia Publishing, 2016).

71. "Rare Biological Specimens," *Santa Cruz News* (California), January 19, 1927, p. 8.

72. Joel W. Hedgpeth, "Ed Ricketts (1897–1948) Marine Biologist," *Steinbeck Newsletter* 9, no. 1 (1995): 17–18.

NOTES TO CHAPTER 2

1. Leland Stanford Junior University, Second Annual Register 1892–1893 (Palo Alto, CA: Leland Stanford Junior University, 1893), 22.

2. Joel Hedgpeth, ed., *The Outer Shores*, vol. 1 (Eureka, CA: Mad River Press, 1978), 28.

3. Hedgpeth, *Outer Shores*, vol. 1, p. 29.

4. Walter K. Fisher, "The New Hopkins Marine Station of Stanford University," *Science* 47, no. 1217 (1918): 410–412.

5. J. P. Baumberger, A. C. Giese, and L. R. Blinks, Memorial Resolution: Fisher, Walter, 1878–1953, Stanford University Faculty Senate Records, 1954, https://exhibits.stanford.edu/stanford-senate/catalog/tq746wm0609.

6. Baumberger et al., Memorial Resolution.

7. Baumberger et al., Memorial Resolution.

8. Walter K. Fisher, "Edward Sandford Burgess," *Science* 67, no. 1742 (1918): 501–502.

9. Ruth Andresen, interview with Tim Thomas, Stanford University Library, 2017.

10. Warder C. Allee, "Concerning Community Studies," *Ecology* 11, no. 4 (1930): 621–630.

11. Walter K. Fisher, "The Hopkins Marine Station," *Stanford Illustrated Review* 20, no. 6 (1919): 288–289.

12. Fisher, "Hopkins," 288–289.

13. Fisher, "Hopkins," 288–289.

14. John Steinbeck and Ed Ricketts, *Sea of Cortez: A Leisurely Journal of Travel and Research* (New York: Viking Press, 1941), 1.

15. "Rediscovered Steinbeck Letter Adds to Turbulent Tale of 'Sea of Cortez' Authorship," *Monterey Herald*, May 15, 2015, https://

www.montereyherald.com/2015/05/14/rediscovered-steinbec
k-letter-adds-to-turbulent-tale-of-sea-of-cortez-authorship/.

16. Edward F. Ricketts, *Pacific Biological Laboratories 1929 Catalogue*
     (Np: np, 1929), 3.

17. "Hopkins Director Confined to Home," *Monterey Peninsula
     Herald* (California), April 8, 1933, p. 1.

18. "Grove to Build Business Block," *Board and Batten: Newsletter of
     the Pacific Grove Heritage Society*, June-July 1988.

19. John Steinbeck, *Cannery Row* (New York: Viking Press, 1945), 1.

20. Anna Maker Ricketts, *Recollections* (Ts. Stanford University
     Library, 1984), 14.

21. Anna Maker Ricketts, *Recollections*, 14.

22. Anna Maker Ricketts, *Recollections*, 14.

23. Anna Maker Ricketts, *Recollections*, 14.

24. Anna Maker Ricketts, *Recollections*, 46.

25. Anna Maker Ricketts, *Recollections*, 47.

26. Anna Maker Ricketts, *Recollections*, 10.

27. Anna Maker Ricketts, *Recollections*, 3.

28. Anna Maker Ricketts, *Recollections*, 8.

29. John Steinbeck, "About Ed Ricketts," in *The Log from Sea of
     Cortez* (New York: Penguin Books, 1951), 230.

30. Edward F. Ricketts and Jack Calvin, *Between Pacific Tides*
     (Stanford, CA: Stanford University Press, 1939), 177.

31. "Carmel," *Monterey Peninsula Herald* (California), August 30,
     1930, p. 3.

32. E. F. Ricketts, Species Identification Report, sent to W. K.
     Fisher, 1930. Edward Flanders Ricketts papers, Department of
     Special Collections, Stanford University Libraries.

33. Ricketts, Species Identification Report.

34. Ricketts, Species Identification Report.

35. Anna Maker Ricketts, *Recollections*, 19.

36. Anna Maker Ricketts, *Recollections*, 11.

37. Walter K. Fisher, "Hopkins Marine Station," *Annual Report of
     the President of Stanford University for the Thirty-Ninth Academic
     Year Ending August 31, 1930* (Stanford, CA: Stanford University
     Press, 1931), 203.

38. Ricketts and Calvin, *Between Pacific Tides*, 96.

39. Torsten Gislén, *Från Hawaiis stränder till New-Yorks skyskrapor;*

minnen från en naturvetenskaplig forskningsfärd (Stockholm: Saxon and Lindström, 1935).

40. Anna Maker Ricketts, *Recollections*, 12.
41. Anna Maker Ricketts, *Recollections*, 15.
42. Warder C. Allee, *Animal Life and Social Growth* (Baltimore, MD: Williams and Wilkins, 1932), 99.
43. Gregg Mitman, *The State of Nature: Ecology, Community and American Social Thought, 1900–1950* (Chicago: University of Chicago Press, 1992), 73.
44. Ricketts and Calvin, *Between Pacific Tides*, 41.
45. Warder C. Allee, *Animal Aggregations* (Chicago: University of Chicago Press, 1931), 9.
46. Warder C. Allee to Anna D. Phillips 1933, as quoted in Mitman, *State of Nature*, 73.
47. Ricketts and Calvin, *Between Pacific Tides*, 41–42.
48. Ricketts and Calvin, *Between Pacific Tides*, 42.
49. Ricketts and Calvin, *Between Pacific Tides*, 42.
50. Anna Maker Ricketts, *Recollections*, 17.
51. Edward F. Ricketts, letter of correspondence to Lucille Lannestock, February 8, 1937, Ed Ricketts Junior Personal Collection.

NOTES TO CHAPTER 3

1. "Death of Mr. James M. Calvin," *Wibaux Pioneer* (Montana), May 7, 1908, p. 1.
2. "Services for Jack Calvin, 83," *Daily Sitka Sentinel* (Alaska), March 12, 1985, p. 3.
3. John Lovejoy, "The Man Who Became a Steinbeck Footnote," *Steinbeck Review* 5, no. 2 (2008): 59–84.
4. Mackenzie Fisher, "Naturalist Jack Calvin's 'Square-Rigged' Returns to Shelves," *Juneau Empire* (Alaska), June 22, 2017, https://www.juneauempire.com/life/naturalist-jack-calvins-squar e-rigged-returns-to-shelves/.
5. Fisher, "Naturalist."
6. "People Talked About," *Carmel Pine Cone* (California), December 11, 1931, p. 13.
7. Sandy McClung, Jack Calvin's "Fisherman 28," Sitka Sound Science Center, July 14, 2020, https://Sitkascience.Org/ Jack-Calvins-Fisherman-28.

8.   Jack Calvin, interview with Richard Astro, August 1971.

9.   "Sitkans Hail 40th Year of Unique Marine Classic," *Daily Sitka Sentinel* (Alaska), April 10, 1979, p. 6.

10. "People Talked About," *Carmel Pine Cone*, December 11, 1931, p. 13.

11. "People Talked About," *Carmel Pine Cone*, December 11, 1931, p. 13.

12. Lovejoy, "Man Who Became a Steinbeck Footnote," 59–84.

13. Lovejoy, "Man Who Became a Steinbeck Footnote."

14. Lovejoy, "Man Who Became a Steinbeck Footnote."

15. Lovejoy, "Man Who Became a Steinbeck Footnote," 59–84.

16. Correspondence from John Cage to Adolph Weiss (early summer, 1935), in *The Selected Letters of John Cage*, ed. Laura Kuhn, 25 (Middletown, CT: Wesleyan University Press, 2016).

17. Lovejoy, "Man Who Became a Steinbeck Footnote."

18. Ritchie Lovejoy, "Between Pacific Tides: Ricketts and Calvin. Published by Stanford University Press. $6.00," Round and About, *Monterey Peninsula Herald* (California), 1948.

19. Ritchie Lovejoy, Round and About, *Monterey Peninsula Herald* (California), September 29, 1952, p. 6.

20. Lovejoy, "Man Who Became a Steinbeck Footnote," 59–84.

21. Lovejoy, "Man Who Became a Steinbeck Footnote."

22. Will Rogers, "Last Report from Alaska, Eskimos Are Very Clever Craftsmen, Fur Market Is Down," *Fresno Bee* (California), September 15, 1935, p. 2.

23. *Milwaukie Sentinel*, May 21, 1960, "Proposal to Name the New Alaska State Library, Archives & Museum Facility in Juneau Father Andrew P. Kashevaroff Library, Archives & Museum," http://www.akleg.gov/basis/get_documents.asp?session=29&docid=4573.

24. Jack Calvin, "*Nakwasina* Goes North: A Man, a Woman, and a Pup Cruise from Tacoma to Juneau in a 17-Foot Canoe," *National Geographic Magazine*, July 1933, pp. 1–42.

25. Joseph Campbell, interview with Pauline Pearson. Salinas, California, November 28, 1983.

26. Stephen Larsen and Robin Larsen, *Joseph Campbell: A Fire in the Mind: The Authorized Biography* (New York: Simon and Schuster, 2002), 3.

27. Larsen and Larsen, *Joseph Campbell*, 155.

28. Donald Newlove, "The Professor with a Thousand Faces," *Esquire*, September 1977, pp. 99–103, 132–136.

29. Larsen and Larsen, *Joseph Campbell*, 170.

30. Larsen and Larsen, *Joseph Campbell*, 177.

31. Larsen and Larsen, *Joseph Campbell*, 172.

32. Katherine A. Rodger, ed., *Breaking Through: Essays, Journals and Travelogues of Edward F. Ricketts* (Berkeley: University of California Press, 2006), 95.

33. Larsen and Larsen, *Joseph Campbell*, 185.

34. Winston Elstob, "The Meeting of 3 Minds," *Alta Vista Magazine*, July 1, 1980, pp. 16–17.

35. Larsen and Larsen, *Joseph Campbell*, 197–198.

36. Fraser Boa, *The Way of the Myth: Talking with Joseph Campbell* (Boston: Shambhala, 1994).

37. Newlove, "The Professor," 99–103, 132–136.

38. Edward F. Ricketts, "Notes and Observations, Mostly Ecological Resulting from Northern Pacific Collecting Trips Chiefly in Southeastern Alaska, with Special Reference to Wave Shock as a Factor, in Littoral Ecology," in *Ed Ricketts from Cannery Row to Sitka, Alaska: Science, History, and Reflections along the Pacific Coast: A Compilation of Essays*, ed. Janice M. Straley, 43–72 (67) (Juneau, AK: Shorefast Editions, 2015).

39. Edward F. Ricketts and Jack Calvin, *Between Pacific Tides* (Stanford, CA: Stanford University Press, 1939), v.

40. Ricketts, "Notes and Observations," 43–72 (47).

41. Ricketts, "Notes and Observations," 47.

42. Larsen and Larsen, *Joseph Campbell*, 204.

43. Jamake Highwater, "A Conversation with Joseph Campbell," *Quadrant: The Journal of the C. G. Jung Foundation* 18, no. 1 (1985): 97–102.

44. Newlove, "The Professor," 99–103, 132–136.

45. Joseph Campbell, "Letter of correspondence to E. F. Ricketts. December 26, 1941," *Correspondence: 1927–1987. Collected Works of Joseph Campbell* (Novato, CA: New World Library, 2019), 48.

46. George E. MacGinitie, "Between Pacific Tides by Edward F. Ricketts; Jack Calvin," *American Midland Naturalist* 21, no. 3 (1939): 768.

47. Ricketts and Calvin, *Between Pacific Tides*, v.
48. Willard Bascom, "John Dove Isaacs, III," National Academy of Sciences, Biographical Memoirs: V.57 (Washington, DC: National Academies Press, 1987).
49. Ricketts and Calvin, *Between Pacific Tides*, 247.
50. Ricketts and Calvin, *Between Pacific Tides*, 176.
51. Anna Maker Ricketts, *Recollections*, 2.
52. Bruce Ariss, *Inside Cannery Row: Sketches from the Steinbeck Era in Words and Pictures* (San Francisco: Lexikos, 1988), 33.
53. Clarence M. Pruitt, "Myrtle Elizabeth Johnson," *Science Education* 51, no. 5 (1967): 424–427.

NOTES TO CHAPTER 4

1.   Edith Ronald Mirrielees, *Stanford: The Story of a University* (New York: G.P. Putnam's Sons, 1959), 36.
2.   Alex Shashkevich, "Stanford University Press Celebrates Its 125-Year History," *Stanford News Service*, November 9, 2017, https://news.stanford.edu/2017/11/09/press-celebrates-125th-anniversary.
3.   John W. Dodds, Leon E. Seltzer, and George F. Sensabaugh, "Memorial Resolution: Davis, William, 1880–1962," Stanford University Faculty Senate Records, 1963, https://exhibits.stanford.edu/stanford-senate/catalog/rn338rd9965.
4.   Richard Astro and Joel W. Hedgpeth, eds., *Steinbeck and the Sea: Proceedings of a Conference Held at the Marine Science Center Auditorium, Newport, Oregon, May 4, 1974* (Corvallis: Oregon State University, Sea Grant College Program, 1975), 30.
5.   Astro and Hedgpeth, *Steinbeck and the Sea*, 30.
6.   Astro and Hedgpeth, *Steinbeck and the Sea*, 30.
7.   Astro and Hedgpeth, *Steinbeck and the Sea*, 30.
8.   Edward F. Ricketts and Jack Calvin, *Between Pacific Tides* (Stanford, CA: Stanford University Press, 1939), v.
9.   Internal Memo, Stanford University Press, March 24, 1930, Stanford University Press records, Department of Special Collections (hereafter SUPR), re "Between Pacific Tides," by Ed Ricketts and Jack Calvin, 1930–1994, Stanford University Libraries.
10. Internal Memo, Stanford University Press, March 24, 1930, SUPR, Stanford University Libraries.

11. Correspondence from Edward F. Ricketts to William Hawley Davis, June 27, 1930, SUPR, Stanford University Libraries.

12. Edward F. Ricketts, "'Zoological Introduction' to Between Pacific Tides," in *Breaking Through: Essays, Journals, and Travelogues of Edward F. Ricketts,* ed. Katherine A. Rodger, 85 (Berkeley: University of California Press, 2006).

13. Joel W. Hedgpeth, "Philosophy on Cannery Row," in *Steinbeck: The Man and His Work,* ed. Richard Astro and Tetsumaro Hayashi, 89–129 (Corvallis: Oregon State University Press, 1971).

14. Joel Hedgpeth, ed., *The Outer Shores,* vol. 1 (Eureka, CA: Mad River Press, 1978), 5.

15. Max Walker De Laubenfels, "The Sponges of California" (thesis, Stanford University, 1929).

16. Max Walker De Laubenfels, "The Marine and Freshwater Sponges of California," *Proceedings of the United States National Museum* 81, no. 4 (1932): 1–140.

17. Max Walker De Laubenfels, "Dinosaur Extinction: One More Hypothesis," *Journal of Paleontology* 30 (1956): 207–212.

18. John Steinbeck, *The Log from the Sea of Cortez* (New York: Penguin Books, 1995), 26.

19. Steinbeck, *Log from the Sea,* 26.

20. John Steinbeck to Carl Wilhelmson, Pacific Grove (late 1930), in *Steinbeck: A Life in Letters,* ed. Elaine Steinbeck and Robert Wallsten, 30 (New York: Penguin Books, 1989).

21. Correspondence from Jack Calvin to William Hawley Davis, October 30, 1930, SUPR, Stanford University Libraries.

22. Correspondence from Jack Calvin to William Hawley Davis, October 30, 1930, SUPR, Stanford University Libraries.

23. Correspondence from Edward F. Ricketts to William Hawley Davis, August 18, 1931, SUPR, Stanford University Libraries.

24. Dean Storey to William Hawley Davis, internal memo, September 17, 1931, SUPR, Stanford University Libraries.

25. Dean Storey to William Hawley Davis, internal memo, September 17, 1931, SUPR, Stanford University Libraries.

26. E. V. Coan and M. G. Kellogg, "The Malacological Contributions of Ida Shepard Oldroyd and Tom Shaw Oldroyd," *The Veliger* 33, no. 2 (1990): 174–184.

27. Correspondence from Edward F. Ricketts to Walter K.

Fisher, November 25, 1931, Edward Flanders Ricketts papers, Department of Special Collections, Stanford University Libraries.

28. Correspondence from Walter K. Fisher to William Hawley Davis, February 29, 1936, SUPR, Stanford University Libraries.

29. Walter K. Fisher, "The Hopkins Marine Station," *Stanford Illustrated Review* 20, no. 6 (1919): 288–289.

30. "Pure Science Is Hit by War: Director Claims Technical Application Now Used," *Pittsburgh Press* (Pennsylvania), July 16, 1943, p. 12.

31. Correspondence from Walter K. Fisher to William H. Davis, February 29, 1936, SUPR, Stanford University Libraries.

32. Fisher to William H. Davis, February 29, 1936, SUPR, Stanford University Libraries.

33. Ricketts and Calvin, *Between Pacific Tides*, 97–98.

34. Ricketts and Calvin, *Between Pacific Tides*, 95.

35. Ricketts and Calvin, *Between Pacific Tides*, 20.

36. Ricketts and Calvin, *Between Pacific Tides*, 23

37. Ricketts and Calvin, *Between Pacific Tides*, 106.

38. Ricketts and Calvin, *Between Pacific Tides*, 120.

39. Ricketts and Calvin, *Between Pacific Tides*, 121.

40. Correspondence from Edward F. Ricketts to Walter K. Fisher, November 25, 1931, Edward Flanders Ricketts papers, Department of Special Collections, Stanford University Libraries.

41. Steinbeck, *Log from the Sea*, 62.

42. Ralph Buchsbaum, "A Handbook of the Common Invertebrates of the Pacific Coast," *Ecology* 1, no. 1 (1940): 93–94.

43. George E. MacGinitie, "Between Pacific Tides, by Edward F. Ricketts; Jack Calvin," *American Midland Naturalist* 21, no. 3 (1939): 768.

44. Internal Memo from William A. Friend to William Hawley Davis, February 2, 1932, SUPR, Stanford University Libraries.

45. Correspondence from William H. Davis to Edward F. Ricketts, February 16, 1932, SUPR, Stanford University Libraries.

46. Correspondence from Edward F. Ricketts to William Hawley Davis, March 17, 1932, SUPR, Stanford University Libraries.

47. Internal memo from William A. Friend to William Hawley

Davis, April 5, 1932, SUPR, Stanford University Libraries.

48. Correspondence from William H. Davis to Edward F. Ricketts, April 11, 1932, SUPR, Stanford University Libraries.

49. Jack Calvin, interview with Richard Astro, July 1971.

50. Correspondence from Edward F. Ricketts to William Hawley Davis, April 14, 1932, SUPR, Stanford University Libraries.

51. Correspondence from Edward F. Ricketts to Torsten Gislén, May 27, 1932, Torsten Gislén archive (hereafter TGA), Lund University Library, Sweden.

52. Correspondence from Edward F. Ricketts to Torsten Gislén, August 8, 1932, TGA, Lund University Library, Sweden.

53. Ricketts to Torsten Gislén, August 8, 1932, TGA, Lund University Library, Sweden.

54. Correspondence from Edward F. Ricketts to Walter K. Fisher, August 18, 1932, Edward Flanders Ricketts papers, Department of Special Collections, Stanford University Libraries.

55. Correspondence from Edward F. Ricketts to William Hawley Davis, October 5, 1932, SUPR, Stanford University Libraries.

56. Internal memo from William A. Friend to William Hawley Davis, October 10, 1932, SUPR, Stanford University Libraries.

57. Correspondence from Edward F. Ricketts to Walter K. Fisher, October 15, 1932, Edward Flanders Ricketts papers, Department of Special Collections, Stanford University Libraries.

58. Ricketts to Walter K. Fisher, October 15, 1932, Edward Flanders Ricketts papers, Department of Special Collections, Stanford University Libraries.

59. Internal memo from William A. Friend to William Hawley Davis, October 18, 1932, SUPR, Stanford University Libraries.

60. Correspondence from William H. Davis to E. F. Ricketts, October 18, 1932, SUPR, Stanford University Libraries.

61. Correspondence from Edward F. Ricketts to Torsten Gislén, October 21, 1932, TGA, Lund University Library, Sweden.

62. Ricketts to Torsten Gislén, October 21, 1932, TGA, Lund University Library, Sweden.

63. Correspondence from Edward F. Ricketts to Torsten Gislén, May 2, 1933, TGA, Lund University Library, Sweden.

64. Edward F. Ricketts, "The Tide as an Environmental Factor Chiefly with Reference to Ecological Zonation on the California

Coast," in *The Outer Shores*, vol. 2, ed. Joel W. Hedgpeth, 63–68 (Eureka, CA: Mad River Press, 1978).

65.   Ricketts, "Tide as an Environmental Factor," in *The Outer Shores*, vol. 2, pp. 63–68.

66.   James T. Carlton, ed., *The Light and Smith Manual: Intertidal Invertebrates from Central California to Oregon*, 4th ed. (Berkeley: University of California Press, 2007), 11.

67.   Ricketts and Calvin, *Between Pacific Tides*, 3.

68.   Ricketts and Calvin, *Between Pacific Tides*, 3.

69.   Ricketts and Calvin, *Between Pacific Tides*, 4.

70.   Ricketts and Calvin, *Between Pacific Tides*, 4.

71.   Ricketts and Calvin, *Between Pacific Tides*, 6.

72.   Ricketts and Calvin, *Between Pacific Tides*, 6.

73.   Isabella Gordon, "Obituary Notices: Theodor Mortensen," *Proceedings of the Linnean Society of London* 165, no. 1 (1954): 90.

74.   Correspondence from Edward F. Ricketts to Th. Mortensen, June 7, 1933, 4°-Letters from E. F. Ricketts to Th. Mortensen, Royal Library, Copenhagen-NKS 4591.

75.   Correspondence from Edward F. Ricketts to Elisabeth Deichmann, October 2, 1933, Special Collection Archives ARC 79, Deichmann, Elisabeth, 1896–1975, Ernst Mayr Library, Museum of Comparative Zoology Archives, Harvard University.

76.   Correspondence from Edward F. Ricketts to Torsten Gislén, December 18, 1933, TGA, Lund University Library, Sweden.

77.   Correspondence from Edward F. Ricketts to Walter K. Fisher, Summer 1934, Edward Flanders Ricketts papers, Department of Special Collections, Stanford University Libraries.

78.   Correspondence from Edward F. Ricketts to Elisabeth Deichmann, August 31, 1934, Special Collection Archives ARC 79, Deichmann, Elisabeth, 1896–1975, Ernst Mayr Library, Museum of Comparative Zoology Archives, Harvard University.

NOTES TO CHAPTER 5

1.   Correspondence from Edward F Ricketts to Torsten Gislén, April 9, 1935, Torsten Gislén archive (hereafter TGA), Lund University Library, Sweden.

2.   Ricketts to Torsten Gislén, April 9, 1935, TGA, Lund University Library, Sweden.

3.   Ricketts to Torsten Gislén, April 9, 1935, TGA, Lund University

Library, Sweden.

4. Correspondence from Stanley M. Croonquist to Edward F. Ricketts and Jack Calvin, May 13, 1935, Stanford University Press records, Department of Special Collections (hereafter SUPR), re "Between Pacific Tides," by Ed Ricketts and Jack Calvin, 1930–1994, Stanford University Libraries.

5. Correspondence from Edward F Ricketts to Torsten Gislén, April 9, 1935, TGA, Lund University Library, Sweden.

6. Correspondence from Stanley M. Croonquist to Edward F. Ricketts and Jack Calvin, May 13, 1935, SUPR, Stanford University Libraries.

7. HB Baker, "Henry Augustus Pilsbry: 1862–1957," *Nautilus* 71, no. 3 (1958): 73–83.

8. Correspondence from Walter K. Fisher to William H. Davis, January 17, 1936, SUPR, Stanford University Libraries.

9. Fisher to William H. Davis, February 29, 1936, SUPR, Stanford University Libraries.

10. Edward F. Ricketts, List of Specialists Provided to Stanford University Press, SUPR, Stanford University Libraries.

11. Correspondence from William Hawley Davis to E. F. Ricketts, March 13, 1936, SUPR, Stanford University Libraries.

12. *Collecting Net* 11, no. 92 (1936), Stanford University Press.

13. "Books Roll Off Stanford University Press," *Stanford Daily* (California), July 30, 1936, p. 1.

14. Fred Strong interview with Richard Astro, August 1972.

15. Katherine A. Rodger, ed., *Renaissance Man of Cannery Row: The Life and Letters of Edward F. Ricketts* (Tuscaloosa: University of Alabama Press, 2002), 2.

16. Correspondence from Jack Calvin to E. F. Ricketts, December 30, 1936, Edward F. Ricketts Papers (ARC-508), California History Room Archives, Monterey Public Library.

17. Correspondence from Edward F. Ricketts to Lucille Lannestock, February 7, 1938, Ed Ricketts Jr. Personal Collection.

18. Correspondence from Edward F. Ricketts to George E. MacGinitie, March 19, 1937, Ed Ricketts Jr. Personal Collection.

19. Correspondence from Edward F Ricketts to Willis G. Hewatt, March 19, 1937, SUPR, Stanford University Libraries.

20. Willis G. Hewatt, "Ecological Studies on Selected Marine

Intertidal Communities of Monterey Bay" (thesis, Stanford University, 1934), 2.

21. Hewatt, "Ecological," 2.

22. Willis G. Hewatt, "Ecological Studies on Selected Marine Intertidal Communities of Monterey Bay, California," *American Midland Naturalist* 18, no. 2 (1937): 161–206.

23. Correspondence from Edward F. Ricketts to Willis H. Hewatt, March 19, 1937, SUPR, Stanford University Libraries.

24. Torsten Gislén, "Evolutionary Series towards Death and Renewal," *Ark. f. zool. K. Svenska Vetens* 26, no. 16 (1934): 1.

25. Ricketts to Torsten Gislén, March 31, 1937, TGA, Lund University Library, Sweden.

26. Correspondence from Torsten Gislén to E. F. Ricketts, April 23, 1937, Edward Flanders Ricketts papers, Department of Special Collections, Stanford University Libraries.

27. Edward F. Ricketts Collecting Reports: May, 1937, SUPR, Stanford University Libraries.

28. Correspondence from Xenia Cage to Edward F. Ricketts, June 6, 1937, Edward Flanders Ricketts papers, Department of Special Collections, Stanford University Libraries.

29. Correspondence from Edward F. Ricketts to Xenia Cage (Summer 1937), Edward Flanders Ricketts papers, Department of Special Collections, Stanford University Libraries.

30. Correspondence from Sol Felty Light to William H. Davis, June 6, 1937, SUPR, Stanford University Libraries.

31. J. T. Carlton, ed., *The Light and Smith Manual: Intertidal Invertebrates from Central California to Oregon*, 4th ed. (Berkeley: University of California Press, 2007).

32. Sol Felty Light, *Laboratory and Field Text in Invertebrate Zoology* (Berkeley: University of California, Associated Students Store, 1941), 1.

33. Light, *Laboratory*, 2–3.

34. Correspondence from Sol Felty Light to William H. Davis, June 29, 1937, SUPR, Stanford University Libraries.

35. Correspondence from Edward F. Ricketts to Jack Calvin, July 3, 1937, Edward F. Ricketts Papers (ARC-508), California History Room Archives, Monterey Public Library.

36. Correspondence from Jack Calvin to Edward F. Ricketts,

October 4, 1937, Edward F. Ricketts Papers (ARC-508), California History Room Archives, Monterey Public Library.

37. Correspondence from Edward F. Ricketts to George MacGinitie, February 16, 1938, Ed Ricketts Jr. Personal Collection.

38. Anna Maker Ricketts, *Recollections* (Ts. Stanford University Library. 1984), 34.

39. Correspondence from Edward F. Ricketts to George MacGinitie, February 16, 1938, Ed Ricketts Jr. Personal Collection.

40. "Farm Press Calls Year Successful Manager Reports Considerable Rise in Sale of Books," *Stanford Daily* (California), May 27, 1938, p. 1.

41. Correspondence from Edward F. Ricketts to William H. Davis, August 30, 1938, SUPR, Stanford University Libraries.

42. "Three Stanford Press Employees Retire after 20 Years of Service," *Stanford Daily* (California), August 19, 1949, p. 2.

43. Correspondence from Jessie D. Whittern to Edward F. Ricketts, September 9, 1938, SUPR, Stanford University Libraries.

44. "Press Releases Three Volumes during Month," *Stanford Daily* (California), November 17, 1938, p. 2.

45. Ritchie Lovejoy, "Between Pacific Tides: Ricketts and Calvin. Published by Stanford University Press. $6.00," Round and About, *Monterey Peninsula Herald* (California), 1948.

46. Correspondence from Edward F. Ricketts to WH Davis, December 26, 1938, SUPR, Stanford University Libraries.

47. Kenneth Silverman, *Begin Again: A Biography of John Cage* (New York: Alfred A. Knopf, 2010), 33.

48. Gustav Lannestock interview with Richard Astro, August 1972.

49. Correspondence from Edward F. Ricketts to Torsten Gislén, December 27, 1938, TGA, Lund University Library, Sweden.

50. Correspondence from Edward F. Ricketts to WH Davis, December 31, 1938, SUPR, Stanford University Libraries.

NOTES TO CHAPTER 6

1. Correspondence from Stanley M. Croonquist to E. F. Ricketts, February 23, 1939, Stanford University Press records, Department of Special Collections (hereafter SUPR), re "Between Pacific Tides," by Ed Ricketts and Jack Calvin, 1930–1994, Stanford

University Libraries.

2.   Correspondence from Edward F. Ricketts to Jack Calvin, February 24, 1939, Edward F. Ricketts Papers (ARC-508), California History Room Archives, Monterey Public Library.

3.   Correspondence from Edward F. Ricketts to Stanley Croonquist, March 29, 1939, SUPR, Stanford University Libraries.

4.   Correspondence from Jack Calvin to E. F. Ricketts, April 19, 1939, Edward F. Ricketts Papers (ARC-508), California History Room Archives, Monterey Public Library.

5.   Janice M. Straley, ed., *Ed Ricketts from Cannery Row to Sitka, Alaska: Science, History, and Reflections along the Pacific Coast: A Compilation of Essays* (Juneau, AK: Shorefast Editions, 2015).

6.   James Carlton, reviewer comment provided to Oregon State University Press and the authors, October 15, 2020.

7.   Correspondence from Edward F. Ricketts to Virginia Scardigli, April 25, 1939, in *Leopold's Shack and Ricketts's Lab: The Emergence of Environmentalism*, ed. Michael J. Lannoo, 41 (Berkeley: University of California Press, 2010).

8.   Virginia Scardigli, interview with Richard Astro, October 1971.

9.   Correspondence from Joseph Campbell to Edward F. Ricketts, August 22, 1939, in *Joseph Campbell, Correspondence: 1927–1987*, Collected Works of Joseph Campbell (Novato, CA: New World Library, 2019), 34.

10.   Campbell to E. F. Ricketts, August 22, 1939, in *Joseph Campbell*.

11.   Correspondence from Edward F. Ricketts to Joseph Campbell, October 7, 1939, in *Renaissance Man of Cannery Row: The Life and Letters of Edward F. Ricketts*, ed. Katherine A. Rodger, 45–46 (Tuscaloosa: University of Alabama Press, 2002).

12.   Ricketts to Joseph Campbell, October 7, 1939, in Rodger, *Renaissance Man*.

13.   Correspondence from Edward F. Ricketts to Xenia Cage, October 9, 1939, in Rodger, *Renaissance Man*, 46.

14.   Correspondence from Edward F. Ricketts to Pat Covici, December 23, 1939, in Rodger, *Renaissance Man*, 54–55.

15.   Correspondence from Edward F. Ricketts to Peg Fitzgerald, February 6, 1940, in Rodger, *Renaissance Man*, 56.

16.   Correspondence from Walter K. Fisher to Edward F. Ricketts, January 31, 1940, Edward Flanders Ricketts papers, Department

of Special Collections, Stanford University Libraries.

17. Richard Astro, "Steinbeck and Ricketts: Escape or Commitment in the Sea of Cortez?" *Western American Literature* 6, no. 2 (1971): 109–121.

18. Correspondence from Edward F. Ricketts to Joel Hedgpeth, November 18, 1941, in Rodger, *Renaissance Man*, 131–133.

19. Correspondence from Edward F. Ricketts to Joel Hedgpeth, August 22, 1945, Edward Flanders Ricketts papers, Department of Special Collections, Stanford University Libraries.

20. Correspondence from Edward F. Ricketts to Xenia Cage, December 11, 1943, in Rodger, *Renaissance Man*, 185–187.

21. Edward F. Ricketts (1945), PBL Survey Card, Typed directions for purpose of the 3x5 PBL Survey Card and 5x7 PBL Species Cards, Edward Flanders Ricketts papers, Department of Special Collections, Stanford University Libraries.

22. Edward F. Ricketts, Permanent Expedition Notebook, Edward Flanders Ricketts papers, Department of Special Collections, Stanford University Libraries.

23. "Ritch Lovejoy, A Unusual Man," *Monterey Peninsula Herald* (California), July 11, 1956, p. 1.

24. John Straley, "Ricketts, Calvin and the Charisma of Place," in *Ed Ricketts from Cannery Row to Sitka, Alaska: Science, History, and Reflections along the Pacific Coast: A Compilation of Essays*, ed. Janice M. Straley, 89–97 (92–93) (Juneau, AK: Shorefast Editions, 2015).

25. Correspondence from Jack Calvin to Floris Hartog, May 32, 1948, Edward Flanders Ricketts papers, Department of Special Collections, Stanford University Libraries.

26. Straley, "Ricketts, Calvin and the Charisma," in *Ed Ricketts*, 89–97 (92–93).

27. Correspondence from Joel Hedgpeth to Grant Barnes, May 22, 1985, Edward Flanders Ricketts papers, Department of Special Collections, Stanford University Libraries.

28. "In Memoriam: Jack Calvin," the Alaska Legislature, *Ravencall Southeast Alaska Conservation Council* 9, no. 1 (1985): 10.

29. A. L. Lundy, *Real Life on Cannery Row: Real People, Places and Events That Inspired John Steinbeck* (Santa Monica, CA: Angel City Press, 2008), 120.

30. John Steinbeck, *Cannery Row* (New York: Viking Press, 1945), 30.

31. Webster Street, "John Steinbeck: A Reminiscence," in *Steinbeck: The Man and His Work,* ed. Richard Astro and Tetsumaro Hayashi, 35–41 (Corvallis: Oregon State University Press, 1971).

32. Richard Brusca, telephone interview with Richard Astro, May 25, 2020.

33. Michael J. Lannoo, *Leopold's Shack and Ricketts's Lab: The Emergence of Environmentalism* (Berkeley: University of California Press, 2010), vi.

34. Richard Brusca, telephone interview with Richard Astro, May 25, 2020.

35. David Starr Jordan, "President Jordan's Address: The Inauguration of President Wheeler," *University Chronicle* 2, no. 4 (Berkeley: University of California, 1899).

36. Laurel Chesky, "Rafe Sagarin," *Monterey County Weekly,* June 1, 2015, https://www.montereycountyweekly.com/milestones/obitu-aries/rafe-sagarin/article_cb38c632-0887-11e5-86ae-8b9eff1b7e49.html.

37. William Jefferson Clinton, "Remarks by the President to the National Oceans Conference," San Carlos Park, Monterey, California, June 12, 1998

38. William Jefferson Clinton, "Remarks by the President to the National Oceans Conference," San Carlos Park, Monterey, California. The White House, Office of the Press Secretary, June 12, 1998, https://clintonwhitehouse2.archives.gov/WH/New/html/19980615-12921.html.

39. Mary Ellen Hannibal, *Citizen Scientist* (New York: Experiment Press, 2016), 24–25.

index